ADVANCED

Physical Education & Sport

FOR AS-LEVEL

SECOND EDITION

JOHN HONEYBOURNE,
MICHAEL HILL AND HELEN MOORS

First published in 1996 by:
Stanley Thornes (Publishers) Ltd
Second edition 2000

Reprinted in 2002 by:
Nelson Thornes Ltd
Delta Place
27 Bath Road
CHELTENHAM
GL53 7TH
United Kingdom

02 03 04 05 06 / 10 9 8 7 6 5 4 3

A catalogue record for this book is available from the British Library

ISBN 0 7487 5303 6

Illustrations by Angela Lumley, Oxford Designers and Illustrators, Shaun Williams, Florence Production
Cover Photograph: Zefa Pictures Ltd
Page make-up by Florence Production

Printed and bound in Italy by Canale

Contents

iii

Revision guides

Introduction

Physical Education continues to be one of the largest growth subjects at A level. Following the government initiative *Learning to Succeed*, new AS-level and A-level syllabuses or specifications have been developed. The new AS in Physical Education has been warmly received and this text is designed specifically for this level. To complete the full A level, or A2 as it is now called, students have to study the AS level first. You can be confident in the knowledge that this text covers the content of all the AS-level specifications, including OCR, EDEXCEL, AQA and WJEC.

We have written this book for students to use as a no-nonsense resource. We have all had considerable experience in teaching A-level Physical Education, sports studies, GCSE Physical Education, GNVQ Leisure and Tourism and GNVQ Health and Social Care. We are all senior examiners at A level for three of the four examination boards.

Students and teachers who use this book will realise that the aim is to give only information that is relevant and clearly expressed. This book will give students enough information to pass the AS-level examination or to build a portfolio for GNVQ work.

The book is clearly set out in sections and chapters. Each section covers the main areas of the subject at AS level and represents the content of all syllabuses in this area at the time of writing. There are three parts to the book. Part 1 deals with anatomy and physiology. Part 2 covers skill acquisition. Part 3 deals with the social issues in physical education and sport.

At the beginning of each chapter, *Learning objectives* clearly state what is to be covered. There are *Activity boxes,* which include ideas to reinforce learning, and *In practice boxes,* which look at the application of theory to practical situations. All the AS-level examinations and the work required for GNVQ demand that the student can apply theory to practice. To help understanding there has also been included *Definition boxes,* which expand on some key words and phrases. At the end of each chapter there is a list of *Key terms* that need to be learned and understood by the student, along with *Revision boxes,* which will focus students' attention on the key concepts that are important for passing the examination. We have also included a *Revision guide* for each section and *Examination-style questions* that will help to prepare students for the written examinations. There is a *Glossary* of the main key terms included at the back of the book, which can again be used for revision purposes.

This is a fascinating and rewarding subject area and should be studied with a view to applying theoretical principles to practical situations. We hope that students and teachers will get maximum benefit from this textbook and share our enjoyment of studying and teaching Physical Education and Sport.

This is a book that will not go out of date and will give students the background that is vital for examination success.

About the authors

John Honeybourne is the Head of Sixth Form at Baverstock School in Birmingham. He has been Chief Examiner for the AEB, Principal Examiner for OCR and is currently question setter for OCR. He is the Chair of Examiners for EDEXCEL.

Michael Hill is Director of Physical Education at the City of Stoke on Trent Sixth Form College. He has been Reviser and Senior Examiner for the AEB and is currently Chief Examiner for EDEXCEL.

Helen Moors teaches A-level Physical Education at the City of Stoke on Trent Sixth Form College. She has been a Senior Examiner for the AEB and Principal Examiner and question setter for OCR. She has been Chair of Examiners for OCR and Reviser for EDEXCEL.

Acknowledgements

The authors and publishers are grateful to the following for permission to reproduce previously published material:
- British Olympic Association for permission to reproduce their logo – page 150
- Central Council of Physical Recreation for permission to reproduce their logo – page 150
- National Coaching Foundation for permission to reproduce their logo – page 150
- SportsAid for permission to reproduce their logo – page 150

Every attempt has been made to contact copyright holders, and we apologise if any have been overlooked. Should copyright have been unwittingly infringed in this book, the owners should contact the publishers, who will make corrections at reprint.

Photo credits
- Allsport (UK) Ltd – pages 40 (bottom), 84, 96 (top), 133 (left), 161 and 170.
- Associated Press – page 167.
- Associated Sports Photography – pages 88, 188 and 189.
- Graham Bool – page 87.
- Hulton Getty Picture Library – pages 130 and 131 (bottom).
- J. Allan Cash Ltd – page 172.
- Mark Leech Sports Photography – pages 164, 165 (left) and 195 (left and right).
- Mary Evans Picture Library – pages 131 (top) and 132.
- Mike Brett – pages 36, 40 (top), 101, 120, 123, 133 (right), 140 (top), 147, 178 and 190.
- Pictor International – page 114 (bottom).
- Scottish Sports Council – page 181.
- Supersport – pages 80 (Sport Presse Photo), 81 (left and right), 86, 90, 92 (top), 102, 103, 108, 114 (top), 117, 121, 122, 124, 128, 140 (bottom) and 183 (Karine Hoskyns).
- The Broadgate Club – page 159.

Anatomy, biomechanics and physiology

This part of the book contains:

The following chapters provide an introduction to anatomy, physiology and, in particular, to the systems that play a significant role in the production of skilled human movement – the skeletal, muscular, cardiovascular and respiratory systems. It is important to know both the structure of these systems and how they function, including basic biomechanics, in order to develop a better understanding of how the body works and to appreciate the body's capabilities and limitations in performance of sport.

1 Introduction to the skeletal system

Learning objectives

- To have a general understanding of the structure of the skeletal system.
- To be aware of the main functions of the skeletal system.
- To know the structure and type of the major joints of the body.
- To know the types of movement that can be produced around each joint.

The skeletal system needs to be studied and understood by any person interested in human movement. The skeletal system provides the system of leverage required for human movement. Each joint is structured in a way that best suits its function, for example the structure of the knee joint allows movement in one plane only. This is because although free movement of the knee is desirable, stability is also needed. The skeletal system provides ths basis of attachment for most muscles, enabling them to work together in order to produce efficient and coordinated movement. It helps to provide the strength and stability that is needed in order to stay balanced and upright, and provides protection for many vital organs.

1.1 The skeletal system

The skeletal system is made up of two kinds of tissue: *bone* and *cartilage*.

1.1.1 Bone

There are five different types of bone, which are classified by their shape rather than their size.
Long bones, such as the femur
Short bones, for example the metatarsals
Irregular bones: the vertebrae are examples of these
Flat bones, for example the scapula
Sesamoid bones, such as the patella

Examples of each type of bone are shown in Figure 1.1.
Bone is the hardest connective tissue in the body, mainly because it contains deposits of calcium phosphate and calcium carbonate. Bone acts as a store for calcium, and as a result of regular exercise more calcium is deposited, increasing bone density. The bone matrix also contains *collagen*. Collagen gives bone tissue a flexible strength, allowing it to cope with a certain amount of impact. As you get older the bone contains less collagen and the bone is less dense, resulting in brittle bones that are quite easily damaged. *Hard*, or *compact*, bone makes up the outer layer of all bones, giving them strength. *Cancellous*, or *spongy*, bone is typically found at the ends of the long bones. Cancellous bone is not as dense as hard bone because it contains cavities filled with bone marrow.

1.1.2 Ossification

The process of bone formation is known as *ossification*. The skeletal frame is initially made out of cartilage, which is gradually replaced by bone. An outline of the structure of a typical long bone can be seen in Figure 1.2. The ossification process begins in the *diaphysis* (the primary ossification centre) and then occurs in the *epiphyses* (the secondary sites of ossification). A plate

Definition

OSSIFICATION

Ossification is the process of bone formation.

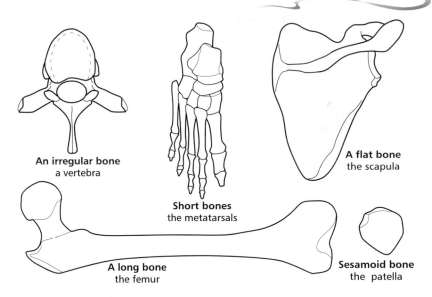

An irregular bone
a vertebra

Short bones
the metatarsals

A flat bone
the scapula

A long bone
the femur

Sesamoid bone
the patella

Figure 1.1 *Classification of bones*

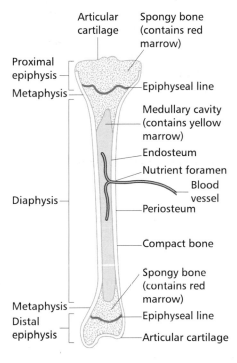

Articular cartilage

Spongy bone (contains red marrow)

Proximal epiphysis

Metaphysis

Epiphyseal line

Medullary cavity (contains yellow marrow)

Endosteum

Nutrient foramen

Blood vessel

Diaphysis

Periosteum

Compact bone

Spongy bone (contains red marrow)

Metaphysis

Epiphyseal line

Distal epiphysis

Articular cartilage

Figure 1.2 *Structure of a typical long bone*

of cartilage is left between the diaphysis and each epiphysis; this is where bones grow in length until maturation takes place (endochondral ossification). The plate is known as the *epiphyseal plate* and when growth stops this plate fuses and becomes bone. A long bone also has to increase in diameter; this is achieved by depositing a new layer of bone on the surface. This process is known as *appositional growth*.

IN TRAINING

As bones do not fully mature until ossification is complete, young athletes can run the risk of damaging the epiphysis and/or the epiphyseal plate. If the epiphyseal plate slips this can result in the hip giving way under the stress of movement and can lead to one leg eventually being shorter than the other. Activities such as swimming (swimmer's shoulder) and tennis (tennis elbow) can put strain on young bones and joints.

1.1.3 Cartilage

There are three types of cartilage:

Yellow elastic cartilage, which is soft and slightly elastic. Examples may be found in the ear lobe and epiglottis.

White fibrocartilage, which is tough and slightly flexible. This cartilage acts as a shock absorber, helping to prevent damage to the bone. The cartilage between the vertebrae is white fibrocartilage.

Hyaline or *articular cartilage*, which is solid and smooth. Hyaline cartilage protects the bone from the constant wear and tear of moving and can be found on the articulating surface of bones.

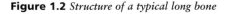

Definition

ARTICULATION

The place where two or more bones meet to form a joint. The articulating surface is the point of contact between the bones.

IN TRAINING

Exercise has a positive effect on bone tissue. It stimulates an increase in the amount of calcium salts deposited in the bone, making it stronger.

ACTIVITY

Examine the bones of a skeleton and see if you can classify the following bones: the parietal bone (part of the skull), the ilium (part of the pelvis), phalanges, the sternum, the ulna and the metatarsals.

1.2 The skeleton

The skeleton is made up of 206 bones (Figure 1.3). It comprises the axial skeleton and the appendicular skeleton.

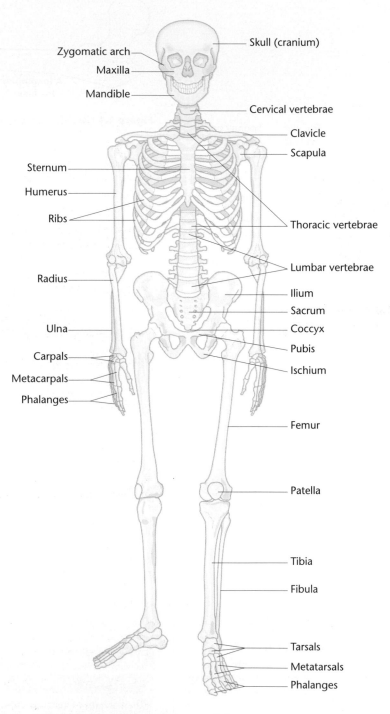

Figure 1.3 *The bones making up the human skeleton*

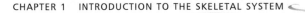

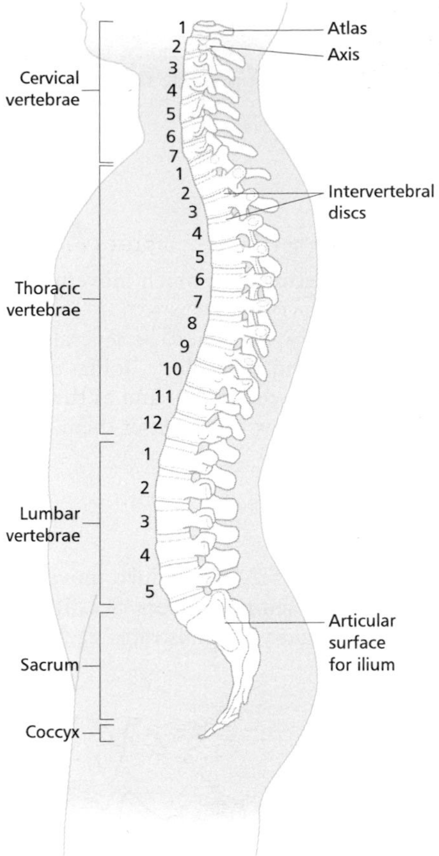

1.2.1 The axial skeleton

This is made up of the skull, the vertebral column, the sternum and the ribs.

1.2.2 The appendicular skeleton

The appendicular skeleton is composed of the shoulder girdle, the hip girdle, the bones of the arms and hands and the bones of the legs and feet.

Although you do not need to know about the individual bones which make up the head and face or the hands and feet for your courses, a more detailed knowledge of the spine is useful. This is outlined in Figure 1.4.

IN TRAINING

The size of an athlete's skeletal frame is largely genetically determined, but exercise and a well balanced diet can help to ensure proper bone growth.

1.2.3 Function of the skeletal system

The skeletal system has four main functions:
- to provide support for the body;
- to provide protection for vital organs;
- to produce blood corpuscles (cells);
- to provide attachment for muscles.

For sport enthusiasts it is the last of these functions which is the most interesting. In order for us to perform the sophisticated movements demanded by many sports, we need a sophisticated system of joints and levers capable of producing a wide range of movements. As you will see, we have been very well designed to do this.

1.3 Joints

Joints can be classified in two ways: by considering their structure, or by considering how much movement they allow.

1.3.1 Classification by structure

The following classification of joint by structure should be used.

Fibrous

These joints have no joint cavity and the bones are held together by fibrous connective tissue. Examples are the sutures of the skull bones.

Cartilaginous

Cartilaginous joints also have no joint cavity. There is cartilage between the bones of the joint. Cartilaginous joints may be found between the vertebrae of the spine.

Synovial

A synovial joint has a fluid-filled cavity surrounded by an articular capsule. The articulating surfaces of the bones are covered in hyaline cartilage. The hinge joint of the knee is a synovial joint.

1.3.2 Classification by movement allowed

When it comes to classifying joints by the movement they allow the following terms are applied.

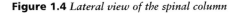

Cervical vertebrae

1 — Atlas
2 — Axis
3
4
5
6
7

Thoracic vertebrae

1
2
3 — Intervertebral discs
4
5
6
7
8
9
10
11
12

Lumbar vertebrae

1
2
3
4
5

Sacrum

Coccyx

Articular surface for ilium

Figure 1.4 *Lateral view of the spinal column*

Fibrous joint or synarthrosis

This type of joint does not allow any movement. When you consider where these joints occur this makes sense as some parts of the body, such as the brain, need protection. A moveable joint could not provide this protection.

Cartilaginous joint or amphiarthrosis

This joint allows limited movement.

Synovial joint or diarthrosis

A synovial joint allows free movement, or certainly as much movement as the shape of the articulating surfaces permits.

As you may have gathered by now, there always seem to be several types of everything you come across in anatomy and physiology. Joints are no exception. There are six different types of synovial joint – and as these are the joints that allow movement, we need to know more about them.

1.4 Synovial joints

The synovial joints allow movement to take place. How much movement is permitted depends on the shape of the articulating surfaces. Six different joint constructions have been identified. Figure 1.5 illustrates each joint type.

Hinge joint **Condyloid joint** **Gliding joint**

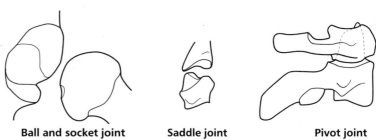

Ball and socket joint **Saddle joint** **Pivot joint**

Figure 1.5 *The six types of synovial joint*

Ball and socket: a ball-like head fits into a cup-shaped depression – an example of this is the shoulder joint.
Hinge: a convex surface articulates with a concave surface. The elbow is a typical hinge joint.
Pivot: part of a bone fits into a ring-like structure. The most well known pivot joint is the atlas and axis (cervical 1 and 2: see Figure 1.4).
Saddle: a bone fits into a saddle-shaped surface on another bone – the thumb is a good example.
Gliding: two relatively flat surfaces slide over one another – this may be seen at the articular processes of the vertebrae.
Condyloid: a convex surface fits into an elliptical cavity – the wrist joint is a condyloid joint.

The six types of synovial joint differ in the amount of movement they allow, but are very similar in structure and share common features.

Figure 1.6 highlights the common features of a synovial joint, using the hinge joint of the knee as an illustration.

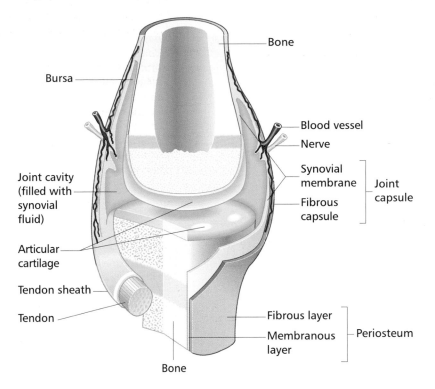

Figure 1.6 *Structure of a synovial joint*

The *articular/joint capsule* is a fibrous tissue encasing the joint, forming a capsule.
The *synovial membrane* acts as a lining to the joint capsule and secretes synovial fluid.
Articular/hyaline cartilage covers the ends of the articulating bones.
Synovial fluid fills the joint capsule and nourishes and lubricates the articular cartilage.
Ligaments are white fibrous connective tissues joining bone to bone, making the joint more stable.
Bursa is found where tendons are in contact with bone. The bursa forms a fluid-filled sac between the tendon and the bone and helps to reduce friction.
Articular discs of cartilage act as shock absorbers.
Pads of fat act as buffers to protect the bones from wear and tear.

IN TRAINING

When organising young children into teams, it is important to match players by size as well as ability, to avoid potential damage to joints due to contact/impact injuries.

ACTIVITY

Try to construct a joint by taking the appropriate bones and fastening them together. For example, you could use tape to represent the ligaments and felt or moulding clay for the articular cartilage. If you don't have any bones, improvise!

1.5 Movement terminology

Later in Part 1 we will look at the structure of some joints in more detail, but here we will consider the range of movement that the body can perform. There are a lot of terms that you need to be familiar with, and you will remember the terms much more easily if you put them into practice.

The terms that you are most likely to use are given below, and are illustrated in Figure 1.7.

Flexion: a decrease in the angle around the joint.

Extension: an increase in the angle around the joint.

Abduction: movement away from the midline of the body.

Adduction: movement towards the midline of the body.

Rotation: movement of a bone around its longitudinal axis. Rotation can be inward (medial) or outward (lateral).

Circumduction: the lower end of the bone moves in a circle. It is a combination of flexion, extension, adduction and abduction.

Lateral flexion: bending the head or trunk sideways.

Elevation: moving the shoulders upwards.

Depression: moving the shoulders downwards.

Plantarflexion: bending the foot downwards, away from the tibia.

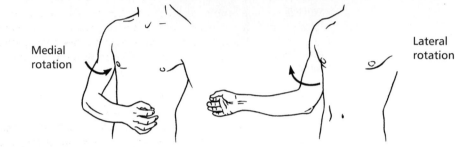

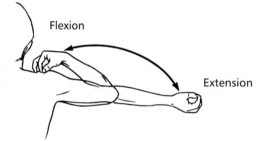

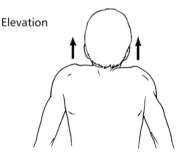

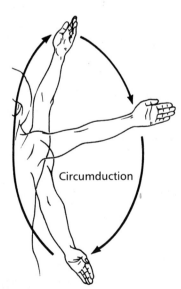

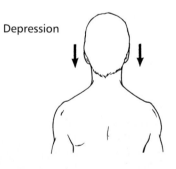

Figure 1.7 *Movement terminology*

Dorsiflexion: bending the foot upwards, towards the tibia.
Pronation: facing the palm of the hand downwards.
Supination: facing the palm of the hand upwards.

More simply, *flexion* occurs when you bend a limb and *extension* occurs when you straighten it. For example, the movement at the elbow joint when you do press-ups involves both flexion and extension. When performing star jumps, as you move your arms outwards you are *abducting* the shoulder joint and as you bring your arms back to the side of your body you are *adducting* the shoulder joint. As a ballet dancer moves into first position he or she must *rotate* their hip joints laterally. When bowling, a cricketer moves the arm in a full circle – this is *circumduction* of the shoulder joint. Remember: movement occurs around a joint and not a body part, so it is incorrect to say (for example) 'flexion of the leg'. You must refer to the actual joint involved, as in flexion of the hip, knee or ankle joint. Be precise.

When you take part in your next practical session, break down the skills you attempt into simple phases and try to identify the specific movements. It is quite difficult to begin with, but with practice becomes very straight-forward. If the joints have a similar structure, then their pattern of movement will be the same: for example, flexion of the hip is the same as flexion of the shoulder joint.

ACTIVITY

Look back to the list of synovial joints. Working with a partner, locate each of the joints given as examples and determine the types of movement that can take place at each. For example, the elbow joint can flex and extend.

Key revision points

There are six types of synovial joint: ball and socket, hinge, pivot, gliding, condyloid and saddle. All synovial joints allow some degree of movement and share common features, such as a synovial membrane, synovial fluid, articular cartilage and ligaments.

KEY TERMS

You should now understand the following terms. If you do not, go back through the chapter and find out.

- Abduction
- Adduction
- Appendicular skeleton
- Articulation
- Axial skeleton
- Cartilaginous joint
- Circumduction
- Extension
- Fibrous joint
- Flexion
- Ossification
- Rotation
- Synovial joint

PROGRESS CHECK

1 List the bones that form the axial skeleton.
2 List the bones that form the appendicular skeleton.
3 What are the functions of the skeleton?
4 Where would you find hyaline cartilage?
5 How may joints be classified?
6 Which category of joint allows free movement?
7 Give an example of a gliding joint.
8 List the common features of a synovial joint.
9 Which features of a synovial joint help increase joint stability?
10 List the movements possible at a ball and socket joint and give a brief description of each movement.
11 What movements can take place at the ankle joint?
12 Name two joints which allow circumduction and give an example in sport of when this movement occurs.
13 The first two cervical vertebrae form a joint. What type of joint is it, and what type of movement does it allow?
14 The range of movement around a joint can be restricted by a number of factors. List three of these factors.
15 Why isn't it advisable for young athletes to do plyometric training?
16 Name a joint that is susceptible to injury when participating in contact sports. Give reasons for your answer.

Chapter 2

Joints and muscles

Learning objectives

- To know the bones that articulate at the major joints of the body.
- To be able to identify the muscles that act as prime movers at each major joint.
- To know the type of movement that the prime movers can produce.
- To be able to analyse sporting actions in terms of the joint and muscle used and the movement produced.

A joint cannot move by itself – it needs muscles to manoeuvre the bones into the correct position. Muscles are attached to bones by connective tissue and we refer to the ends of the muscle as the *origin* and the *insertion*. The origin is the more fixed, stable end and the insertion is usually attached to the bone that moves.

When a muscle contracts it shortens and the insertion moves closer to the origin, creating movement around a joint. For example, biceps brachii causes flexion of the elbow. The origin of this muscle is on the scapula and the insertion is on the radius. When the muscle contracts the radius is pulled upwards towards the shoulder, as the insertion moves closer to the origin.

The muscle directly responsible for creating the movement at a joint is called the *prime mover*. There is usually more than one prime mover at a joint, and other muscles can assist the movement. The number of muscles involved depends on the type and amount of work being carried out.

Any sports performer, at whatever level, should have a working knowledge of joint and muscle action. The human body is very complex and is made up of hundreds of muscles acting on numerous joints – see Figure 2.1. As an introduction we will look at the joints most involved in the production of gross motor skills in more detail.

IN TRAINING

Many athletes train in order to increase the amount of force that their muscles can generate. Strength training involves working the muscle against a resistance to the extent that adaptations occur within the muscle resulting in hypertrophy. In addition, neural adaptations include an improvement in coordination of motor unit activation and the recruitment of additional motor units. Both adaptations result in an increase in muscular strength. Weight-training sessions are planned to develop strength in the muscles specific to the needs of the athlete and their chosen activity. Free weights, a multi-gym, or the athlete's own body weight can be used to provide the resistance.

Definition

HYPERTROPHY

Where an increase in cell size leads to an increase in tissue size.

IN PRACTICE

When throwing a ball underarm the radioulnar joint is supinated and when throwing a ball overarm the radioulnar joint is pronated.

IN PRACTICE

A warm-up is useful only if you are warming up the muscles and joints that you are about to use. When preparing a training schedule the exercises you choose should reflect the movement pattern you will be performing in competition.

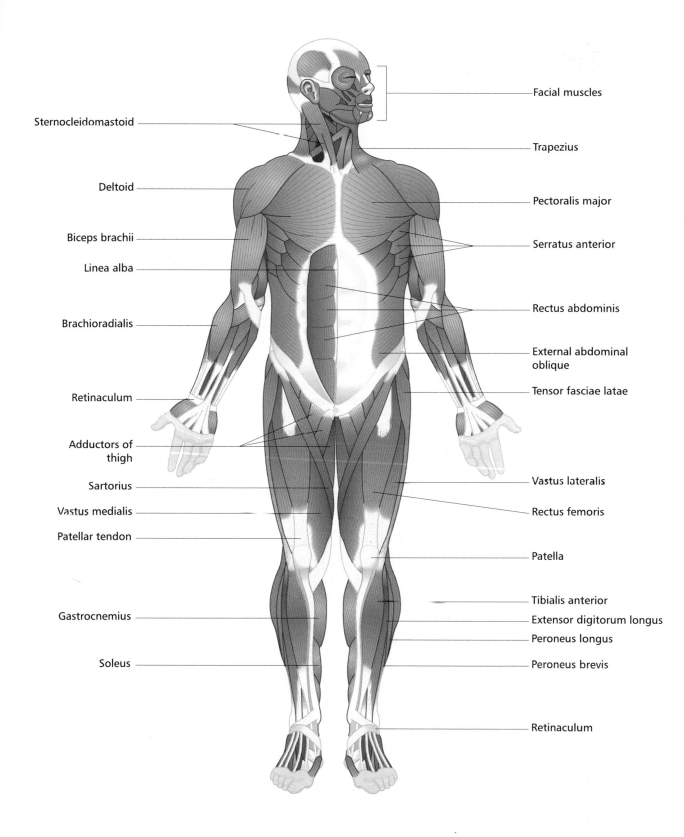

Sternocleidomastoid

Deltoid

Biceps brachii

Linea alba

Brachioradialis

Retinaculum

Adductors of
thigh

Sartorius

Vastus medialis

Patellar tendon

Gastrocnemius

Soleus

Facial muscles

Trapezius

Pectoralis major

Serratus anterior

Rectus abdominis

External abdominal
oblique

Tensor fasciae latae

Vastus lateralis

Rectus femoris

Patella

Tibialis anterior

Extensor digitorum longus

Peroneus longus

Peroneus brevis

Retinaculum

Figure 2.1 *The muscles of the human body. (a) Anterior view*

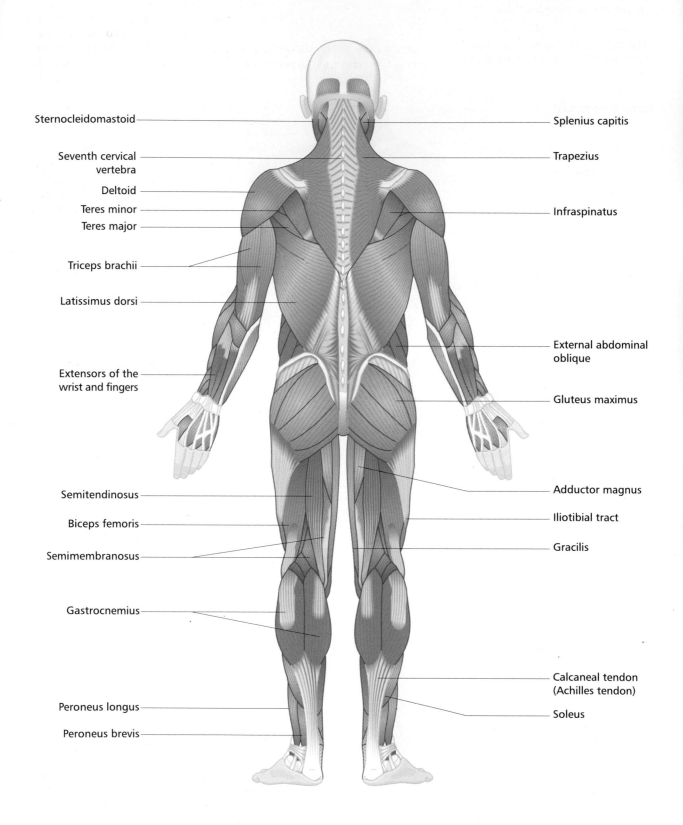

Sternocleidomastoid

Seventh cervical
vertebra

Deltoid

Teres minor

Teres major

Triceps brachii

Latissimus dorsi

Extensors of the
wrist and fingers

Semitendinosus

Biceps femoris

Semimembranosus

Gastrocnemius

Peroneus longus

Peroneus brevis

Splenius capitis

Trapezius

Infraspinatus

External abdominal
oblique

Gluteus maximus

Adductor magnus

Iliotibial tract

Gracilis

Calcaneal tendon
(Achilles tendon)

Soleus

Figure 2.1 *The muscles of the human body. (b) Posterior view*

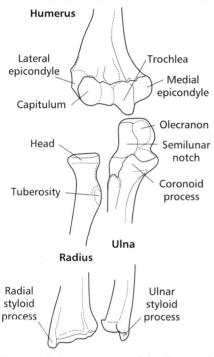

Figure 2.2 *Bony structures of the elbow and radioulnar joints. Surface markings such as bumps and grooves are visible, usually where a tendon inserts or where a joint articulates*

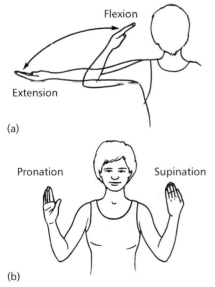

Figure 2.3 *Movements of the elbow and radioulnar joints. (a) Flexion and extension; (b) right radioulnar joint pronated, left radioulnar joint supinated*

2.1 The elbow joint, the radioulnar joint and the wrist joint

The elbow is a hinge joint, with the *distal* end of the humerus articulating with the *proximal* end of both the radius and the ulna. On the proximal end of the ulna is the olecranon process and this fits into the olecranon fossa on the distal end of the humerus. This feature of the joint prevents the elbow joint from hyperextending. The joint is strengthened by four ligaments. Movement is possible in one plane only, allowing flexion and extension to take place.

Also within the elbow joint capsule the radius articulates with the ulna to form a pivot joint. This radioulnar joint allows pronation and supination of the lower arm (medial and lateral rotation).

Figure 2.2 shows the bones that articulate at the elbow joint.

The movements possible at the elbow and radioulnar joints are shown in Figure 2.3. The muscles that create these movements are outlined in Table 2.1 and illustrated in Figure 2.4. The specific origins and insertions are not given, but a general location of the muscle is provided to help with future movement analysis.

Table 2.1 *Muscles of the elbow joint*

Movement	Prime mover(s)	Origin	Insertion
Elbow (hinge)			
Flexion	Biceps brachii	Scapula	Radius
	Brachialis	Humerus	Ulna
Extension	Triceps brachii	Scapula and humerus	Ulna
	Anconeus	Humerus	Ulna
Radioulnar (pivot)			
Pronation	Pronator teres	Humerus and ulna	Radius
Supination	Supinator	Humerus and ulna	Radius

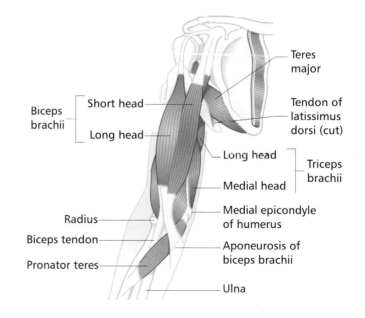

Figure 2.4 *Prime movers of the elbow and radioulnar joints*

The wrist is a condyloid joint, where the distal end of the radius and ulna articulate with three of the carpal bones – the navicular, lunate and triquetrum bones. It is a common misconception that the wrist joint can rotate. This is not the case – the wrist joint can only flex, extend, abduct and adduct (and can therefore circumduct). At 'A' level it is not necessary to

CONDYLE

A large knuckle-shaped articular surface, e.g. lateral condyle of the femur.

HEAD

A ball-shaped articular surface, e.g. the head of the femur.

SPINOUS PROCESS

A long slender projection, e.g. the processes of the vertebrae.

TUBEROSITY

A large rounded surface, for example on the proximal end of the radius.

FORAMEN

A hole – e.g. the vertebral foramen allows the spinal cord to pass through.

FOSSA

A depression, e.g. the olecranon fossa of the humerus.

analyse the movement of the wrist in any great detail, nor is any detailed knowledge of the muscles of the wrist expected. Usually it is sufficient to talk about the muscles collectively as either flexors or extensors of the wrist.

IN TRAINING

Multi-gym weight training exercise to develop strength in the biceps brachii (and brachialis and brachioradialis): **the *biceps curl*** (Figure 2.5). Start with your elbows extended and then move the bar upwards, flexing your elbow. Do not allow your elbows to touch your body and keep your back straight. Lower to the start position and repeat. The biceps will be working concentrically during the upward phase and eccentrically on the downward phase (see page 35).

Multi-gym exercise to develop strength in the triceps: **the *triceps curl*** (Figure 2.6). Flex the elbow and keep your elbows in contact with the side of your body as you pull the bar down towards your thigh until the elbow is extended. Return to start position, keeping your back straight.

Figure 2.5 *The biceps curl*

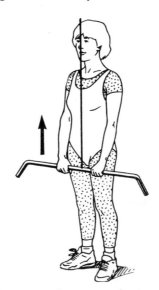
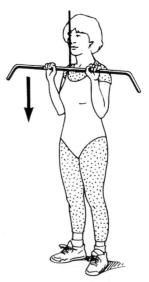

Figure 2.6 *The triceps curl*

2.2 The shoulder joint and the shoulder girdle

The structure of the shoulder joint and the shoulder girdle are shown in Figure 2.7.

2.2.1 The shoulder girdle

The shoulder girdle is a gliding joint (with slight rotation) where the clavicle articulates with the scapula, usually moving as a unit. We are not particularly aware of the involvement of the shoulder girdle in the numerous arm actions we perform (these are illustrated in Figure 2.8).

The prime movers of the shoulder girdle are outlined in Table 2.2 and illustrated in Figure 2.9.

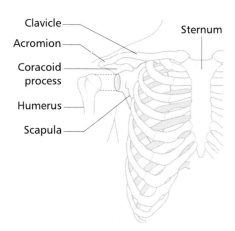

Figure 2.7 *Anterior view of the shoulder joint and shoulder girdle*

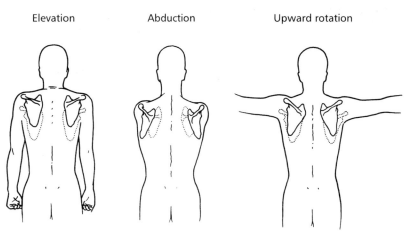

Elevation   Abduction   Upward rotation

Figure 2.8 *Possible movements of the shoulder girdle*

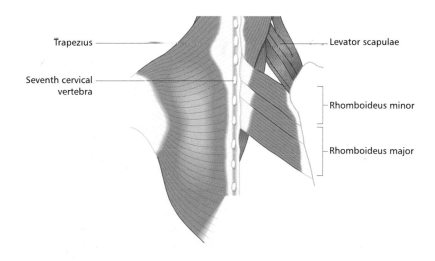

Figure 2.9 *Prime movers of the shoulder girdle*

Table 2.2 *Muscles of the shoulder girdle*

Movement	Prime mover(s)	Origin	Insertion
Elevation	Trapezius part one	Skull	Clavicle
Depression	Trapezius part four	Thoracic vertebrae	Base of spine
Upward rotation	Trapezius part two	Ligaments of the neck	Acromion process
Downward rotation	Rhomboids	Cervical and thoracic vertebrae	Scapula
Abduction	Serratus anterior	Side of ribs	Scapula
Adduction	Trapezius part three	Cervical and thoracic vertebrae	Scapula

ACTIVITY

Work with a partner. Place your hand over your partner's scapula and note what happens when he or she lifts their arms above their head, to the side, etc. You should be able to see that the shoulder girdle can abduct, adduct, rotate upwards and downwards, elevate and depress.

2.2.2 The shoulder joint

The shoulder joint is a ball and socket joint, with the head of the humerus fitting into a very shallow cavity on the scapula called the glenoid fossa. The shoulder joint is the most mobile joint in the body but also one of the most unstable because the shallow cavity gives little support to the head of the humerus. Stability has to be provided by ligaments and muscles.

The movements possible at the shoulder joint are shown in Figure 2.10. They include flexion, extension, horizontal flexion and extension, abduction, adduction, external and internal rotation and circumduction.

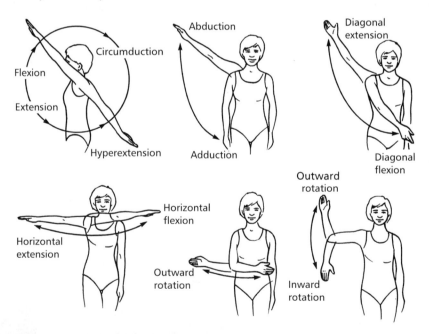

Figure 2.10 *Movements possible at the shoulder joint*

IN PRACTICE

Lack of stability of the shoulder means that in contact sports, such as rugby, a dislocated shoulder is a very common injury.

For some skills analysis of the shoulder movement is quite straightforward, for example lifting the arms above the head in preparation for a handstand clearly involves flexion of the shoulder joint and upward rotation of the shoulder girdle. Unfortunately, most of the actions we perform in sport, for example a tennis serve, are a combination of several movements and are therefore quite difficult to analyse. Students at 'A' level are not expected to attempt complex movement analysis – but have a go at the next activity.

ACTIVITY

Describe the movement pattern at the shoulder and elbow joints during each phase of the javelin throw.

Table 2.3 *Muscles of the shoulder joint*

Movement	Prime mover(s)	Origin	Insertion
Flexion	Anterior deltoid	Clavicle, scapula and acromion process	Humerus
Extension	Latissimus dorsi	Ilium, lumbar and thoracic vertebrae	Humerus
Abduction	Middle deltoid	Clavicle, scapula and acromion	Humerus
Adduction	Pectoralis major	Clavicle, ribs and sternum	Humerus
Inward rotation	Subscapularis	Scapula	Humerus
Outward rotation	Infraspinatus	Scapula	Humerus

Table 2.3 details the muscles and movements of the shoulder joint and the prime movers are illustrated in Figure 2.11

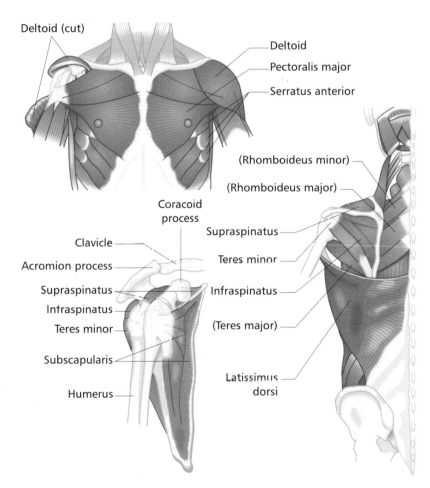

Figure 2.11 *Prime movers of the shoulder joint*

IN TRAINING

Multi-gym weight training exercise to improve strength in the trapezius and rhomboids: **the *shoulder shrug*** (Figure 2.12). Keeping a straight back, lift your shoulders then roll them back and downwards and forward and up. Make sure that the movement is smooth and controlled.

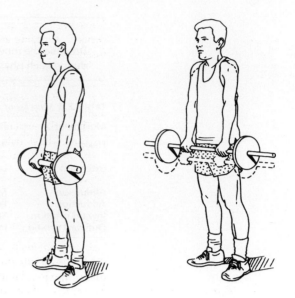

Figure 2.12 *The shoulder shrug*

IN TRAINING

The *military press* or *overhead press* is a free-weight exercise to improve strength in the deltoid, pectoralis major and triceps brachii (Figure 2.13). Use the overhand grip and with your elbows flexed hold the bar at chest level. Raise the bar above your head, making sure that your elbows are fully extended. Keeping the bar under control lower the bar back to the starting position.

Figure 2.13 *Overhead press*

2.3 The spine

The spinal column has to fulfil many functions. It has to be weight bearing, provide stability and support, act as a shock absorber, protect the spinal cord and allow movement. Although there are five regions of the spine (look back to Figure 1.4 to refresh your memory) we will consider the cervical, thoracic and lumbar regions here, as the sacrum and coccyx are fused together.

The spinal column has three types of joint:
a *cartilaginous* joint between the individual vertebrae;
a *gliding* joint between the vertebral arches; and
a *pivot* joint formed by the first two cervical vertebrae (the atlas and axis). The atlas articulates with the occipital bone of the skull and allows flexion and extension, as in nodding. The atlas and axis articulate and allow rotation, as in shaking your head.

To make the column more stable several ligaments hold the vertebrae together.

2.3.1 Movement at the spine

The movements possible at the spine are shown in Figure 2.14. Overall the spine allows flexion, extension, lateral flexion and rotation. The combination of flexion, lateral flexion and hyperextension results in circumduction. Movement is not uniform throughout the three regions and before you read on try to decide which region moves more freely.

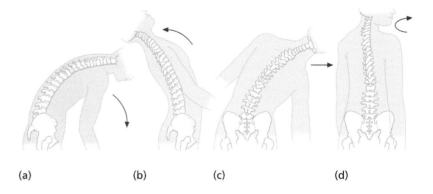

(a)   (b)   (c)   (d)

Figure 2.14 *Movements of the spinal column. (a) Flexion; (b) hyperextension; (c) lateral flexion to the right; (d) rotation to the right*

Definition

HYPEREXTENSION

Continuing to extend a limb beyond 180°.

Flexion

Most flexion occurs in the cervical region, with some occurring in the lumbar region. There is little flexion in the thoracic region.

Extension

This is quite free in the cervical and lumbar regions, but very limited in the thoracic region.

Lateral flexion

This takes place in all regions of the spine but more so in the cervical and lumbar regions.

Rotation

This is good in the cervical and upper thoracic regions, but minimal in the lumbar region.

Table 2.4 outlines the prime movers of the spine. These are illustrated in Figure 2.15

Table 2.4 *Muscles of the spine*

Movement	Prime mover(s)	Origin	Insertion
Flexion	Rectus abdominis	Pelvis	Base of sternum and ribs
	External oblique	Lower ribs	Pelvis
	Internal oblique	Pelvis	Lower ribs
Extension	Sacrospinalis	Pelvis, sacrum, lumbar and lower ribs	Ribs, base of skull and all vertebrae
Lateral flexion	External oblique	Lower ribs	Pelvis
	Internal oblique	Pelvis	Lower ribs
	Sacrospinalis	Pelvis, sacrum, lumbar and lower ribs	Ribs, base of skull and all vertebrae
Rotation to the same side	Internal oblique	Pelvis	Lower ribs
Rotation to the opposite side	External oblique	Lower ribs	Pelvis

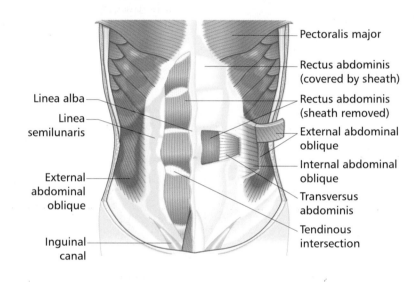

Pectoralis major

Rectus abdominis (covered by sheath)

Linea alba

Linea semilunaris

Rectus abdominis (sheath removed)

External abdominal oblique

Internal abdominal oblique

External abdominal oblique

Transversus abdominis

Tendinous intersection

Inguinal canal

Figure 2.15 *Prime movers of the spine*

IN TRAINING

Free-weight-training exercise to improve the strength of the erector spinae (sacrospinalis): **dead lift** (Figure 2.16). Start in an upright position, holding the bar in your hands. Bend over, making sure that you keep your elbows and knees extended, until the bar touches the floor. Then return to the start position.

Multi-gym exercise to improve the strength of the abdominal muscles: **sit-up** (Figure 2.17). Select the angle of the board depending on your fitness level. Start lying on your back, with your knees flexed and hands behind your head. Sit up so that your elbows make contact with your knees and then lower your body back to the start position.

Figure 2.16 *The dead lift*

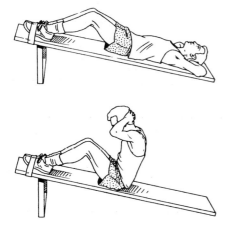

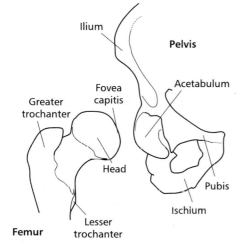

Figure 2.17 *Sit-ups*

ACTIVITY

In warm-up sessions the muscles of the spine are often neglected. Devise a series of exercises that would involve all possible movements of the spine, and therefore would involve all the prime movers of the spine.

2.4 The hip joint

The hip joint is another ball and socket joint, where the head of the femur fits into a deep cavity, called the acetabulum, on the pelvic bone (Figure 2.18). Although it is desirable to have a wide range of movement at this joint, it is perhaps more desirable to have stability. The cavity on the pelvis is much deeper than the cavity on the scapula, so the hip joint is much more stable (but less mobile) than the shoulder joint. The hip joint is also reinforced by extremely strong ligaments, making it much more difficult to dislocate the hip than the shoulder even though they are similar in structure.

Movements possible at the hip include flexion, extension, abduction, adduction, rotation and circumduction – see Figure 2.19.

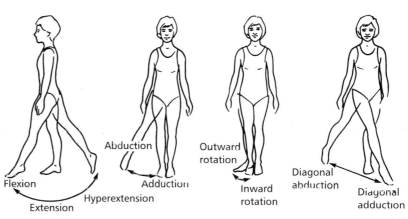

Figure 2.18 *The hip joint*

Figure 2.19 *Movements possible at the hip joint*

ACTIVITY

Using a goniometer or a 360° angle measurer, work with a partner and measure the range of movement possible at both the shoulder and hip joints. Compare your results with those of other people in your group: is there a significant difference between males and females, or between gymnasts and footballers?

The prime movers of the hip joint are outlined in Table 2.5, and these are illustrated in Figure 2.20.

Table 2.5 *Muscles of the hip joint*

Movement	Prime mover(s)	Origin	Insertion
Flexion	Iliopsoas	Pelvis and lumbar vertebrae	Femur
Extension	Gluteus maximus	Pelvis and sacrum	Femur
Abduction	Gluteus maximus	Pelvis	Femur
Adduction	Adductors longus, brevis and magnus	Pelvis	Femur
Inward rotation	Gluteus minimus	Pelvis	Femur
Outward rotation	Gluteus maximus	Pelvis and sacrum	Femur

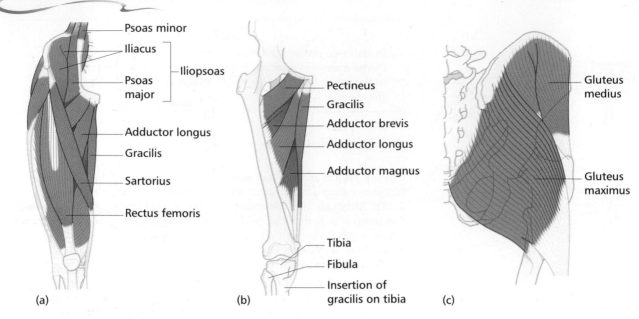

Figure 2.20 *Prime movers of the hip. (a) Anterior view; (b, c) posterior views*

Figure 2.21 *Hip flexors*

IN TRAINING

Multi-gym exercise to strengthen the hip flexors: ***hip flexors*** (Figure 2.21). Support your weight on your forearms and keep your back in contact with the back rest. The start position is with your knees either extended or flexed, but as this exercise can put a lot of strain on the back it is better to have the knees flexed. Flex your hip by raising either one leg at a time or both legs simultaneously and then return to the start position.

ACTIVITY

Analyse the movements of a hurdler and compare the actions at the hip of the lead leg with the actions at the hip of the trail leg.

2.5 The knee joint

The knee joint (shown in detail in Figure 1.6) is referred to as a hinge joint but it is not a true hinge joint because, although it allows both flexion and extension, it also allows slight medial and lateral rotation (to facilitate full extension and locking of the knee – see Figure 2.22).

The condyles of the femur articulate with the proximal end of the tibia. The patella, attached to the quadriceps tendon, helps to provide a better angle of pull, and is a functional part of the knee joint (Figure 2.23). The fibula is not part of the knee joint and therefore the tibia bears all the weight. The weight-bearing function of the knee is considerable and it is important that the ankle, knee and hip are aligned properly to allow the line of stress to pass through the centre of the knee joint.

The strong ligaments surrounding the knee and the large muscle groups of the thigh help to maintain the most mechanically efficient position.

The prime movers of the knee are outlined in Table 2.6, and illustrated in Figure 2.24.

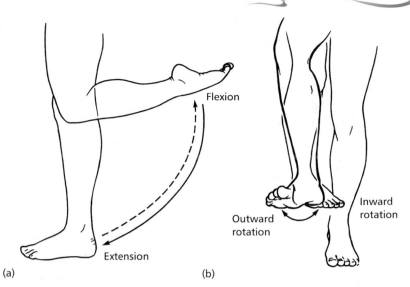

Figure 2.22 *Movements possible at the knee joint. (a) Flexion and extension; (b) inward and outward rotation (in a flexed, no-weight-bearing position)*

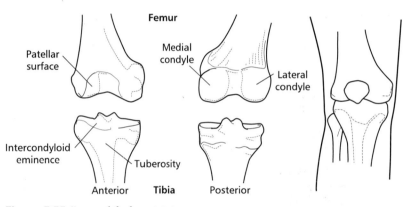

Figure 2.23 *Bones of the knee joint*

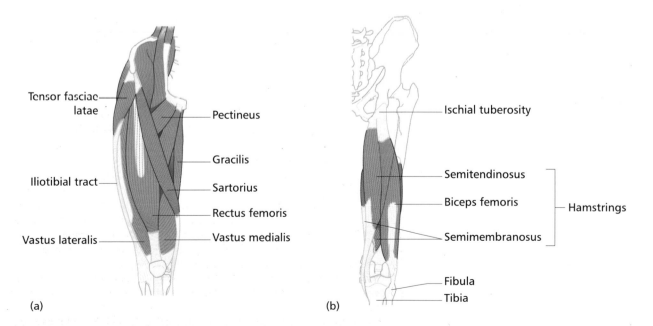

Figure 2.24 *Prime movers of the knee. (a) Anterior view; (b) posterior view*

Table 2.6 *Muscles of the knee joint*

Movement	Prime mover(s)	Origin	Insertion
Flexion	Biceps femoris	Pelvis and femur	Tibia and fibula
	Semimembranosus	Pelvis	Tibia
	Semitendinosus	Pelvis	Tibia
Extension	Rectus femoris	Pelvis	Patella
	Vastus lateralis	Femur	Tibia
	Intermedius lateralis	Femur	Tibia
Inward rotation	Popliteus	Femur	Tibia
Outward rotation	Biceps femoris	Pelvis and femur	Tibia and fibula

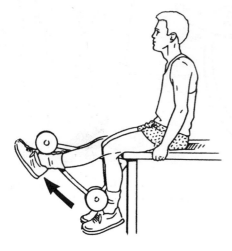

Figure 2.25 *Knee extension*

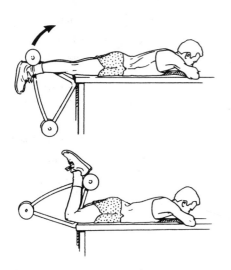

Figure 2.26 *Hamstring curl*

IN TRAINING

Multi-gym weight-training exercise to improve strength in the quadriceps: *knee extension* (Figure 2.25). Sit on the end of the bench with your kenes flexed and your feet placed under the bar. Move your lower leg upwards until the knee is extended, and then lower back to the start position.

The *hip sled* (leg and hip press) also works the hip and knee extensors.

Multi-gym weight-training exercise to improve strength in the hamstrings: *hamstring curl* (Figure 2.26) Lie on your stomach on the bench with your knees extended and with the back of your ankles under the bar. Lift the lower leg upwards until your knees are fully flexed, and then lower back to the start position.

ACTIVITY

Analyse the three hurdling positions shown in Figure 2.27. Describe the movements taking place at the hip and knee joints and name the prime mover responsible for each movement.

Figure 2.27

2.6 The ankle joint

The ankle joint (shown in Figure 2.28) is a hinge joint, the talus articulating with the tibia and fibula. This allows both flexion and extension – at the ankle this is referred to as *dorsiflexion* and *plantarflexion* (Figure 2.29). As in all synovial joints, ligaments provide additional stability. On the medial (inner) side of the ankle there are five ligaments and on the lateral (outer) side of the ankle there are three ligaments.

Figure 2.30 illustrates the prime movers of the ankle outlined in Table 2.7.

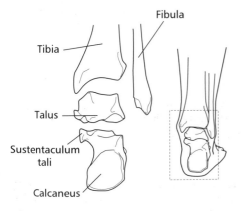

Figure 2.28 *Bones of the ankle and subtalar joints*

Fibula

Tibia

Talus

Sustentaculum tali

Calcaneus

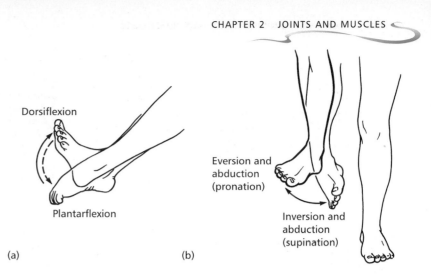

Figure 2.29 *Movements possible at the ankle and tarsal joints. (a) Dorsiflexion and plantarflexion; (b) supination and pronation (tarsal joint only)*

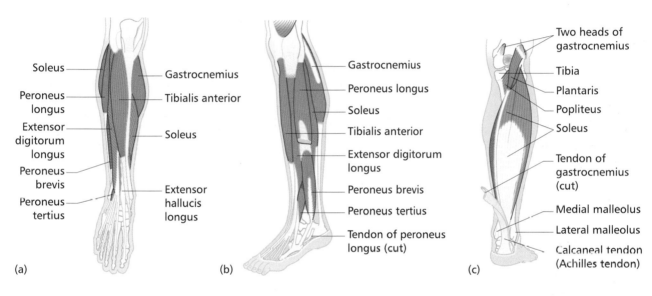

Figure 2.30 *Prime movers of the ankle and foot*

Table 2.7 *Muscles of the ankle joint*

Movement	Prime mover(s)	Origin	Insertion
Dorsiflexion	Tibialis anterior	Tibia	Tarsal bone
Plantarflexion	Soleus	Tibia and fibula	Tarsal bone
	Gastrocnemius	Femur	Tarsal bone

IN TRAINING

Multi-gym or free-weight exercise to strengthen the gastrocnemius and the soleus: *heel raise* (Figure 2.31). The bar is rested across the shoulders and behind the neck, and the back is kept straight. The balls of your feet should be on a raised ledge – the heels should not be *on* the ledge. Move up onto your toes and then lower your heels to the floor. Return to the start position.

ACTIVITY

Identify the major prime movers used in either your game or individual activity, and design a weight training circuit that would improve the strength of each prime mover.

This section of the book is meant only as an introduction to kinesiology. It therefore takes a very simplified view of the joints, and in particular the muscles, used in sporting activities, as a basis for further study. A reading list is suggested at the end of this part of the book.

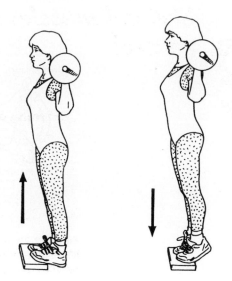

Figure 2.31 *Heel raise*

Key revision points

Movement takes place around a joint and at least one prime mover is responsible for each type of movement that can be produced at a specific joint. You need to know the name and location of the prime mover for each movement possible around the major joints outlined in this chapter.

KEY TERMS

You should now understand the following terms. If you do not, go back through the chapter and find out.

Condyle
Distal
Foramen
Fossa
Hyperextension
Hypertrophy
Insertion
Origin
Prime mover
Process
Proximal
Tuberosity

PROGRESS CHECK

1 The first two cervical vertebrae form a joint. What type of joint is it and what type of movement does it allow?
2 What regions of the spine allow rotation?
3 Apart from rotation, what movements are possible at the spine?
4 List three functions of the spine.
5 If you broke your fibula would you still be able to walk? Justify your answer.
6 Where would you find the glenoid fossa?
7 Which bones articulate at the following joints:
   a the shoulder
   b the elbow
   c the hip
8 Name three hinge joints.
9 Does the proximal or distal end of the tibia articulate with the femur?
10 Which of the following statements are true, and which false?
   a Biceps femoris flexes the elbow.
   b Iliopsoas flexes the hip.
   c Latissimus dorsi originates on the radius.
   d Rectus femoris extends the knee.
   e The posterior deltoid abducts the shoulder.
   f Pectoralis major adducts the shoulder.
   g Tibialis anterior dorsiflexes the ankle.
11 Identify a weight-training exercise that would develop strength in the following muscles:
   a biceps brachii
   b quadriceps
   c pectoralis major.

Skeletal muscle: structure, function and control

Learning objectives

- To know the structure of skeletal muscle.
- To know the characteristics of the three muscle fibre types.
- To understand the role of the nervous system in muscular control.
- To be aware of the different functions of muscle.
- To know the different types of muscular contraction.

Muscles produce the force required for movement within the body. The nervous system coordinates the muscular contractions of the muscles to allow us to carry out everyday tasks and bodily functions. Movement can be caused by the contraction of *skeletal muscle*, resulting in the movement of the body or body part, it can be caused by the contraction of *smooth muscle*, resulting in such things as food being moved through the digestive system, or it can be the contraction of *cardiac muscle*, resulting in the movement of blood through the cardiovascular system. This chapter will mainly concentrate on the structure and function of skeletal muscle because of its relevance to the production of movement of the body.

3.1 Muscle tissue

Muscle tissue has four main characteristics: excitability, contractility, extensibility and elasticity. This means that muscles react to a stimulus, contract and apply force, stretch and return to their original length.

There are three types of muscle tissue found in the body:
Cardiac muscle is a very specialised tissue located in the wall of the heart.
Smooth/visceral muscle is found in tubular structures such as blood vessels.
Skeletal muscle is usually attached to bone, or in some cases to other muscles. Skeletal muscle creates movement around a joint, but can also act to hold a body part in a stable position. Unlike cardiac or smooth muscle skeletal muscle is under voluntary/conscious control – we know what we are going to do and when we are going to do it.

> ### Definition
>
> **TENDON**
>
> *A round cord or band of connective tissue joining muscle to bone.*
>
> **APONEUROSIS**
>
> *A fibrous sheet of connective tissue joining muscle to bone or muscle to muscle.*

3.2 Structure of skeletal muscle

Skeletal muscle is made up of individual *muscle fibres* (muscle cells) grouped together to form bundles (*fasciculi*), which in turn are grouped together to form the muscle itself (Figure 3.1). Each element of the muscle is covered by connective tissue to help provide shape and add strength. The muscle fibre is covered by the *endomysium*, the fasciculi by the *perimysium* and the muscle by the *epimysium*. More connective tissue, in the form of a tendon or an aponeurosis, joins the muscle to bone or another muscle.

3.2.1 Skeletal muscle fibres

> ### Definition
>
> *Anatomy and physiology can be very confusing because of the vast amount of terminology that has to be learnt. It is useful to know that there are common prefixes and suffixes that can help our understanding of this subject.*
>
> *For example: epi means upon or on; peri means around; endo means within; myo means muscle.*

In order to understand how a muscle can shorten we need to take a more detailed look at the structure of each individual muscle fibre. There are lots of terms to remember here, so keep going over the text and referring back to the diagrams – don't expect to understand it first time through.

IN TRAINING

DOMS (the delayed onset of muscle soreness) is often experienced by athletes one or two days after training or competing. This soreness is usually associated with the discomfort experienced after eccentric strength training. Contrary to popular belief, the pain is not caused by a build up of lactic acid, but is associated with actual structural damage to the muscle. Excessive tension on the muscle causes structural damage to the muscle fibre (Z lines pulled apart) and damage to the sarcolemma, affecting the balance of the cell contents. DOMS can be reduced by avoiding eccentric work early in the training programme and by starting at a low intensity and gradually increasing the stress placed on the muscle.

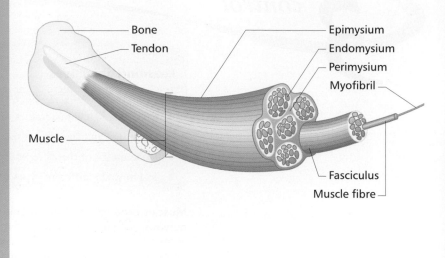

Figure 3.1 *The basic structure of a muscle*

The muscle fibre is surrounded by a membrane called the *sarcolemma* and within the cell are *myofibrils*, long tubular structures running the length of the muscle fibre. Other organelles of the cell such as the mitochondria are found between the myofibrils. The myofibrils are embedded in the cell's *sarcoplasm* (muscle tissue's equivalent to cytoplasm). Surrounding the myofibrils within the sarcoplasm is the *sarcoplasmic reticulum*, a series of channels that store and secrete calcium (this is essential for muscle contraction). Also in the sarcoplasm are *transverse tubules/T vesicles* that transmit the nerve stimulus from the sarcolemma into the cell, causing the sarcoplasmic reticulum to release calcium. Figure 3.2 shows the structure of a skeletal muscle fibre.

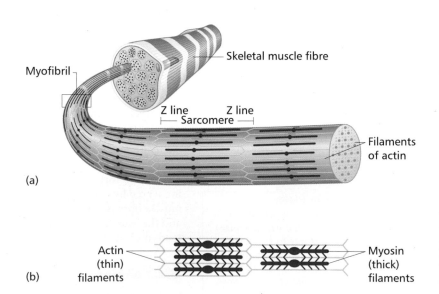

Figure 3.2 *The microsturcture of a muscle. Note the striations in the fibre and the myofibril. These are alternating light and dark bands caused by the geometric arrangement of the filaments of actin and myosin*

3.2.2 Myofibrils

Figure 3.3 shows the structure of a myofibril. The myofibrils are an arrangement of separate units connected end on to form long strands. These units are called *sarcomeres* and are the contractile units of the muscle. Within the sarcomeres are two protein filaments called *myosin* and *actin*, the myosin filament being the thicker of the two filaments. The myosin and actin filaments run adjacent to each other but at rest are not attached. The sarcomere is the area between the two *Z lines*, the *I band* contains only the thin filaments of actin, the *H zone* contains only myosin filaments and the *A band* contains both actin and myosin filaments.

When a muscle contracts the actin and myosin filaments slide over each other, rather like a pair of patio doors. As the actin filaments are attached to the Z lines the result is to pull the two Z lines closer together, shortening the sarcomere. This process will be discussed in more detail in Section 3.4.

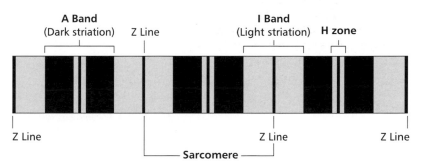

Figure 3.3 *Sarcomeres and myofibril bands*

3.3 Neuromuscular control

All skeletal muscle reacts to an electrical stimulus, which is conducted from the brain to the muscle via nerves. The brain and spinal cord are referred to as the *central nervous system* and nerves that carry information from the central nervous system to skeletal muscle are called *motor* or *efferent* nerves. Motor nerves form part of the *somatic nervous system*, which in turn forms part of the *peripheral nervous system*. Figure 3.4 gives an overall view of the nervous system.

Motor neurones (nerves) are made up of three parts: the *cell body*, the *dendrites* and the *axon*. The structure of a motor neurone is shown in Figure 3.5. Stimuli are received from the central nervous system by the dendrites and passed on via the axon. At the end of the axon is the *axon terminal*, which connects with the motor end plate of the muscle to form the *neuromuscular junction*.

As there are so many muscle fibres it would take a lot of internal 'wiring' to connect them all to a separate motor neurone, so instead one motor neurone branches off and stimulates between 15 and 2000 muscle fibres – this is called a *motor unit*. The number of muscle fibres in a motor unit depends on the type of work the muscle performs and the degree of muscular control required. Once the motor unit is stimulated then all the fibres in it will contract. This is known as the 'all or none' law.

ACTIVITY

Name a muscle that you think might have motor units containing a lot of muscle fibres and one muscle that may only have a few muscle fibres per unit. Give reasons for your answer.

29

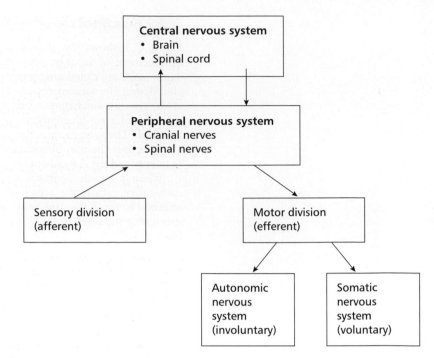

Figure 3.4 *The nervous system*

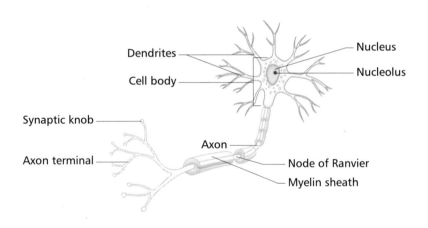

Figure 3.5 *A motor neurone and its structure*

3.3.1 The nerve impulse

Information is relayed from the brain to the muscle via a nerve impulse. A nerve impulse is an electrical current running the length of the nerve, starting at the brain and passing down the spinal column to the relevant cell body. The cell bodies of individual motor neurones are located in various regions of the anterior horn of the spinal column. These collections of cell bodies are referred to as *motor neurone pools*. The cell bodies are positioned in relation to the muscle they stimulate, for example the circumflex nerve, which stimulates the deltoid, is found in the fifth cervical vertebra, whereas the sciatic nerve (stimulates biceps femoris) is found in the fifth lumbar vertebra.

The nerve impulse is passed along the axon of the motor neurone. If you refer back to Figure 3.5 you will notice that the axon is covered in a myelin sheath. This sheath is mostly made up of fat and acts to insulate the nerve; however, it is not continuous. Where there is a gap in the myelin sheath there is a node of Ranvier. The impulse is passed from one node of Ranvier to the next, rather than along the whole length of the axon. This means that the impulse can travel more quickly. This method of nerve impulse propagation is called *saltatory conduction* and the thicker the myelin sheath the faster the nerve impulse that can be conducted.

When the impulse reaches the axon terminal the nerve transmits the information to the muscle by releasing a chemical transmitter, called *acetylcholine*, at the neuromuscular junction.

3.4 The sliding filament theory

The muscle responds to a nerve impulse by shortening. The sliding filament theory was put forward to explain how a muscle alters its length.

When a muscle contracts three things can be observed.
1   The I band shortens (the I band is the area in the sarcomere that contains only actin filaments).
2   The A band remains the same length (the A band is the area in the sarcomere that is equal to the length of the myosin filaments).
3   The H zone disappears (the H zone is the area in the sarcomere that contains only myosin filaments).

These three events can be explained by the myosin pulling the actin across so that the two filaments slide closer together, rather than either of the two filaments physically getting shorter.

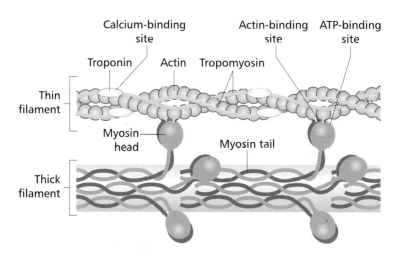

Figure 3.6 *The relationship between troponin, tropomyosin, myosin cross-bridges and calcium*

3.4.1 Cross-bridges

The myosin filaments have small projections called myosin heads, which extend towards the actin but are not actually attached to it. A protein called tropomyosin, bound to the active sites of the actin filament, prevents the myosin heads forming cross-bridges with the actin filament. Another protein bound to actin, troponin, can neutralise the effect of tropomyosin, but only in the presence of calcium (Figure 3.6). When the nerve impulse is transmitted down the transverse tubules it stimulates the release of calcium from the sarcoplasmic reticulum. The troponin is then able to move the tropomyosin from the active site so that cross-bridges form between the myosin and the actin filament to produce actomyosin. Coupling of acto-myosin stimulates the breakdown of ATP, releasing energy. The cross-bridges swivel towards the middle of the sarcomere, pulling the actin over the myosin and making the muscle shorter. More specifically, the myosin head couples with the active site on the actin. The myosin head swivels and collapses and then reforms on another active site further along the actin, rather like the rowing action in a boat, pulling the actin along the myosin towards the middle of the sarcomere. When the stimulus from the nerve stops the calcium ions diffuse back into the sarcoplasmic reticulum and the muscle returns to its normal resting state.

Figure 3.7 summarises the sliding filament theory of muscle contraction.

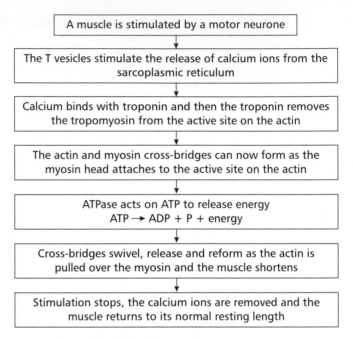

Figure 3.7 *Summary of the sliding filament theory*

ACTIVITY

Try to produce a flow chart showing the chain of events from the start of the nerve impulse in the brain to the point where the muscle releases calcium.

3.5 Types of muscle fibre

Why are some people able to run so much faster than others, while some people may run slower but can keep going for hours? One reason for this is that there are three different types of muscle fibre and any one individual will have a different mix of these fibre types. As the fibres have distinct characteristics this will affect performance in certain sporting activities. The mix of fibres in your physiological make-up is genetically determined.

The three fibre types are referred to as *type I slow oxidative* (SO), *type IIa fast oxidative glycolytic* (FOG) and *type IIb fast glycolytic* (FG). Each muscle contains all three types but not in equal proportions. The fibres are grouped in motor units – you will find only one fibre type in any given motor unit. Usually the proportion of each fibre type found in the muscle of the legs is very similar to the mix of fibre type found in the muscles of the arms.

3.5.1 Type I slow oxidative fibres

These fibres are known as *slow twitch fibres* because they contract more slowly than the type II (*fast twitch*) fibres. The myelin sheath of the motor neurone stimulating the muscle fibre is not as thick as that of the fast twitch unit, and this reduces the amount of insulation, slowing down the nerve impulse. Slow twitch fibres do not produce as much force as fast twitch fibres but can easily cope with prolonged bouts of exercise. They are more suited to aerobic work as they contain more mitochondria and myoglobin and have more blood capillaries than fast twitch fibres. Slow twitch fibres have the enzymes necessary for aerobic respiration and are able to break down fat and carbohydrate to carbon dioxide and water. This is a slower process than releasing energy anaerobically but it does not produce any fatiguing by-products.

3.5.2 Type IIa fast oxidative glycolytic fibres

The motor neurone stimulating the type IIa fibre has a thicker myelin sheath than the slow twitch fibre, so it can contract more quickly and exert more force. The amount of force produced by the type IIa fibre is greater than the type I fibre because there are more muscle fibres in each motor unit. This fibre type can produce energy both aerobically and anaerobically by breaking down carbohydrate to pyruvic acid but it is much more suited to anaerobic respiration, which means it can release energy very quickly. The rapid build up of lactic acid (a by-product of anaerobic respiration) lowers the pH and has a negative affect on enzyme action, causing the muscle fibre to fatigue quickly.

3.5.3 Type IIb fast glycolytic fibres

These muscle fibres are also very quick to contract and can exert a large amount of force. They rely heavily on anaerobic respiration for releasing energy as they have very few mitochondria. This means energy is rapidly released but also that the muscle fibre is quick to fatigue. The motor neurones supplying this fibre type are large and this increases the contractile speed. The neurone also activates a greater number of muscle fibres meaning that each motor unit can produce much more force than slow oxidative motor units.

Table 3.1 summarises the characteristics of the different fibre types.

IN TRAINING

It has been generally assumed that the percentage distribution of fibre type is genetically determined and that training would only enhance the capacity of the existing fibre types. More recent research has suggested that fibre type conversion is possible and that with specific training a fibre may adopt the characteristics of another. Type IIa seems to be the most versatile, adopting either more aerobic or more anaerobic characteristics depending on the type of training undertaken. At the moment the research is far from conclusive but watch this space!

ACTIVITY

Study Table 3.1 and decide which fibre type you think would be predominantly recruited for the following activities: a 5000 m run, a diving save from a goalkeeper, a 400 m hurdle race and a fast break in basketball.

Table 3.1 *Characteristics of muscle fibres*

Characteristics of muscle fibres	Slow oxidative fibres (type I)	Fast oxidative glycolytic fibres (type IIa)	Fast glycolytic fibres (type IIb)
Structural			
Fibres per motor neurone	10–180	300–800	300–800
Motor neurone size	Small	Large	Large
Type of myosin ATPase	Slow	Fast	Fast
Sarcoplasmic reticulum development	Low	High	High
Functional			
Aerobic capacity	High	Moderate	Low
Anaerobic capacity	Low	High	Very high
Contractile speed	Slow	Fast	Fast
Fatigue resistance	High	Moderate	Low
Motor unit strength	Low	High	High

Table amended from *Physiology of Sport and Exercise*, by JH Wilmore and DL Costill

IN TRAINING

Muscular strength usually refers to the maximum force that a muscle can generate in one contraction, referred to as one repetition maximum. Elastic (explosive) strength or power is a combination of strength and speed, and strength endurance is the ability of a muscle to sustain repeated muscular contractions. Every activity demands a different mix of strength components and each athlete should tailor their training to the specific demands of their activity. An athlete can do very little to enhance their speed of movement but they can improve their strength. Appropriate training will lead to muscular adaptations that can lead to as much as 100% improvement in strength.

Table 3.2 shows how elite athletes are genetically well suited to their chosen sporting activity. The proportion of fibre type found in their muscles means that they have the potential to match the physical demands of their activity.

Table 3.2

Athlete	Gender	Muscle	Percentage of slow twitch muscle	Percentage of fast twitch muscle
Sprint runner	Male	Gastrocnemius	24	76
	Female	Gastrocnemius	27	73
Distance runner	Male	Gastrocnemius	79	21
	Female	Gastrocnemius	69	31
Swimmer	Male	Posterior deltoid	67	33
Shot putter	Male	Gastrocnemius	38	62
Non-athlete	Male	Vastus lateralis	47	53

Table amended from *Physiology of Sport and Exercise*, by JH Wilmore and DL Costill

IN TRAINING

One widely known strength training effect is muscle hypertrophy. This hypertrophy is attributed to an increase in size of the myofibrils, with more actin and myosin filaments. More filaments means that more cross-bridges can be formed and therefore more strength can be achieved. Recent research offers another explanation for strength gains as a result of training: *fibre hyperplasia*. Fibre hyperplasia is a term used to describe fibre splitting. It suggests that, instead of every muscle fibre increasing in size, the fibres actually separate first and then increase in size. The research in humans is so far inconclusive but research involving cats has been verified.

3.6 Muscle function

Muscles can only *actively* contract so when, for example, biceps brachii is stimulated, it contracts and causes the elbow to flex. In order to straighten the arm we need another muscle to contract to complete the opposite action. When triceps brachii is stimulated it causes extension of the elbow joint. These two muscles are said to be working as an *antagonistic pair*. The muscle initiating the movement (shortening) is the *prime mover* or *agonist* and the muscle that is relaxing and returning to its original length is the *antagonist*. When you flex your elbow biceps brachii is the prime mover and triceps brachii is the antagonist. When you extend your elbow triceps brachii is acting as the prime mover and biceps brachii as the antagonist. The muscles work as a unit, which requires a high degree of coordination. This coordination is achieved by nervous control. When the prime mover is being stimulated the nerve impulse to the antagonist is inhibited – this is known as *reciprocal innervation*.

> ## IN PRACTICE
>
> Research has shown that the percentage of slow twitch fibres in the leg muscles of distance runners is high (about 80% of fibres) and that sprinters have a higher percentage of type IIa and type IIb fibres (roughly 50% and 30%, respectively). This research is by no means conclusive as so many other factors contribute to good sporting performance, but certainly some people are more physiologically suited to some activities than others.

> ## IN PRACTICE
>
> When you perform an arm curl during a weights session you can feel the tension in the deltoid muscle as it helps to stabilise the shoulder joint.

ACTIVITY

Identify the muscles that cause flexion and extension of the knee joint and decide which muscles act as the prime mover and which muscles act as the antagonist during both movements.

A muscle may also assist the work of a prime mover at a particular joint, making the movement more efficient. This second muscle is sometimes referred to as a *synergist*. The term can also be used to describe a muscle that acts to counteract an unwanted movement of a prime mover, for example a prime mover that acts around two joints where only one movement is required. Either way, synergistic muscle action is difficult to analyse and is beyond the scope of this book.

The third function of a muscle is to act as a *fixator*. A fixator allows the prime mover to work more efficiently, usually by stabilising the bone where the prime mover originates. The fixator muscle increases in tension but does not allow any movement to take place.

ACTIVITY

Identify the muscles that act as prime movers and as antagonists when you perform a squat thrust. Identify any muscles that you think act as fixators.

3.7 Types of muscular contraction

There are four different ways that a muscle can contract, reflecting the function that the muscle is performing.

3.7.1 Isotonic or concentric contraction

This is the most common form of muscular contraction. It occurs when a muscle is acting as a prime mover and shortening under tension, creating movement around a joint.

3.7.2 Eccentric contraction

> ## IN PRACTICE
>
> In any activity where you are lowering the body, body part, or an object, muscles will be working eccentrically.

This is the opposite of concentric action. In eccentric contraction the muscle acting as the antagonist lengthens under tension (usually returning to its normal resting length). A muscle contracting eccentrically is acting as a 'brake' to help control the movement of a body part during *negative work*. Negative work describes a resistance that is greater than the contractile strength of the muscle, for example gravity.

When you perform a press-up, starting from the floor, you push your body upwards by extending your elbow joints. Triceps brachii works as the prime mover and contracts concentrically (it shortens under tension), while biceps brachii acts as the antagonist, relaxing and returning to its normal length. During the downward phase (lowering the body) you are performing negative work and triceps brachii, working as the antagonist, contracts eccentrically (lengthens under tension) and helps to control the movement.

ACTIVITY

Identify the muscles of the spine involved during a sit-up and complete the table.

Phase	Movement	Muscle used	Function	Type of contraction
Upward				
Downward				

3.7.3 Isometric contraction

The muscle increases in tension but there is no change in its length and therefore no movement. This type of contraction occurs when a muscle is acting as a fixator or when it is working against a resistance that it cannot overcome, for example when two equally strong packs collide in a rugby scrum.

A rugby scrum – muscles are working hard but there is no movement (isometric contraction)

3.7.4 Isokinetic contraction

During this type of contraction the muscle shortens and increases in tension while working at a constant speed against a variable resistance. The muscle works throughout the full range of movement but this can be achieved only by using isokinetic weight-training equipment.

3.8 Gradation of contraction

There is just one more term to introduce: *gradation of contraction*. Put simply, this refers to the strength of contraction exerted by the muscle. Gradation of contraction depends on:

1 The number of motor units stimulated (*recruitment*). If only a few of the motor units within the muscle are stimulated obviously the strength

of contraction will be weak. For maximal contraction to occur all motor units must be stimulated.

2   The frequency of the stimuli (*wave summation*). For a motor unit to maintain a contraction it must receive a continuous string of impulses. Usually a frequency of 80–100 stimuli per second is required. Slow twitch muscle fibres have a lower threshold for activation than fast twitch fibres and so tend to be recruited first.

3   Timing of the stimuli to various motor units (*synchronisation* or *spatial summation*). If all the motor units are stimulated at exactly the same time then maximum force can be applied. If, however, a muscle needs to work over a long period, fatigue can be delayed by rotating the number of motor units being stimulated at any one time.

IN TRAINING

Strength gains are not purely a product of hypertrophy or hyperplasia; neural adaptations make a significant contribution in terms of early strength development. Research has concluded that training helps synchronisation of the recruitment of motor units and increases the number of motor units recruited. In order to achieve maximum strength all motor units involved must be recruited at the same time – obviously an increase in the number of units innervated will increase the amount of strength produced.

Key revision points

Skeletal muscle creates movement by actively contracting and shortening. The muscle is stimulated by a motor neurone. This stimulation results in each individual sarcomere decreasing in length as the actin and myosin filaments slide over each other. The nature of the contraction produced is a result of the fibre type recruited, the number of fibres stimulated and the frequency and timing of the stimuli.

KEY TERMS

You should now understand the following terms. If you do not, go back through the chapter and find out.

Actin
Antagonist
Axon
Fasciculi
Fixator
Myofibril
Myosin
Myosin cross-bridges
Prime mover
Sarcomere
Sarcoplasmic reticulum
Transverse tubules

PROGRESS CHECK

1   Name the two types of connective tissue that attach muscle to bone and muscle to muscle.
2   List four common features of muscle tissue.
3   Why do muscles work in antagonistic pairs?
4   What is the difference between a muscle fibre and a myofibril?
5   What is a sarcomere?
6   Name the two protein filaments responsible for muscle contraction.
7   Sketch and label a diagram showing the structure of a sarcomere.
8   Explain the role of the sarcoplasmic reticulum in muscle contraction.
9   What are the three fibre types found in skeletal muscle?
10   Give four characteristics of each fibre type found in skeletal muscle.
11   Give an example in sport to show when each muscle fibre type would be used.
12   What is the relationship between fibre type distribution and athletic performance?
13   What is the role of a fixator?
14   When would a muscle contract eccentrically?
15   What is meant by gradation of contraction?
16   What is the transmitter substance at the neuromuscular junction called?
17   What is meant by reciprocal innervation?
18   What is the 'all or none' law?
19   What effect does the myelin sheath have on propagation of nerve impulses?
20   What is meant by the term DOMS?
21   What adaptations occur after a period of strength training?

4 The mechanics of movement

Learning objectives

- To know the three orders of levers.
- To understand the effect of the length of lever and the angle of pull on the movement produced.
- To be familiar with and able to apply Newton's laws of motion.
- To understand the effects of the centre of gravity on balance and rotation.

An ability to analyse movements is extremely helpful to both performer and coach. The ability to identify the joints and muscles involved in a movement and their roles enables development of a suitable training programme. Even though an athlete may work out regularly using weights he or she may not be exercising the correct muscles, or might be working them concentrically when some eccentric work is also needed. A basic understanding of the principles of movement can help to identify and correct problems with technique. This chapter provides a brief introduction to the mechanics of movement and shows how this knowledge can be applied to help improve sporting performance.

4.1 Levers and their function

When we think of levers crowbars and wheelbarrows spring to mind rather than ulnas and femurs. The skeleton forms a system of levers that allows us to move. A *lever* is a rigid bar that rotates around a fixed point (a *fulcrum*) and is used to apply force (*effort*) against a *resistance*. In the human body the bones are the levers, the joints the fulcrums, the muscles act as the effort and the weight of the body part, plus anything that it holds, is the resistance.

A single body part, such as an arm, can also act as a lever, providing it works as a rigid unit. Figure 4.1 shows the lever system of the forearm.

A lever has two functions:

- to overcome a larger resistance than the effort applied
- to increase the distance a resistance can be moved by using an effort greater than the resistance.

In other words, a lever provides strength or improves the range of movement. The strength and range of movement of a muscle depend on the position of its insertion (where the effort is applied) relative to the joint it moves (the fulcrum). The greater the distance between the joint and the muscle insertion, the more strength can be generated; the closer the insertion is to the joint the better the range of movement will be.

The type of lever formed by the joint and the surrounding musculature affects the movement produced, but two related factors also need to be considered: the angle of pull and the length of the lever. These will be described below.

4.2 Classification of levers

A lever can be defined as first-order, second-order or third-order. The three classes of lever are illustrated in Figure 4.2. This classification is based on

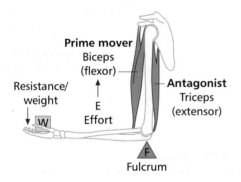

Figure 4.1 *The lever system in the forearm*

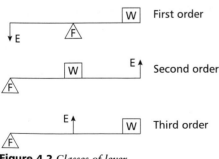

Figure 4.2 *Classes of lever*

the relative positions of the fulcrum (joint), effort (muscle insertion) and resistance (body part or external weight).

4.2.1 First-order levers

A first-order lever is organised like a set of scales, with the fulcrum between the effort and the resistance. The head is a good example of the action of a first-order lever in the body when the head and neck are being flexed and extended, as in nodding (see Figure 4.3).

4.2.2 Second-order levers

When the resistance lies between the fulcrum and the effort a second-order lever is produced. When you raise up on to your toes (plantar flexion of the ankle) you are using a second-order lever. Where the toes are in contact with the floor is the fulcrum, the resistance is at the ankle joint where the body's weight is transferred to the foot and the effort is produced at the position on the ankle where the Achilles tendon inserts onto the calcaneus (see Figure 4.3).

4.2.3 Third-order levers

In a third-order lever the effort lies between the fulcrum and the resistance. This is the most common form of lever in the human body. In terms of applying force this is a very inefficient lever, but it allows speed and range of movement. An example within the body is the forearm during flexion (see Figure 4.3).

4.3 Angle of pull

This refers to the position of the insertion of the muscle relative to the position of the joint, measured in degrees. The angle of pull changes continuously as the limb is moved and these changes have a direct effect on the efficiency of the muscle's pulling force. The most efficient angle of the joint, for most joints, is between 90° and 100°. A decrease or increase in this joint angle results in a reduction in the force that can be applied. Structures within joints can act as pulleys to increase the angle of pull and therefore the efficiency of the muscle. For example, the patella, attached to the quadriceps tendon and the patellar ligament, acts as a pulley at the knee joint. A muscle works most effectively as it nears an angle of pull of 90°–100° (Figure 4.4) and where it is not advantageous the only solution is to increase the strength of the muscle.

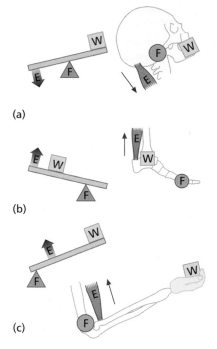

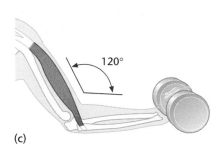

Figure 4.3 *First (a), second (b) and third-order (c) levers in the human body*

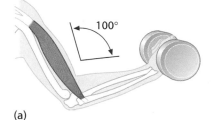

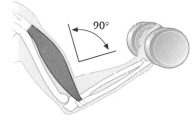

Figure 4.4 *Each joint has an optimal angle of pull (where the force is applied). Biceps brachii has an optimal angle of 100° (a). Decreasing or increasing the joint angle reduces the amount of force produced (b, c)*

IN TRAINING

The muscle's potential to generate force is dependent on several factors:

- how many motor units are recruited
- the type of motor units recruited e.g. fast glycolytic fibres
- the length of the muscle when recruited
- the angle of pull
- the speed of contraction.

If an athlete wants to produce maximum force in a biceps curl the optimal angle of the joint needs to be 100°. Biceps brachii should be stretched 20% before the contraction and the speed of the concentric muscle contraction should be quite slow.

A combination of levers is used in batting

Different golf shots use different joint actions and lever lengths

ACTIVITY

Choose three hand-held weights that you consider to be light, manageable and heavy. Using Figure 4.4 as a guide try to lift each weight using a different angle of pull. Discuss your results with others in your group.

4.4 Length of lever

The longer the lever the greater the change in momentum, and consequently change in velocity, that can be imparted on an object. This can be an advantage in sports in which you hit objects, for example a squash ball can be hit harder when the elbow joint is fully extended rather than flexed; the use of a racket lengthens the lever arm further. To generate a much greater overall force the effects of several levers can be combined, as in batting in cricket where the trunk, upper arm, forearm and bat all work together as one unit.

ACTIVITY

Contrast the length of club and stroke technique used in golf at the tee shot with that used in the approach to a short putt. Your answer should make reference to the choice of joint, joint action and lever arm length.

4.5 Force

Forces can be used to make something move, stop something that is already moving or to prevent something from moving altogether. A force might be internal or external. In the human body, muscles act as internal forces, whereas the effect of gravity is external.

The effect that a force has on a body is influenced by three factors.
- *The size, or magnitude, of the force* is measured in newtons (N) or in pounds. The magnitude of the force refers to the weight of a body, which is a product of its mass and the external force of gravity. A muscle's force is determined by the size and number of the fibres contained within any one muscle.
- *The direction of the force.* If a single force is applied to a body through its centre of gravity the body will move in the same direction as the force.
- *The position of application of the force.* Applying the force slightly off-centre will produce angular motion – e.g. hitting a snooker ball off-centre will create spin (see Figure 4.5).

In sport, a performer must gauge how much force to apply in any given situation. If you are performing a closed skill, for example a free throw in basketball, you are at an advantage in that the amount of force, the

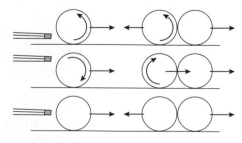

Figure 4.5 *Applying a force slightly off-centre will cause spin*

direction and the application of the force required are the same each time you perform the throw. Therefore practice can lead to a habitual response. In open skills the situation will vary each time and errors can be made – a footballer not connecting with the ball correctly will cause it to veer off to one side, a hockey player with an enthusiastic backswing applying too much force to the ball will over-hit a pass. Errors can be rectified very quickly if a coach is able to point out the basic mechanical weaknesses in a technique.

4.6 Newton's laws of motion

Motion (movement) will occur only if a force is applied; most movement of the body is caused by the internal force created by the muscles. Motion occurs either in a straight line (linear motion) or around an axis (angular motion). Isaac Newton formulated three laws of motion, which can be applied to sports performance.

4.6.1 Newton's first law of motion (law of inertia)

This law states that:

'a body continues in its state of rest or of uniform motion unless a force acts on it.'

A body or an object is said to be in a state of inertia and a force must be applied to it before any change in velocity can occur. The greater the mass of a body the more force is required to overcome its inertia. You can throw a 5 kg weight further than you can throw a 10 kg weight using the same force.

4.6.2 Newton's second law of motion (law of acceleration)

This law states that:

'the acceleration of an object is directly proportional to the force causing it and is inversely proportional to the mass of the object.'

The speed that a person can throw a tennis ball is proportional to the amount of force applied by the muscles. It also depends on the inertia of the ball.

In sport we often refer to the *momentum* of an object. This is a product of velocity × mass. A defender in hockey usually uses a heavier hockey stick than a forward because it allows him or her to transfer more momentum to the ball, and consequently to hit it further. Momentum can also be built up and transferred from one body part to the rest of the body, resulting in more force – for example, swinging the arms backwards and forwards before take-off transfers momentum to the rest of the body for a vertical jump.

IN PRACTICE

Skilled sports performance depends on selecting joint, joint action and lever arm length correctly. To do this requires a combination of good physical preparation and good coaching.

Definition
MASS
Mass is the quantity of matter a body contains.

IN PRACTICE

A medicine ball has greater inertia than a tennis ball and therefore more force is needed to alter its speed.

IN TRAINING

The momentum of a moving body needs to be gradually reduced in order to avoid injury. When landing – e.g. during the performance of a long jump – the momentum of the body can be reduced by flexion of the ankle, knee and hip joints. this allows the eccentric action of the extensor muscles of these joints to act as a brake to help control the movement.

ACTIVITY
Perform a vertical jump with no preparatory arm swings. Note the height of the jump and then perform the jump using your arms to build up momentum. Compare the two heights.

4.6.3 Newton's third law of motion (law of reaction)

This law states:

'for every action there is an equal and opposite reaction.'

When an object exerts a force on a second object, the second object exerts an opposite and equal force back on the first. The most common sporting illustration of this law is when an athlete pushes back against the starting blocks at the beginning of a sprint race (exerting a force on the blocks), causing the opposite and equal reaction of being pushed forward out of the blocks. When in mid air it is possible to move one body part to cause another body part to react in opposition; for example in trampolining a half twist is achieved by swinging the arms to the right, rotating the rest of the body to the left.

4.7 Centre of gravity

The centre of gravity, sometimes referred to as the point of balance, is the point in an object where all its mass is concentrated. The centre of gravity of a performer is continually changing as the body position changes. As the centre of gravity is the point of balance of the body we commonly refer to performers being 'balanced' or 'off-balance'. A gymnast plainly displays good balance when performing a handstand (Figure 4.6), but balance is a less obvious requirement of most sports and we often refer to a games player as being well balanced. Therefore balance has both a static and dynamic dimension.

Figure 4.6

In a uniformly shaped body (such as a snooker ball) the centre of gravity lies at its geometric centre, but the centre of gravity of a non-uniform body is determined by the distribution of its mass and density. When standing upright the centre of gravity of most people is in the hip region, the centre of gravity for males being slightly higher than that for females. As the body's position changes so does its centre of gravity – in some cases it may even be located outside the body (see Figure 4.7).

4.7.1 Maintaining balance

To be in a state of balance the centre of gravity must be over the area of support. For example when you stand upright the area of support is your feet. The larger the area of support, the easier it is to maintain balance. Lowering or raising the centre of gravity will affect stability. By raising your arms above your head you are redistributing your mass, and your centre of gravity will move higher up your body. When you learn to do a headstand you are encouraged to form a triangle with your head and hands because

---

CENTRE OF GRAVITY

The centre of gravity of an object is the point at which the mass of the object is concentrated. It is sometimes referred to as an object's point of balance.

Figure 4.7 *In some body positions the centre of gravity is located outside the body*

Figure 4.8

this position forms a large area of support, making it easier to balance. In the early stages of learning to do a headstand, you bring your legs into a tuck position and hold the balance, rather than extend your legs vertically. It is relatively easy to balance in the tuck position as the centre of gravity is lowered, increasing stability. However, as the legs are extended the centre of gravity is raised, making the position less stable and consequently more difficult to perform.

ACTIVITY

Rank the gymnastic positions shown in Figure 4.8 in order of stability and difficulty.

4.7.2 Use of the off-balance position

Occasionally a performer needs to become off-balance. A sprinter in the 'set' position holds their body so that the line of gravity is as close as possible to the edge of the area of support. On the 'go' signal the sprinter moves out of the area of support, causing loss of balance – literally he or she falls forwards. A new area of support now needs to be established.

As mentioned previously, when a force is applied in line with the centre of gravity this will result in linear motion, but when a force is applied out of line with the centre of gravity or the centre of rotation, then rotation will occur. This is known as eccentric force and is used extensively in gymnastics and trampolining. For example, in order to produce a forward somersault in a gymnastic routine the centre of gravity must be displaced in front of the feet.

4.8 Movement analysis

To complete an anatomical and mechanical analysis (kinesiological analysis) of a motor skill you need to be able to:
1 describe the skill and its purpose
2 evaluate the performance in terms of
   a the joint action, muscle action and function and
   b the mechanical principles applied
3 correct faults where applicable.

The following analysis of the take off phase of the standing broad jump is an example of the detail required at 'A' level and shows how the basic principles of mechanics can be applied to sporting performance.

4.8.1 Description

The standing broad jump is a forward jump to cover as much horizontal distance as possible. The performer takes off from both feet and lands on both feet.

4.8.2 Joint and muscle action during take-off

Definition
KINESIOLOGY
The study of the science of movement.

Joint	Joint type	Movement observed	Main muscle involved	Muscle function	Type of contraction
Elbow	Hinge	Extension	Triceps brachii	Prime mover/agonist	Concentric
Shoulder	Ball and socket	Flexion	Anterior deltoid	Prime mover/agonist	Concentric
Shoulder girdle	Gliding	Upward rotation	Trapezius part 2	Prime mover/agonist	Concentric
		Abduction	Serratus anterior	Prime mover/agonist	Concentric
Spine	Gliding and cartilaginous	Extension	Sacrospinalis	Prime mover/agonist	Concentric
Hip	Ball and socket	Extension	Gluteus maximus	Prime mover/agonist	Concentric
Knee	Hinge	Extension	Quadriceps group	Prime mover/agonist	Concentric
Ankle	Hinge	Plantarflexion	Soleus	Prime mover/agonist	Concentric

4.8.3 Mechanical principles involved in take-off

- The application of force at take-off needs to be in line with the centre of gravity. If it isn't the performer will jump slightly to one side and the horizontal distance jumped will be less.
- The speed of projection depends on the total impulse (force × time) generated at take-off. This is the combination of the forces exerted at the ankle, knee, hip and shoulder joints. How strongly and quickly the musculature around these joints can contract affects the distance jumped. Careful timing of joint action is essential, because if joints act out of sequence the overall force that can be applied will be reduced. For the standing broad jump the hips should initiate the movement, followed by the shoulders, knees and ankles.
- The amount of force that can be generated at take-off will increase the upward reaction force (Newton's third law).
- Preparatory swings of the arms and flexion of the knees will help to overcome inertia (Newton's first law).
- Momentum can be increased by swinging the arms forwards and upwards at take-off (Newton's second law), adding to the overall force of the movement.

ACTIVITY

Observe the action of an athlete who performs a good standing broad jump, and compare it with a person who performs a relatively poor standing broad jump. List any major differences between the two techniques.

Key revision points

A basic kinesiological analysis needs to include three features: a description of the skill; an evaluation of both the joints and muscles used and the mechanical principles applied; and identification and correction of any faults.

KEY TERMS

You should now understand the following terms. If you do not, go back through the chapter and find out.

Angle of pull
Angular motion
Application of force
Centre of gravity
Fulcrum
Inertia
Kinesiology
Length of lever
Lever
Linear motion
Magnitude of force
Momentum
Reaction force
Resistance

PROGRESS CHECK

1 Give examples within the body of a first-order lever, a second-order lever and a third-order lever.
2 What two functions can a lever perform?
3 Which type of lever allows the greatest range of movement?
4 Give an example from sport, other than batting in cricket, where the effects of several levers are combined to form one unit in order to generate more force.
5 What is the optimum angle of pull for a muscle?
6 What is the advantage of lengthening the lever arm?
7 How can a person raise their centre of gravity?
8 What benefit is gained by lowering your centre of gravity?
9 Give an example from sport where a performer might deliberately lower their centre of gravity.
10 Why is it easier to perform a headstand than a handstand?
11 What benefit does an athlete gain by performing preparatory swings with the arm before throwing the discus?
12 What happens if a force is applied in line with an object's centre of gravity?
13 Describe the three factors that determine the effect that a force will have on a body.
14 Complete a kinesiological analysis of a vertical jump.
15 What stance should you adopt when catching a medicine ball? Give reasons for your answer.
16 Why should you bend the joints of the legs when landing from a jump?

5 *Structure and function of the heart*

Learning objectives

- To know the structure of the heart and be able to describe the flow of blood through the heart.
- To describe and explain the structure and function of the conduction system of the heart.
- To understand the relationship between stroke volume, heart rate and cardiac output.
- To be able to describe how the body regulates heart rate.
- To be aware of the effects of exercise on heart rate.

The heart forms part of the *cardiovascular system*; 'cardio' meaning heart and 'vascular' meaning the circulatory networks of the blood vessels. The cardiovascular system ensures constant distribution of blood to the body to help meet the demands of the body's tissues. During exercise the role of the cardiovascular system is extremely significant, in that the efficiency of this system helps to determine the amount of oxygen that can reach the cells. Figure 5.1 gives an overview of the cardiovascular system.

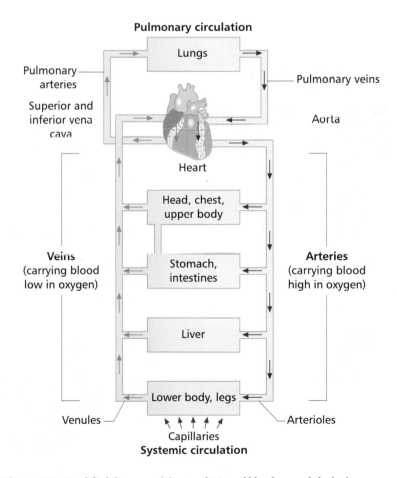

Figure 5.1 *Simplified diagram of the circulation of blood around the body*

The heart acts as two completely separate pumps. The pump at the right side of the heart sends deoxygenated blood to the lungs and the pump on the left side sends oxygenated blood round to the body's tissues. The two sides of the heart are separated by a muscular wall called the *septum*.

5.1 Structure of the heart

The heart is about the size of a closed fist and lies within the *pericardial cavity*. The pericardial cavity forms part of the *mediastinum*, which in turn forms part of the thoracic cavity.

The heart is made up of four chambers. The two top chambers are the *atria* and the bottom two are the *ventricles*.

The close proximity of the heart to the lungs means that the right side of the heart has very little work to do compared with the left side. This is reflected in the size and shape of the heart, as the left side is larger.

The heart is surrounded by a closed sac known as the *pericardium* and is bathed in pericardial fluid within the pericardium. As the heart is continually moving this fluid is needed to reduce the effects of friction on the heart wall (Figure 5.2).

The heart wall is made up of three different layers.
- The *endocardium* is the inner layer. It is made up of very smooth tissue to allow uninterrupted flow of blood through the heart.
- The *myocardium*, the middle layer, is made up of cardiac muscle tissue. Cardiac muscle cells are similar to skeletal muscle cells in that they appear striated but they are highly specialised. Cardiac muscle cells have a single nucleus and contain many mitochondria (Figure 5.3). This is because the heart needs a good supply of ATP to avoid fatigue. Unlike skeletal muscle cells, cardiac muscle cells are connected by intercalated discs. This connection allows a coordinated wave of contraction to occur when the heart muscle is stimulated.
- The *epicardium* is the outer layer of the heart and also forms the inner layer of the pericardium. The outer layer of the pericardium is made of strong fibrous tissue that helps to protect the heart.

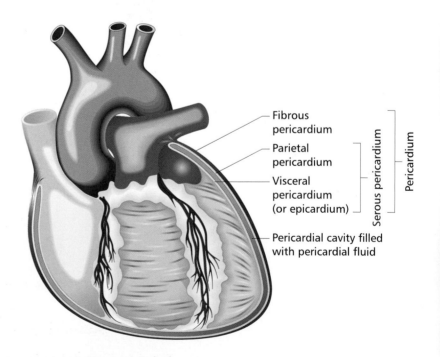

Fibrous pericardium

Parietal pericardium

Visceral pericardium (or epicardium)

Serous pericardium

Pericardium

Pericardial cavity filled with pericardial fluid

Figure 5.2 *The pericardium*

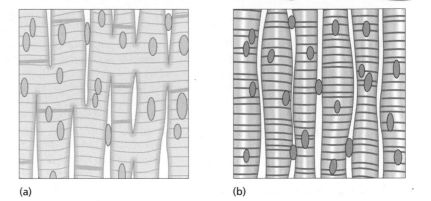

(a)   (b)

Figure 5.3 *Cardiac (a) and skeletal (b) muscle. Note how both muscle types are striated but only cardiac fibres are connected by intercalated discs*

5.1.1 Arteries and veins of the heart

Numerous blood vessels are attached to the heart, bringing blood to the heart or taking blood away from it (Figure 5.4). Blood enters the heart via the atria and exits through the ventricles. To be more precise, the inferior and superior *venae cavae* bring deoxygenated blood from the body to the right atrium and the four *pulmonary veins* bring oxygenated blood from the lungs to the left atrium. The *pulmonary artery* carries deoxygenated blood from the right ventricle to the lungs and the *aorta* carries oxygenated blood from the left ventricle round the body.

The heart itself requires a good blood supply and the *coronary artery*, which branches from the aorta, distributes oxygenated blood to the heart through an extensive network of capillaries. Deoxygenated blood is returned by the veins of the heart directly into the right atrium through the *coronary sinus*.

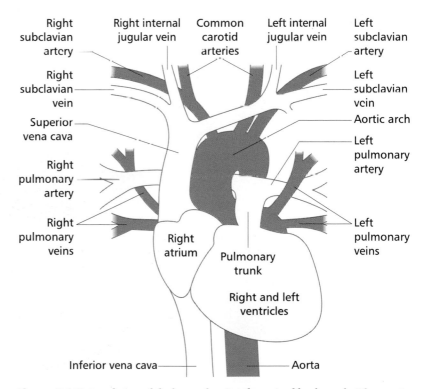

Figure 5.4 *External view of the heart, showing the major blood vessels. The vessels shown in red carry oxygenated blood*

5.1.2 Chambers of the heart

As already mentioned, the two pump units of the heart are separated by a muscular wall called the septum; each unit has an atrium and a ventricle. The atria have relatively thin muscular walls as the force needed to push the blood from them into the ventricles is quite small. The ventricles, as the mechanism pumping blood around the whole body, need much thicker, stronger, muscular walls. The wall of the right ventricle usually exerts a pressure of 25 mmHg, whereas the left ventricle exerts a pressure of about 120 mmHg at rest. This difference is because the right ventricle pumps blood only as far as the lungs, but the left ventricle needs to provide sufficient force to carry the blood round the systemic circulation.

IN TRAINING

After a period of endurance training changes to the left ventricle are the most significant. The interior volume of the left ventricle increases, allowing greater filling during diastole. The left ventricular wall also increases in size and the hypertrophy of the ventricular wall increases the contractility of the muscle. This means that more blood can be ejected out of the heart during systole.

5.1.3 Valves of the heart

The flow of blood through the heart needs to be regulated so that blood flows only in one direction. Four valves inside the heart help to control blood flow through the heart – two separating the atria from the ventricles and two in the arteries carrying blood from the ventricles. The valves operate only one way and when properly closed prevent backflow of blood. The valves between the atria and the ventricles are known collectively as the *atrioventricular valves*, the valve between the right atrium and right ventricle is the *tricuspid valve* and that between the left atrium and the left ventricle is the *bicuspid valve*. Blood flowing from the atria into the ventricles pushes the valves open, and they are closed by thin connective tissues called the *chordae tendineae*. The chordae tendineae are attached to the papillary muscles, which are attached to the walls of the ventricle. When the ventricles contract so do the papillary muscles, causing the chordae tendineae to tighten and preventing the valves from collapsing inwards.

IN PRACTICE

The closing of the valves creates the heart sounds that can be heard through a stethoscope. The sound is described as 'lubb dupp', the 'lubb' corresponding to the closing of the atrioventricular valves and the 'dupp' to the closing of the semilunar valves. A muffled sound usually indicates a malfunction of one of the valves and is known as a heart murmur.

The *aortic valve* is found between the left ventricle and the aorta and the *pulmonary valve* lies between the right ventricle and the pulmonary artery. These two valves are known collectively as the *semilunar valves*. Ejection of blood from the ventricles forces the semilunar valves open. When the ventricles relax backflow of blood is prevented because the semilunar valves, like the atrioventricular valves, operate in only one direction. The internal structure of the heart is shown in Figure 5.5.

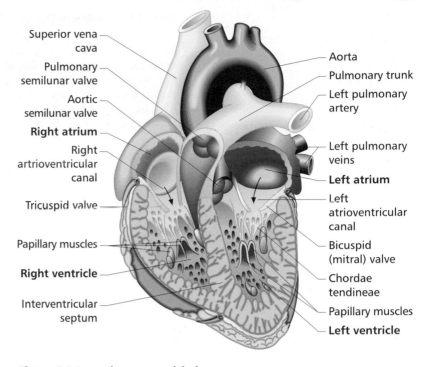

Figure 5.5 *Internal structures of the heart*

ACTIVITY

Borrow a stethoscope and, working in pairs, try to pick up your partner's heart sounds.

5.2 Flow of blood through the heart and the cardiac cycle

Deoxygenated blood flows into and fills the right atrium from the superior and inferior venae cavae. At the same time, oxygenated blood enters the left atrium via the pulmonary veins from the lungs. As the left and right ventricles relax blood flows from both atria into them. The atria contract to ensure that the ventricles are completely filled. The ventricles then contract (when this happens the atrioventricular valves close to prevent backflow of blood into the atria) and the blood is pushed out of the ventricles through the semilunar valves into the pulmonary artery and the aorta. When the ventricles relax the semilunar valves close, preventing backflow. The atria relax and begin to fill again – and the whole process repeats itself.

This process is known as the *cardiac cycle* and at rest takes approximately 0.8 seconds. The cardiac cycle involves rhythmic contraction and relaxation of the heart muscle. The contraction phase is known as *systole* and takes about 0.3 seconds at rest, the relaxation phase (*diastole*) lasts roughly 0.5 seconds at rest. Note: these terms are usually used to refer to the contraction and relaxation phases of the *ventricles*.

ACTIVITY

On a copy of Figure 5.5 illustrate the flow of blood through the heart. Then complete the flow chart below to show the journey of a red blood cell through the heart and the circulatory systems.

Inferior and superior venae cavae → ? → Tricuspid valve → ? → ? → Pulmonary artery → Lungs → ? → Left atrium → ? → Left ventricle → ? → ? → Tissues of the body → Inferior and superior venae cavae.

5.3 The conduction system of the heart

The muscular pump of the heart needs a stimulus to make it contract. Unlike skeletal muscle, cardiac muscle needs to create a wave-like contraction so that the atria contract before the ventricles. An added problem is that blood needs to flow downwards from the atria into the ventricles and then flow upwards out of the aorta and pulmonary artery. The system of nerves that stimulate the heart is shown in Figure 5.6.

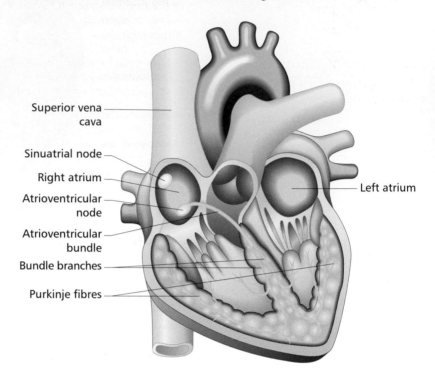

Superior vena cava

Sinuatrial node

Right atrium

Atrioventricular node

Atrioventricular bundle

Bundle branches

Purkinje fibres

Left atrium

Figure 5.6 *The conduction system of the heart*

The wave of contraction is initiated by a specialised node in the wall of the right atrium, called the *sinuatrial* (SA) *node* or *pacemaker*. The SA node is controlled by the autonomic nervous system (the regulation of the heart rate will be discussed later in this chapter). The nerve impulse spreads through the cardiac muscle tissue, rather like a 'Mexican wave', as all the muscle fibres are interconnected. This causes the atria to contract, pushing the blood into the ventricles. The impulse then spreads over the ventricles from the bottom (the *apex*) of the heart. This is achieved by a second node sited in the atrioventricular septum, known as the *atrioventricular* (AV) *node*. The impulse travels across the atria to the AV node and then down a specialised bundle of nerve tissue in the septum (the *bundle of His*). The nerve impulse is carried to the apex of the heart, where the specialised fibres branch out into smaller bundles, called *purkinje fibres*. The purkinje fibres extend upwards and across the ventricles, causing the ventricles to contract and push blood up and out of the heart. Once the ventricles have completely relaxed another impulse is initiated at the SA node and the cycle is repeated.

5.3.1 The electrocardiogram

The electrical activity of the heart's conduction system can be measured by electrodes on the skin of the chest. The information is recorded in the form of a trace such as that illustrated in Figure 5.7. This trace is an *electrocardiogram* (also known as an ECG). The P wave occurs just before the atria

IN PRACTICE

The ECG is used extensively in the medical profession as a diagnostic tool as it will highlight any problems with the conduction system of the heart.

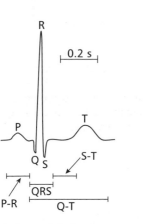

Figure 5.7 *Some of the important events on an ECG*

contract, the QRS complex occurs just before the ventricles contract and the T wave corresponds to repolarisation of the ventricles before ventricular diastole.

5.4 Cardiac output

The amount of blood the heart manages to pump out per minute is known as the cardiac output ($\dot{Q}$). The cardiac output is a product of the stroke volume × heart rate.

$$\dot{Q} = SV \times HR$$

Heart rate (HR) is the number of times the heart actually beats per minute and the stroke volume (SV) is the amount of blood ejected by the ventricle each contraction.

IN PRACTICE

For the amount of energy required at rest 5 litres of blood ensures an adequate supply of oxygen. If the body becomes more active and uses up more energy more oxygen will be required and the cardiac output will increase.

The stroke volume is measured in millilitres of blood per beat, the heart rate is measured in beats per minute, giving a cardiac output in litres per minute.

Definition

STROKE VOLUME

The volume of blood pumped out of the heart by each ventricle during one contraction.

Stroke volume can vary due to the following factors:
1 How much blood is being returned to the heart (venous return).
2 How far the ventricles will stretch (remember that muscle tissue is elastic).
3 The contractility of the ventricles.
4 The pressure in the main arteries leading from the heart.

The first two factors relate to how much blood can enter the ventricles and the last two relate to how much blood can be ejected from the heart during systole.

IN TRAINING

One of the adaptations of aerobic training is that the heart muscle increases in size (hypertrophies). This means that the ventricles can stretch further and contract with a greater force, resulting in an increase in both resting and maximal stroke volumes.

At rest the average stroke volume is 70 ml and the average heart rate 72 beats per minute, giving an overall cardiac output of just over 5 litres/min.

Definition

HYPERTROPHY

Growth of a tissue through an increase in cell size.

The resting heart rate of an individual can vary greatly, although we all need to produce roughly the same cardiac output at rest. If a person does a lot of aerobic work (prolonged periods of submaximal exercise) their resting pulse rate often drops to 60 beats per minute or lower. In order to produce the same cardiac output, the stroke volume must increase to compensate for this drop in heart rate.

$$\dot{Q} \qquad = SV \times HR$$
$$5 \text{ litres} \quad = ? \times 60 \text{ (beats/min)}$$

END-DIASTOLIC VOLUME

The amount of blood in the ventricles just before the contraction phase (systole).

The heart subjected to regular exercise does not have to beat as often as an untrained heart to produce the same cardiac output at rest. This also means that the maximum cardiac output will increase.

A person's maximum heart rate is estimated as being 220 minus their age, so the maximum heart rate of an athlete aged 20 will be about 200 beats per minute. The maximum SV reached during exercise increases with training – from 110–120 ml per beat for an untrained male to 150–170 ml per beat for an endurance athlete.

IN TRAINING

Cardiac output at rest remains relatively unchanged as a result of endurance training. In contrast, the maximum cardiac output after endurance training shows a marked increase. This increase is due to the big increase in maximum stroke volume.

ACTIVITY

Take the resting pulse of all the members of your group and discuss the amount and type of exercise that each person participates in. Is there a relationship between exercise and resting heart rate?

By rearranging the equation,

$$SV = \dot{Q}/HR$$
$$= 5 \text{ litres}/60$$
$$83 \text{ ml}$$

IN TRAINING

Some elite endurance athletes have resting heart rates as low as 40 beats per minute.

In this case the stroke volume increases to about 120 ml per beat. In effect, it is the increase in SV that produces the drop in heart rate, and not the other way round, because as the heart gets used to regular exercise it gets bigger (undergoes hypertrophy) and stronger.

This means that the *end-diastolic volume* of the ventricle increases (it can physically hold more blood). The ventricle is thus capable of stronger contraction and able to push more blood out per beat.

In exceptional cases the maximum cardiac output can be as high as 40 litres.

	$HR \times SV$		$\dot{Q}$
Untrained:	200×120 ml	=	24 litres
Trained:	200×170 ml	=	34 litres

This is an obvious benefit because more oxygen can be delivered to the working tissues, enabling them to work harder or for longer periods of time.

The 5 litres of blood pumped out of the heart at rest is circulated around the body. The proportion of the cardiac output distributed to the particular organs is shown in Table 5.1.

Table 5.1 *Distribution of blood to the vital organs*

Organ	Percentage of cardiac output at rest
Bone	5
Brain	15
Heart	5
Kidney	25
Liver	25
Muscle	15
Skin	5
Other	5

When the body starts to exercise the distribution of the blood changes. The main change is that about 85% is now channelled to the working muscles. The flow of blood to the brain is maintained, but flow to the kidneys, liver and the gastrointestinal tract decreases. The effect of exercise on the cardiac output and blood distribution may be seen in Figure 5.8.

5.5 Control of heart rate

Unlike other muscle tissue the heart initiates its own action potentials automatically at the SA node, resulting in rhythmic contractions of the heart. The contractions are at regular intervals but their timing is altered by two extrinsic factors and one intrinsic factor:

1   neural control ⎫
2   hormonal control ⎬ extrinsic factors
3   intrinsic control. ⎭

Of these, neural control is the most important control mechanism.

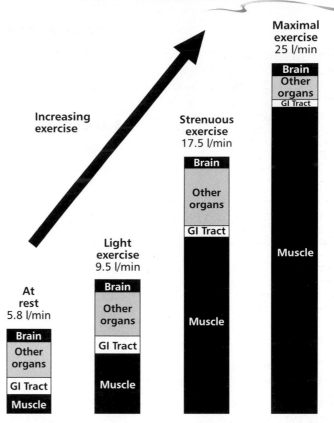

Figure 5.8 *Effect of exercise on cardiac output and blood distribution*

5.5.1 Neural control

Figure 5.6 shows that the SA node (the pacemaker) in the wall of the right atrium is controlled by the autonomic nervous system. Two nerves stimulate this node: the *sympathetic cardiac accelerator nerve*, which speeds up the heart rate, and the *parasympathetic vagus nerve*, which slows it down.

Overall control of the two nerves is coordinated by the cardiac control centre in the medulla of the brain. The cardiac control centre is stimulated by:

- muscle receptors in the muscles and joints that stimulate the cardiac control centre at the onset of exercise
- chemoreceptors in the muscle that respond to changes in muscle chemistry, such as a rise in lactic acid
- emotional excitement
- changes in blood pressure, detected by the baroreceptors in the aorta and carotid arteries – for example a decrease in blood pressure will result in an increase in heart rate and stroke volume
- chemoreceptors in the aorta and carotid arteries that respond to changes in oxygen, carbon dioxide and pH levels.

5.5.2 Hormonal control

Adrenaline is secreted from the adrenal glands into the bloodstream and stimulates the SA node, causing an increase in heart rate. Adrenaline also increases the strength of contraction produced by the myocardium (heart muscle).

5.5.3 Intrinsic control

When any muscle gets warmer the conduction of nerve impulses seems to speed up – this is also true of heart muscle. The heart rate of a warm heart increases, and a drop in temperature reduces the heart rate. In addition, during exercise the amount of blood returning to the heart (the venous return) is increased, stretching the cardiac muscle more than usual. This stimulates the SA node and increases the heart rate – it also increases the force of contraction. The relationship between an increase in venous return and an increase in stroke volume is known as *Starling's law*.

5.6 Exercise and control of heart rate

The heart rate needs to increase during exercise in order to increase the supply of oxygen to working muscle and to remove waste products such as carbon dioxide and lactic acid. Before you even begin to exercise your heart rate will start to increase. This *anticipatory rise* in heart rate is caused by the release of adrenaline acting directly on the heart and the impact of emotional excitement on the medulla. As soon as exercise begins the heart rate rises rapidly, mainly due to a nerve reflex response, initiated by the muscle receptors, that stimulates the cardiac control centre. Also within the muscles chemoreceptors respond to the increase in lactic acid and other chemical changes by sending messages to the cardiac control centre to increase heart rate. As the body continues to exercise the heart muscle begins to get warmer and venous return increases, increasing the heart rate further – see above.

When you stop exercising the muscle receptors stop stimulating the cardiac control centre and the heart rate begins to fall quite rapidly. The activity of the chemoreceptors also reduces and this, combined with the reduced levels of adrenaline, the drop in venous return and the drop in body temperature returns the heart rate to normal within a matter of minutes. Figure 5.9 shows a typical response of the heart to submaximal exercise.

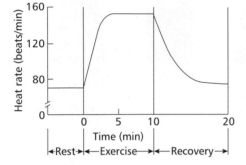

Figure 5.9 *Change in heart rate with submaximal exercise*

ACTIVITY

For this activity work in groups of four. You will need access to a cycle ergometer and a pulse meter. Monitor the heart rate of each subject for two minutes before the activity, for a six minute work period and for a six minute recovery period.

- *Subject one* works at 60 r.p.m., with a constant resistance of 1.0 kg.
- *Subject two* works at 60 r.p.m., with an initial load of 0.5 kg for two minutes, increasing to 1.0 kg after two minutes, and finishing with 1.5 kg for the third two minutes.
- *Subject three* works at 60 r.p.m. with 1–1.5 kg, increasing to 2–3.0 kg after two minutes, and to 3–4.5 kg for the last two minutes. The choice of load will depend on the age, sex, weight and fitness of the subject. If at any time a subject becomes uncomfortable or distressed they should stop the exercise immediately.

Plot the results on to a graph and compare the heart rate response of each subject

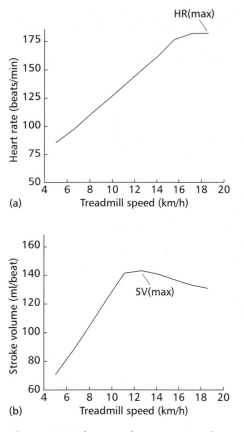

Figure 5.10 *Changes in heart rate (a) and stroke volume (b) during a progressive treadmill workout*

Definition

MAXIMUM HEART RATE

Maximum heart rate is the highest heart rate you can achieve when you work to exhaustion.

The heart rate increases in direct proportion to the increase in exercise intensity. Initially the cardiac output increases as a result of both the heart rate and the stroke volume increasing, but maximum stroke volume is achieved during submaximal work and any increase in cardiac output during maximal exercise is due solely to an increase in heart rate. Figure 5.10 shows the changes in both heart rate and stroke volume during a progressive treadmill workout. As the workload is increased the heart rate steadily rises until a maximum heart rate is reached. By this stage most of the energy is being produced anaerobically and you will soon have to stop exercising because of fatigue. If you are working submaximally your heart rate will usually rise until you reach a point where the oxygen delivered to the working muscles is sufficient to release enough energy aerobically to cope with the demands of the exercise. The heart rate will then reach a plateau. This is known as 'steady state' exercise.

IN TRAINING

As you get older your maximum heart rate drops by 5–7 beats per minute per decade and the maximal stroke volume decreases due to an increase in peripheral resistance. This in turn contributes to a reduction in aerobic capacity. If athletes continue to do regular aerobic exercise the decrease in VO_2(max) is significantly smaller than that found in non-athletes.

ACTIVITY

Using a pulse meter to monitor your heart rate response go for a jog/run and adjust your pace so that you run at a steady state, first with a heart rate of 100 beats per minute then increasing to 120 and finally to 140. Compare your heart rate response and pace with those of other members of your group. Suggest reasons for any differences.

When you stop exercising your heart rate does not immediately return to normal but takes a number of minutes to recover. This is because you need to maintain an elevated rate of aerobic respiration in order to replenish some of the energy stores you have used during the exercise and also to remove some of the waste products that have accumulated, for example lactic acid and carbon dioxide (Figure 5.9).

IN TRAINING

It has usually been accepted that resistance training will not lead to cardio-vascular adaptations. Some recent research, however, has shown some reduction in resting heart rate, and this has been attributed to an increase in heart wall size leading to an increase in contractility. The adaptations noted were not as significant as those achieved through endurance training and not all studies have substantiated the change in heart rate.

Key revision points

The heart acts as two separate pumps, distributing oxygenated blood round the body. Deoxygenated blood returns to the heart via the pulmonary and systemic circulatory systems. The heart responds to the demands made on the body when exercising by increasing the heart rate and stroke volume to increase the overall cardiac output.

KEY TERMS

You should now understand the following terms. If you do not, go back through the chapter and find out.

Atrioventricular node
Atrioventricular valve
Bundle of His
Cardiac control centre
Cardiac output
Diastole
End-diastolic volume
Mediastinum
Myocardium
Pericardial cavity
Purkinje fibres
Semilunar valve
Sinuatrial node
Stroke volume
Systole

PROGRESS CHECK

1 Name the two circulatory systems.
2 Where would you find the pericardium?
3 What centre controls the heart rate and where is it situated in the body?
4 List three factors that directly affect the control centre resulting in a change of heart rate.
5 Which nerve speeds up the heart rate?
6 Describe how the wave of excitation spreads through the heart muscle.
7 Briefly describe the cardiac cycle.
8 Define 'cardiac output' and give typical values at rest and during exercise.
9 How does stroke volume affect cardiac output?
10 Where would you find the papillary muscle? What is its function?
11 List four ways in which cardiac muscle fibre differs from skeletal muscle fibre.
12 What is Starling's law?
13 What name is given to the heart's own blood supply?
14 List three factors that affect cardiac output during the first few moments of exercise and explain what they do.
15 Briefly describe the pathway of a drop of blood through the heart.
16 When someone has trained aerobically for over three months their resting pulse drops. Why?
17 Explain 'steady state' in terms of heart rate and workload.
18 How and when during the cardiac cycle are the heart sounds generated?

6 *Structure and function of the vascular system*

Learning objectives

- To know the major constituents of blood.
- To describe the structure and function of the arteries, capillaries and veins.
- To know the major arteries and veins of the body.
- To describe the factors influencing venous return.
- To understand the role of the vasomotor centre in regulation of blood flow and blood pressure.
- To know how blood pressure changes within the circulatory system and what changes occur during exercise.

As mentioned in Chapter 5, the blood vessels are part of the cardiovascular system and form the body's transport network. It is essential that a sports performer has an efficient vascular system, to deliver oxygen and food supplies to the working muscles and to remove waste products such as carbon dioxide. The blood carries all the vital ingredients needed for the muscles to work and the blood vessels form a *closed circulatory network*, allowing distribution of blood to all cells. During exercise there is a dramatic change in the distribution of blood round the body, with up to 85% of the total cardiac output going to the working muscles. The heart, vascular and respiratory systems all work together to coordinate the increase in oxygen delivery needed to cope with the increased demand for energy.

6.1 Constituents of the blood

The blood accounts for about 8% of the total body weight. It is made up of *blood cells* and *platelets* floating in the *plasma*.

The plasma makes up 55% of the blood volume. Approximately 90% of the plasma is water. The following substances may be found dissolved in the plasma:
- salts
- glucose and fatty acids
- blood proteins
- waste products
- enzymes
- hormones
- gases such as oxygen and carbon dioxide.

The blood cells make up 45% of total blood volume. There are three types of blood cell.

Red blood cells (*erythrocytes*) are biconcave discs just small enough to pass through a capillary. These form about 95% of the blood cells. The main function of the erythrocytes is to transport oxygen and carbon dioxide round the body. They contain a protein called *haemoglobin*, which has a high affinity for carbon monoxide, carbon dioxide and oxygen. Haemoglobin is capable of carrying up to four oxygen molecules and transports 97% of the oxygen in the body (the remaining 3% is dissolved in the plasma). Oxygen is carried bound to the haemoglobin as *oxyhaemoglobin*. Haemoglobin can also carry carbon dioxide (about 20% of the carbon dioxide is transported this way, the rest is dissolved in the plasma). However, haemoglobin has highest affinity for carbon monoxide and will pick up carbon monoxide in preference to either carbon dioxide or oxygen.

White blood cells (*leukocytes*). There are five different types of leukocytes but they basically all have the same function of protecting the body from bacteria, viruses and foreign bodies.

Platelets are small cell fragments that help clot the blood.

IN PRACTICE

Cigarette smoke contains carbon monoxide so the oxygen-carrying capacity of a smoker's blood is reduced as the haemoglobin binds to the carbon monoxide. This impairs any performance in aerobic activities until the effects of the cigarette have worn off.

IN TRAINING

One of the advantages of aerobic training is that the total blood volume increases (by about 8% at rest) because the amount of plasma and the number of erythrocytes increase. More erythrocytes means that more oxygen can be transported to the cells, allowing more aerobic respiration to take place. Another way of increasing the number of erythrocytes is to train at high altitude – at higher altitudes the blood oxygen levels decrease, stimulating the body to produce more erythrocytes. A banned performance enhancing drug called RhEPO (recombinant erythropoietin) artificially stimulates the increased production of red blood cells and is reportedly used by some endurance athletes. An untrained male would expect to have a hematocrit of about 43%, but the use of RhEPO can result in a hematocrit of nearer 50%.

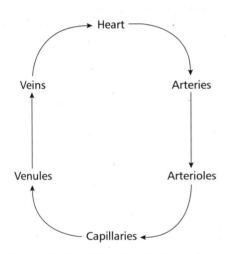

Figure 6.1 *Blood flow through the vessels*

6.2 Blood vessels

Five different types of blood vessels in the body link together to form the vascular system. The flow of blood around the body through these vessels is shown in Figure 6.1.

All blood vessels are basically a muscular wall surrounding a central *lumen*, or opening. The walls of the blood vessels (except those of the capillaries) comprise three layers (Figure 6.2).

The *tunica interna* forms the inner lining of the vessel. It contains endothelial cells and collagen.

The *tunica media*, or middle layer, is made up of smooth muscle and elastin fibres. The smooth muscle is stimulated by the sympathetic nerves of the autonomic nervous system.

The *tunica externa* is made up mostly of collagen with some elastin fibres. Vessel walls need to be elastic as they have to cope with large fluctuations in blood volume.

6.2.1 Arteries and arterioles

Arteries always carry blood away from the heart. The major arteries in the human body are shown in Figure 6.3. As the arteries branch and become smaller they eventually form arterioles. The largest arteries contain a lot of elastin fibres but as they get smaller the muscular middle layer becomes much thicker and the amount of elastin relatively less. The smaller, more muscular, arteries and the arterioles are used to control blood flow. Contraction of the smooth muscle in these vessels narrows their lumen and restricts blood flow.

6.2.2 Capillaries

The arterioles transport blood to the capillaries. The capillaries are the smallest of the blood vessels and their walls are extremely thin – the exchange of gases and nutrients takes place here. Although capillaries are small they form an extensive network, particularly around skeletal muscle, the heart and the lungs. Capillaries are so small that blood cells can only

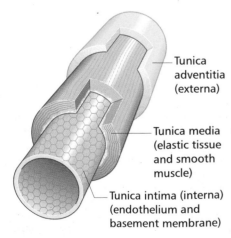

Tunica adventitia (externa)

Tunica media (elastic tissue and smooth muscle)

Tunica intima (interna) (endothelium and basement membrane)

Figure 6.2 *Structure of an elastic artery*

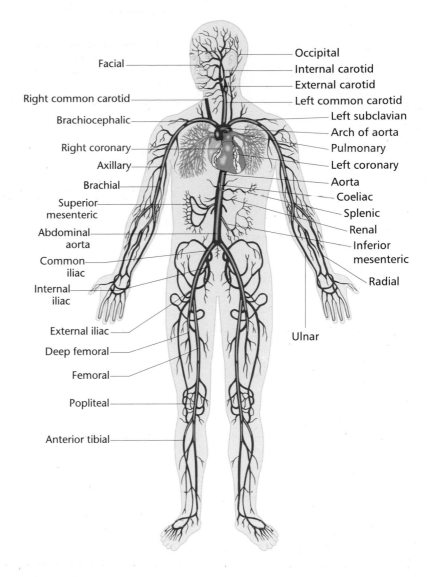

Figure 6.3 *The major arteries of the human body*

pass through one at a time. The flow of blood through the capillaries is controlled by *precapillary sphincters*. Capillaries ensure a constant supply of blood to all cells.

IN TRAINING

After a period of endurance training there is an increase in capillarisation in the muscle tissue and greater opening of existing capillaries. Both these factors contribute to an increase in blood flow to the working muscle.

6.2.3 Veins and venules

Blood flows from the capillaries into the venules. As the venules decrease in number they increase in size and eventually form veins. Veins have much thinner inner and middle layers than arteries and the larger veins contain valves. These valves allow blood to flow only in one direction – back towards the heart – helping venous return.

6.3 Venous return

As we mentioned in Chapter 5, stroke volume depends on venous return. If the venous return decreases the stroke volume will decrease, reducing the overall cardiac output.

A vein has quite a large lumen and offers very little resistance to blood flow. However, by the time blood enters the veins the blood pressure is low, and active mechanisms are needed to ensure venous return.

6.3.1 The skeletal muscle pump

This is the most important mechanism of venous return. When we are moving our muscles contract, squeezing and compressing nearby veins. This action pushes the blood back towards the heart as the valves in the vein allow the blood to flow in one way only, therefore preventing back-flow and pooling (Figure 6.4).

6.3.2 The respiratory pump

When air is breathed into and out of the lungs the volume of the thoracic cavity changes, creating changes in pressure. During inspiration the pressure around the abdomen increases as the diaphragm lowers to increase the volume of the thoracic cavity. This pressure squeezes the blood in the abdominal veins back towards the heart. During expiration the pressure in the thoracic region increases as the diaphragm and ribs move back to reduce the volume of the thoracic cavity. This has a similar squeezing effect on the veins.

6.3.3 The valves

Obviously the valves play an important role in venous return as they direct the flow of blood towards the heart.

Another consideration in venous return is the effect of gravity, especially on veins returning blood from areas above the heart.

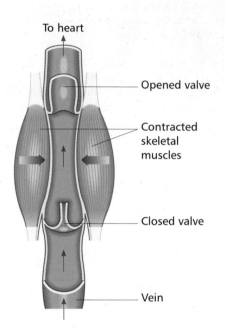

Figure 6.4 *The skeletal muscle pump helping blood return to the heart*

To heart

Opened valve

Contracted skeletal muscles

Closed valve

Vein

6.4 Vasomotor control

The flow and pressure of blood are controlled by the *vasomotor centre* in the medulla of the brain. The vasomotor centre is stimulated by baroreceptors (which respond to changes in blood pressure) in the aorta and carotid arteries. Most blood vessels are stimulated by sympathetic nerves of the autonomic nervous system. Blood vessels receive a continual low-frequency impulse that is known as the *vasomotor tone*. The vasomotor centre controls this stimulus by

- increasing vasomotor tone, causing *vasoconstriction* (the lumen decreases in size, resulting in an increase in blood pressure and a reduction in blood flow) or
- decreasing vasomotor tone, causing *vasodilatation* (the lumen increases in size, resulting in a decrease in blood pressure and an increase in blood flow).

As the arterioles have a relatively thick tunica media they are responsible for most of the changes in blood flow and blood pressure.

There is also a degree of local control of blood distribution, called *autoregulation*. The arterioles in some areas of the body react directly to chemical changes in the tissues that they supply. An increased demand by the tissue for oxygen seems to trigger the response of vasodilatation of the surrounding arterioles, so do increases in carbon dioxide and lactic acid.

Definition

VASOCONSTRICTION

A decrease in the size of the lumen of a blood vessel as the smooth muscle in the tunica media contracts.

VASODILATATION

An increase in the size of the lumen of a blood vessel as the smooth muscle in the tunica media relaxes.

AUTOREGULATION

The local control of blood distribution within the tissues of the body in response to chemical changes.

6.4.1 The vascular shunt

During exercise the demand for oxygen from the skeletal muscles increases dramatically and more oxygenated blood must flow to them to meet this demand. The increase in stroke volume and heart rate helps to increase the overall cardiac output and therefore increases oxygen supply, but this in itself is not enough. Blood must also be redistributed so that more goes to the skeletal muscles and less to the other organs. This is known as the *vascular shunt*.

The vascular shunt involves two mechanisms:

1   Vasodilatation of the arterioles supplying the skeletal muscles increases the blood flow to them. Vasoconstriction of the arterioles supplying the other organs, such as the kidneys and liver, reduces blood flow to these organs.
2   Opening of the precapillary sphincters in the capillary network supplying skeletal muscle and closure of the precapillary sphincters in the capillary networks supplying the other organs increases the flow of blood to the skeletal muscles and decreases flow to the other organs.

The net effect is to substantially increase the percentage of the cardiac output going to the muscles. Figure 6.5 shows the flow of blood through a muscle at rest and during exercise.

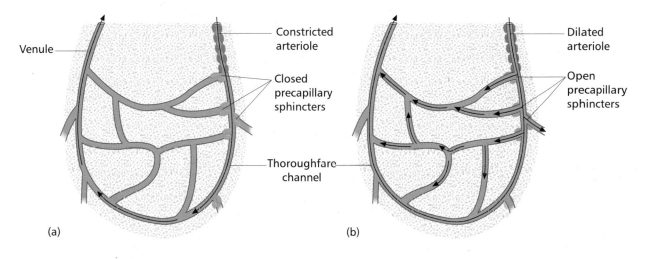

Figure 6.5 *Local blood flow through skeletal muscle (a) at rest; (b) in exercising muscle*

The vascular shunt mechanism doesn't only increase blood flow to working muscles. If you are involved in strenuous or prolonged periods of exercise you begin to get hot. The body's response to overheating is to dilate the blood vessels near the skin, increasing the blood flow to the skin and allowing heat to escape from the body.

6.5 Blood flow and blood pressure

Blood, like any other fluid, flows from areas of high pressure to areas of low pressure. The area of high pressure in the human body is the pressure created by contraction of the ventricles, which forces blood out of the heart into the aorta. Blood pressure is equal to blood flow × resistance. The resistance is caused by the friction between the blood and the vessel walls.

During ventricular contraction (systole) the blood pressure at rest for a young adult is about 120 mmHg and during relaxation of the ventricles (diastole) the pressure drops to about 80 mmHg. A doctor normally uses a

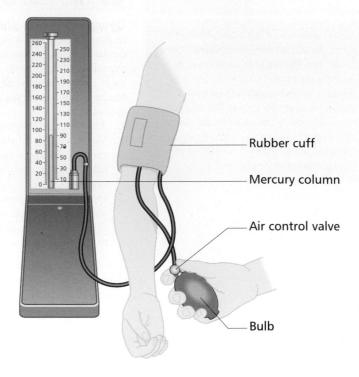

Figure 6.6 *Measurement of blood pressure using a sphygmomanometer*

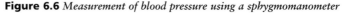

> ### Definition
>
> ## BLOOD PRESSURE
>
> *Blood pressure = blood flow ×*
> *resistance.*

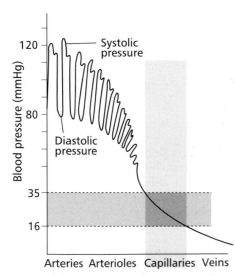

Figure 6.7 *Pressure changes in the systemic circulation*

> ### Definition
>
> ## HYPERTENSION
>
> *The clinical name given to high blood pressure.*

sphygmomanometer, shown in Figure 6.6, to monitor blood pressure. Blood pressure is usually quoted as systolic pressure 'over' diastolic pressure, for example '120 over 80'. Various factors (such as exercise, stress and pregnancy) can affect blood pressure and the blood pressure varies between individuals. However, a resting blood pressure of 150 over 90 mmHg or above would cause concern because it is indicative of *hypertension*.

ACTIVITY

Using a sphygmomanometer and a stethoscope attempt to measure your partner's blood pressure. Place the stethoscope over the brachial artery and inflate the cuff to about 180 mmHg, then slowly decrease the pressure. As soon as you detect the sound of the blood through the stethoscope make a note of the pressure: this is the systolic blood pressure. Continue to decrease the pressure until the sound of the blood disappears: this will be the diastolic blood pressure.

As blood flows into the large arteries the blood pressure is quite high because they have relatively large lumens and offer little resistance to blood flow. When the blood reaches the arterioles the pressure drops suddenly because the resistance exerted by the vessel walls is much greater. By the time blood reaches the capillaries the blood pressure has dropped to about 35 mmHg. As the blood passes back through the venous system the pressure continues to fall, and is almost zero by the time the blood enters the right atrium (Figure 6.7).

The arterioles play a significant role in regulating blood pressure. By changing the diameter of the lumen (vasoconstriction or vasodilatation) of these vessels their resistance can be increased or decreased, which in turn increases or decreases the blood pressure.

6.6 Velocity of blood flow

At rest a blood cell will take about a minute to be carried round the circulatory system, but the velocity of the blood flow is far from constant as it passes from one vessel to another. The velocity of the blood flow is affected by the cross-sectional area of the blood vessels. Blood travels through the aorta at about 40 cm/s. As it travels through the smaller arteries and arterioles the *total* cross-sectional area of these vessels increases (although the cross-sectional area of the individual vessels decreases, there are a great many of them), decreasing the velocity of the blood. The greatest *total* cross-sectional area is found in the capillary network as there are so many capillaries. In the capillary network the velocity of the blood is only 0.1 cm/s, slow enough to allow exchange of gases, nutrients and waste products. The blood then flows back through the venules and veins, where the *total* cross-sectional area decreases, resulting in an increase in velocity. The relationship between blood velocity and total cross-sectional area of the vessels is shown graphically in Figure 6.8.

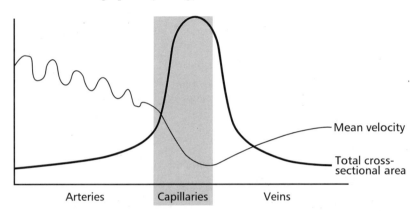

Figure 6.8 *The velocity of blood flow varies inversely with the total cross-sectional area of the vessel*

6.7 Effects of exercise on blood pressure and blood volume

Overall, systolic blood pressure tends to increase during exercise. The vasodilation that occurs in skeletal muscle causes a drop in blood pressure because of the decrease in resistance, but the cardiac output increases significantly and negates the effect of this vasodilatation. During exercise there is very little change in diastolic pressure; diastolic pressure only increases during isometric work because of the resistance to blood flow caused by the contracting muscle.

After a period of exercise it is much better to perform a series of cooling-down activities rather than to stop abruptly. If you do stop suddenly the blood 'pools' in the working muscles. During heavy exercise about 85% of the cardiac output is distributed to working muscle. The skeletal pump mechanism is largely responsible for maintaining venous return and if you stop exercising the venous return will instantly drop. The knock-on effect is that less blood enters the heart during diastole which means that the stroke volume will be much lower. The overall result is a drastic reduction in blood pressure causing the performer to fell dizzy and sick (Figure 6.9).

Blood volume can change during exercise, but whether it increases or decreases depends on the type of activity and the fitness of the individual. A decrease in volume is mostly caused by plasma moving out of the capillaries into the surrounding tissues. This increases the viscosity of the blood and therefore increases the peripheral resistance. After a period of aerobic training the usual trend identified is an increase in blood volume. This is of great benefit to athletes as it increases their capacity to carry oxygen.

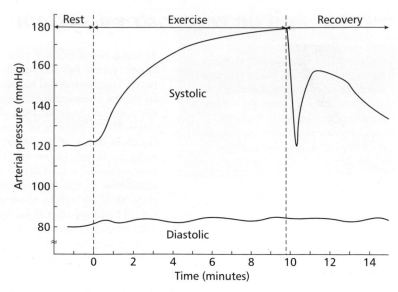
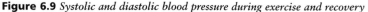

Figure 6.9 *Systolic and diastolic blood pressure during exercise and recovery*

Key revision points

Five different types of vessel form the closed circulatory network that distributes blood to all cells. The distribution of the cardiac output is controlled by the vasomotor centre and is achieved by altering the flow and pressure of the blood. This is mainly brought about by opening or closing of the arterioles and the pre-capillary sphincters.

KEY TERMS

You should now understand the following terms. If you do not, go back through the chapter and find out.

Arteries
Blood pressure
Capillaries
Erythrocyte
Haemoglobin
Leukocyte
Lumen
Precapillary sphincter
Sphygmomanometer
Vascular shunt
Vasoconstriction
Vasodilatation
Vasomotor tone
Veins
Venous return

PROGRESS CHECK

1 Describe how the different blood vessels link together to form the circulatory system.
2 Give one structural and one functional difference between arteries, capillaries and veins.
3 What is the role of haemoglobin?
4 What is meant by venous return?
5 Describe three factors that help maintain venous return.
6 What is the average resting blood pressure?
7 What happens to blood pressure when you start to exercise?
8 If you have a heart problem, or suffer from high blood pressure, what kind of exercise should you avoid?
9 Why does the velocity of the blood change as it passes through the vascular system?
10 Which vessel is mostly responsible for the control of blood flow and blood pressure?
11 What is a precapillary sphincter and what function does it perform?
12 How does smoking affect your capacity for transporting oxygen?
13 Why is it important to perform cooling-down exercises?
14 Name the three layers that form the wall of a blood vessel.
15 What is one of the effects of training at high altitude?
16 What is the function of the vasomotor centre?
17 During exercise a lot more blood is distributed to the working muscles. How is this achieved?
18 What effect does endurance training have on blood flow?

7 The respiratory system

Learning objectives

- To be able to describe the structures of the respiratory system.
- To understand the process of respiration.
- To describe and explain the mechanics of breathing, both at rest and during exercise.
- To know the definitions and capacities of the pulmonary volumes and how these volumes change with exercise.
- To be able to describe the control mechanisms of the respiratory system.

In order to stay alive, we need a continuous supply of oxygen. We use oxygen to break down food to release energy and produce carbon dioxide as a waste product. We need to continually take in oxygen from the air and expel carbon dioxide into the air. This process of exchanging gases is known as *respiration*. Respiration involves all of the following processes:

- Physically moving air into and out of the lungs – *ventilation*.
- The gaseous exchange that takes place between the lungs and the blood – *external respiration*.
- Transport of gases in the blood.
- Exchange of gases between the blood and the cells, known as *internal respiration*.

'Respiration' is also used to describe the process occurring in the mitochondria that uses oxygen to produce ATP. This is usually referred to as *cellular respiration*. The respiratory system has to coordinate with the actions of the cardiovascular system to ensure adequate delivery of oxygen to the cells and efficient removal of carbon dioxide from the cells.

7.1 Structure of the respiratory system

Air taken from the atmosphere passes through several structures before it reaches the bloodstream (Figure 7.1).

7.1.1 The nose

Air enters the body through the nose where hairs and mucus help to filter it. The air is also warmed.

7.1.2 The pharynx

Air passes from the nose into the pharynx. Both food and air pass through the pharynx. At the bottom of the pharynx air is directed through the larynx and food is directed down the oesophagus.

7.1.3 The larynx

The larynx is commonly known as the 'voice box' as it contains the vocal folds. A flap of elastic cartilage, the *epiglottis*, covers the opening of the larynx during swallowing and prevents food entering the lungs.

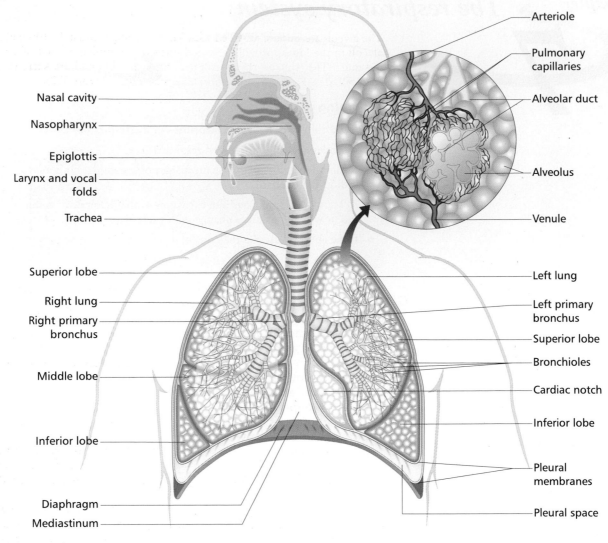

Figure 7.1 *The respiratory system*

7.1.4 The trachea

The trachea (or windpipe) is just over 10 cm long and is kept open and protected by C-shaped pieces of cartilage. The trachea is lined with mucus-secreting and ciliated cells. These cells remove foreign particles by pushing them back up towards the larynx. The trachea divides at the bottom to form the left and right bronchi.

7.1.5 Bronchi

The right bronchus enters the right lung and the left bronchus enters the left lung. From there the bronchi subdivide to form smaller branches called bronchioles. This structure is known as the *bronchial tree* and carries the air deep into the lungs.

7.1.6 Bronchioles

The walls of the bronchioles, unlike those of the bronchi, are not reinforced with cartilage but do contain smooth muscle. When this smooth muscle contracts, as occurs during an asthma attack, it can create severe breathing difficulties. The bronchioles continue to divide, forming *terminal bronchioles* that supply each lobule of the lungs. The terminal bronchioles merge into *respiratory bronchioles* that lead to alveolar air sacs, which contain the alveoli.

ACTIVITY

Rearrange the following terms so that they correctly show the passage of air from the atmosphere to the alveoli:

alveolar air sacs, trachea, nose, terminal bronchiole, epiglottis, pharynx, respiratory bronchiole, larynx, bronchi, alveoli

7.1.7 Alveoli

The alveoli are minute air-filled sacs. There are approximately 300 million alveoli in the lungs, providing a total surface area similar to that of a tennis court. The walls of the alveoli are extremely thin and are surrounded by capillaries. External respiration takes place here (Figure 7.2).

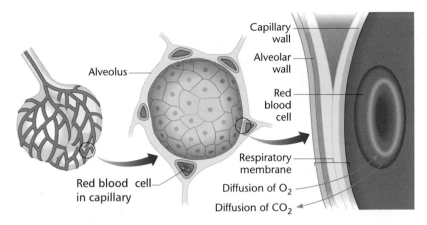

Figure 7.2 *The exchange of oxygen and carbon dioxide between an alveolus and capillary bed*

7.2 The lungs

The two lungs lie in the thoracic cavity. The right lung has three lobes and the left lung two. The heart nestles between the lungs in the mediastinum. Each lobe of a lung is further divided into lobules, which are completely separate units.

Each lung is surrounded by a serous membrane, known as the *pleural membrane*, which lines the *pleural cavity*. The outer layer of the membrane is called the *parietal pleura* and is attached to the wall of the thoracic cavity. The inner layer is known as the *visceral pleura* and covers the lungs.

The pleural cavity contains *pleural fluid*, which holds the two membranes together and acts as a lubricant, reducing friction.

The lower part of the lung is bordered by the *diaphragm*, which separates the thoracic cavity from the abdominal cavity. The diaphragm is a sheet of skeletal muscle and plays an important role in the mechanics of breathing. The lungs receive deoxygenated blood from the heart via the right and left pulmonary arteries and return oxygenated blood to the heart via the pulmonary veins. The lung's own supply of oxygenated blood is delivered by the bronchial artery.

7.3 Pulmonary ventilation

Movement of air into and out of the lungs is known as *pulmonary ventilation*. Taking air into the lungs is called *inspiration* and moving air out of the lungs is called *expiration*. The amount of air moved per minute (the minute ventilation, $\dot{V}_E$) varies, depending on the amount of work being performed. As more work is done more energy is required, increasing the demand for oxygen, and so the rate of pulmonary ventilation increases.

At rest, the average rate of breathing is 12–15 breaths per minute and the average amount of air taken in or out per breath (the tidal volume) is 0.5 litres, giving a minute ventilation of 6–7.5 litres per minute.

$$\dot{V}_E = \text{Frequency} \times \text{Tidal volume}$$

MINUTE VENTILATION, $\dot{V}_E$

The amount of air taken into or out of the lungs in one minute. It is calculated by multiplying the number of breaths taken by the amount of air inspired or expired in one breath.

IN PRACTICE

The response of the breathing mechanism to exercise is very similar to the heart rate response (see Chapter 5).

At rest,
$$\dot{V}_E = 12 \times 0.5$$
$$= 6 \text{ litres.}$$

ACTIVITY

Working in pairs, count how many breaths your partner takes in a minute. Why is it difficult to count your own rate of breathing and what does this imply about the breathing mechanism?

During strenuous exercise the volume of air breathed increases dramatically – up to 180 litres is not uncommon for male athletes. This increase is achieved by increasing the rate and depth of breathing. For example
$$\dot{V}_E = \text{Frequency} \times \text{Tidal volume}$$
$$= 45 \times 3.5$$
$$= 157.5 \text{ litres}$$

IN TRAINING

After a period of training pulmonary ventilation will, if anything, be lower at rest, because external respiration becomes more efficient. On the other hand, maximal values increase tremendously. An elite endurance athlete will normally be able to ventilate a maximum of about 180 litres/min. This increase is a combination of an increase in tidal volume and an increase in the rate of respiration.

ACTIVITY

Complete as many sit-ups as you can in a minute. Get your partner to count the number of breaths you take in one minute after completing your exercise. Continue to monitor your rate of breathing until it returns to normal.

As with the heart, there is an *anticipatory rise* in ventilation rate, followed by a steep increase and a plateau (during steady-state exercise) or a steady increase to maximum (during maximal exercise). Recovery after exercise shows a substantial initial drop then a gradual levelling off to normal ventilation rates (Figure 7.3).

7.4 The mechanics of breathing

In order for air to move into the lungs the pressure of air within the lungs must be lower than the pressure of air within the atmosphere. The greater the pressure difference is, the faster the air will flow into the lungs. This is because air always moves from an area of high pressure to an area of low pressure. By changing the volume of your thoracic cavity you can alter the pressure of air in your lungs. Reducing the volume will increase the pressure within the alveoli; increasing it will decrease the pressure within the alveoli. The muscles involved in ventilation are shown in Figure 7.4.

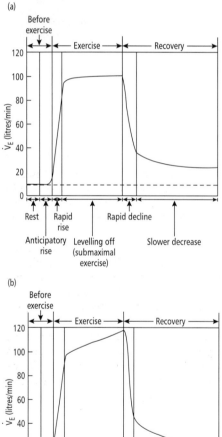

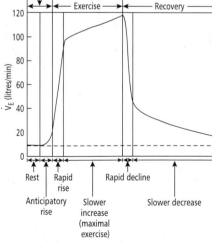

Figure 7.3 *The changes in ventilation rate during (a) submaximal and (b) maximal exercise*

Table 7.1 *Summary of the muscles used in ventilation*

Ventilation phase	Muscles used in quiet breathing	Muscles used in laboured breathing
Inspiration	Diaphragm, external intercostals	Diaphragm, external intercostals, sternocleidomastoid, scalenes, pectoralis minor
Expiration	Passive	Internal intercostals, abdominals

Muscles of inspiration   **Muscles of expiration**

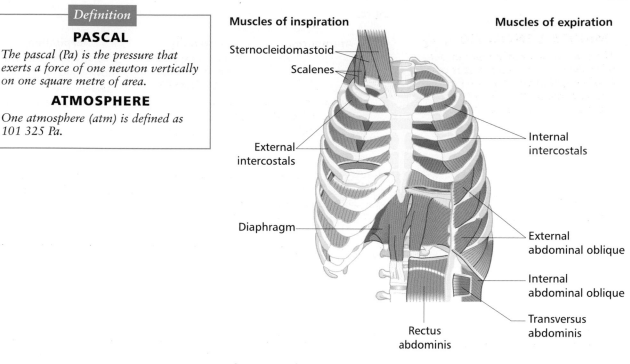

Figure 7.4 *The muscles involved in respiration*

7.4.1 Inspiration

During inspiration the volume of the thoracic cavity must be increased so that the pressure of air within the lungs is lowered. The pressure of atmospheric air is about 100 kPa (760 mmHg) and during inspiration the pressure within the alveoli is lowered to 99.74 kPa (758 mmHg), causing air to move into the lungs.

During quiet inspiration reduction of pressure in the thorax is achieved in part by contraction of the diaphragm. Usually dome-shaped, the diaphragm flattens during contraction, increasing the volume of the thoracic cavity. At the same time the external *intercostal muscles* contract, pulling the ribs upwards and outwards and helping to increase the volume of the thoracic cavity.

When exercising three more inspiratory muscles are involved as the rate and depth of breathing increases: *sternocleidomastoid* lifts the sternum and *scalenes* and *pectoralis minor* both help to further elevate the ribs. As the parietal pleura is attached to the wall of the thoracic cavity and the visceral pleura is attached to the lung tissue, the lung tissue is stretched as the thoracic cavity increases in size.

7.4.2 Expiration

During quiet breathing expiration is passive. The diaphragm and external intercostal muscles relax, reducing the volume of the thoracic cavity and the lung tissue recoils to its normal position. This increases the pressure within the alveoli so that it exceeds atmospheric pressure and forces air out of the lungs.

When exercising expiration becomes active as air has to be forced out of the lungs quickly and effectively. The internal intercostal muscles help pull the ribs back downwards and inwards and the abdominal muscles contract, helping to push the diaphragm back upwards. The net result of this is to reduce the volume of the thoracic cavity (Figure 7.5).

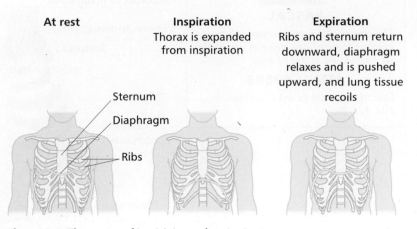

At rest	Inspiration	Expiration
	Thorax is expanded from inspiration	Ribs and sternum return downward, diaphragm relaxes and is pushed upward, and lung tissue recoils

Sternum
Diaphragm
Ribs

Figure 7.5 *The process of inspiration and expiration*

7.5 Respiratory volume

If you breathe normally for a few seconds and then at the end of expiration try to force more air out of your lungs, you will find you are able to breathe out a lot more air. Equally, if you breathe in normally and then continue to inhale as much air as possible you can take in considerably more air. This suggests that we have a 'working' volume of air that we ventilate normally, with a reserve volume available if we need it. This allows a great deal of flexibility in the amount of exercise we can perform, as we have the capacity to increase our ventilation in line with the increase in demand for oxygen. A normal healthy individual can easily ventilate more than enough air for any activity; the limiting factor is the amount of oxygen we can actually transport and use.

Several lung volumes have been identified (Table 7.2) using a spirometer to measure them. Figure 7.6 shows an example of the trace that a spirometer produces. Lung volumes are measured in litres, ml or dm^3. Table 7.3 shows the differences in lung volumes between an average male and an elite endurance runner.

Table 7.2 *Lung volumes*

Volume	Resting value (ml/dm³)	Definition
Tidal volume	500/0.5	The amount of air breathed in or out of the lungs in one breath
Inspiratory reserve volume	3100/3.1	The amount of air that can be forcibly inspired in addition to the tidal volume
Expiratory reserve volume	1200/1.2	The amount of air that can be forcibly expired in addition to the tidal volume
Vital capacity	4800/4.8	The maximum amount of air that can be forcibly exhaled after breathing in as much as possible
Residual volume	1200/1.2	Even after maximal expiration there is always some air left in the lungs to prevent them from collapsing
Total lung capacity	6000/6.0	The vital capacity plus the residual volume

Table 7.3

Respiratory rates and volumes	Average male	Elite endurance runner
Pulmonary ventilation at rest	7 l/min	6 l/min
Maximum pulmonary ventilation	110 l/min	195 l/min
Tidal volume at rest	0.5 l	0.5 l
Maximum tidal volume	2.75 l	3.9 l
Vital capacity	5.8 l	6.2 l
Residual volume	1.4 l	1.2 l

Table amended from *Physiology of Sport and Exercise*, by JH Wilmore and DL Costill

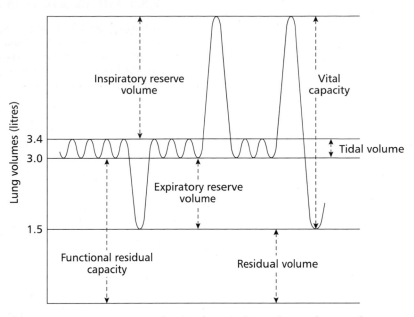

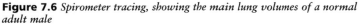

Figure 7.6 *Spirometer tracing, showing the main lung volumes of a normal adult male*

IN PRACTICE

When you start to exercise, your 'working' volume (tidal volume) increases at the expense of your inspiratory reserve volume and your expiratory reserve volume, which decrease. You only rarely use your full vital capacity – for example, when taking a deep breath before swimming under water. Your tidal volume is usually increased in conjunction with an increase in breathing rate – it is not efficient to take fewer breaths and breathe to capacity.

Lung volumes differ with age, sex, body frame and aerobic fitness – but, as already mentioned, in most cases pulmonary ventilation is not a limiting factor in sporting performance.

To summarise,

Vital capacity = Tidal volume + Inspiratory reserve + Expiratory reserve

Total lung capacity = Residual volume + Vital capacity

IN TRAINING

Endurance training does not result in enormous changes to lung volumes. There is a slight increase in vital capacity at the expense of a reduced residual volume. Tidal volume appears to be unchanged at rest but does show an increase during maximal exercise.

ACTIVITY

- If, when you are resting, you inspire 500 ml and inhale every six seconds,
- if, when you forcibly exhale to a maximum having just breathed out, you blow out another 1850 ml,
- if, when you fill your lungs to capacity and breathe out as much as you can, you exhale 4300 ml,

what would be your

1 vital capacity
2 inspiratory reserve volume
3 expiratory reserve volume
4 minute ventilation?

7.5.1 Asthma and pulmonary efficiency

Asthma is becoming increasingly common and many elite and highly successful athletes are asthma sufferers. Asthma attacks occur when the smooth muscle of the bronchiole contracts, restricting the movement of air into the lungs. During an attack the mucous membranes also swell, further aggravating the situation. The person experiences anything from a shortage of breath to a feeling of fighting for breath. In most cases this contraction is triggered by an allergic reaction (for example, to dust or pollen). There is also a form of asthma that is exercise induced, in which an attack happens either shortly after exercise or up to six hours later. Factors that seem to influence exercise induced asthma are:

- *The temperature and humidity of the inspired air.* Cold dry air is more likely to cause an adverse response than warm, moist air.
- *The type of exercise.* Running seems to set off an attack more readily than either cycling or walking. Swimming is less likely to trigger an attack as the inspired air is usually warm and moist (if in an indoor pool).
- *The time lapse between the last medication and the start of exercise.* It is best to keep an inhaler to hand and use it at the first signs of breathing complications.

To help reduce the likelihood of an attack the athlete suffering from asthma should always warm up thoroughly before exercising. The athlete should avoid exercising in cold, dry conditions and should consider cross-training (e.g. instead of running, go for a swim). If the air is cold a scarf can be worn around the lower part of the face to help warm it and retain moisture. Exercise sessions should generally be short in duration and the intensity kept sub-maximal. It should, however, be stressed that asthma sufferers can safely take part in all sports – although it is not considered advisable for an asthma sufferer to go SCUBA diving.

7.6 External respiration

So far we have looked at how air is moved in and out of the lungs but we now need to consider the gaseous exchange that happens at the lung's surface.

Gases flow from an area of high pressure to an area of low pressure. The term *partial pressure* is often used when describing the process of respiration: this refers to the pressure that a particular gas exerts within a mixture of gases and is linked to the concentration of the gas and the barometric pressure. At sea level the barometric pressure of air is 760 mmHg. Oxygen makes up 21% of air so oxygen in the atmosphere exerts a partial pressure of roughly 160 mmHg (21% of 760). By the time air reaches the alveoli the partial pressure of the oxygen has reduced to only 105 mmHg, but the partial pressure of oxygen in the alveoli is significantly higher than the partial pressure of the oxygen in the blood vessel surrounding the lungs, which is only 40 mmHg. This is because oxygen has been removed by the tissues so its concentration in the blood is lower, and its partial pressure is lower. The difference between the two pressures (105 – 40) is known as the *concentration gradient* or *diffusion gradient*. Oxygen will move from the area of higher pressure to the area of lower pressure (down the diffusion gradient) until there is a state of equilibrium. The greater the diffusion gradient is, the faster the diffusion will take place.

In the same way, carbon dioxide diffuses from the capillaries into the alveoli. The partial pressure of carbon dioxide in the alveoli is only 40 mmHg but it is 45 mmHg in the capillaries. Therefore carbon dioxide flows into the air in the alveoli and is expired.

A summary of the movement of the respiratory gases is given in Figure 7.7

Partial pressure (mmHg) in:

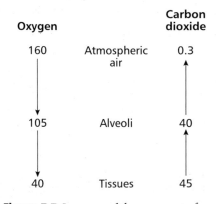

Figure 7.7 *Summary of the movement of gases during external respiration*

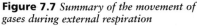

Definition
PARTIAL PRESSURE
The partial pressure of a gas is the pressure it exerts within a mixture of gases.

7.7 Internal respiration

The process described in the last section is reversed at the tissues because the cell is continuously using oxygen to produce ATP. This means that the partial pressure of oxygen is lower in the tissues than in the blood so it diffuses into the cell. At the same time, carbon dioxide is being continuously produced by the cell. This results in a higher partial pressure of carbon dioxide within the cell than in the blood, so it diffuses into the blood.

The lungs are designed to ensure that gaseous exchange takes place as quickly and effectively as possible. The most significant factor in terms of diffusion is the difference in the partial pressures of the gases, but the following factors all contribute to the efficiency of the process:
- the respiratory membrane is extremely thin
- the length of the diffusion path is very short
- the total surface area available for diffusion is very large.

7.8 Transport of respiratory gases

7.8.1 Oxygen

Oxygen diffuses into the capillaries, where 3% dissolves in plasma and about 97% combines with haemoglobin to form oxyhaemoglobin (see Chapter 6). Haemoglobin, when fully saturated, can carry four oxygen molecules and this easily happens at sea level where the pressure gradient between the alveoli and the blood is high. At the tissues the oxygen dissociates from the haemoglobin because of the relatively low pressure of oxygen in the tissues.

7.8.2 Carbon dioxide

Carbon dioxide is transported one of three ways: 7% dissolves in plasma and 23% combines with haemoglobin. The remaining 70% dissolves in water to form carbonic acid. In the plasma this dissociates to hydrogen ions and bicarbonate ions. Hydrogen ions create a more acidic environment and the body needs to regulate the acid–base balance of the body by neutralising or buffering its effects. This is achieved by combining the hydrogen ions with haemoglobin, as haemoglobin acts as a major buffer within the blood:

$$CO_2 + H_2O \longrightarrow H_2CO_3 \longrightarrow H^+ + HCO_3^-$$
$$\text{(carbonic acid)} \quad \text{(bicarbonate ion)}$$

> **Definition**
>
> **BUFFER**
>
> *A substance (e.g. haemoglobin) that combines with either an acid or a base to help keep the body's pH at an optimal level.*

IN TRAINING

An excess of hydrogen ions decreases the body's pH and interferes with ATP production and muscle contractility. Some athletes who perform in highly anaerobic events take sodium bicarbonate to help increase their plasma bicarbonate levels, in order to improve the blood's buffering capacity. This in turn enables the body to remove carbon dioxide and lactic acid more effectively during high-intensity workouts and therefore offset fatigue.

7.8.3 Haemoglobin saturation

The relationship between oxygen and haemoglobin is often represented by the oxyhaemoglobin dissociation curve (Figure 7.8). The level of saturation of oxygen to the haemoglobin is affected by several factors.
- The *partial pressure of oxygen* influences the saturation of haemoglobin with oxygen. The partial pressure of oxygen at sea level is always high enough for full saturation of haemoglobin in the lungs. When the blood

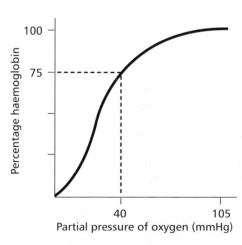

Figure 7.8 *The oxyhaemoglobin dissociation curve at 38°C and pH 7.4*

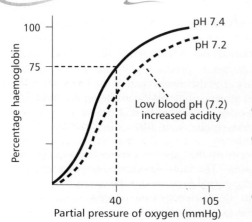

Figure 7.9 *Effect of pH on haemoglobin saturation – the Bohr effect*

arrives at the tissues the partial pressure of oxygen drops, causing the oxygen to dissociate from the haemoglobin and diffuse into the cell. At high altitude the change in barometric pressure causes the partial pressure of oxygen to drop. This means that the haemoglobin is not fully saturated at the lungs and the oxygen-carrying capacity of the blood is decreased. This can cause an athlete working at altitude problems.

- As *body temperature* increases the oxygen dissociates more easily from the haemoglobin.
- The *partial pressure of carbon dioxide*. As this increases the dissociation of oxygen from haemoglobin increases. During exercise the amount of carbon dioxide produced by the cells increases, which helps to increase the diffusion of much-needed oxygen into the cell.
- *Change in pH*. As more carbon dioxide is produced the concentration of hydrogen ions in the blood increases, lowering the pH. A drop in pH causes oxygen to dissociate more easily – this is known as the *Bohr effect* and is shown in Figure 7.9.

A combination of these factors means that as we start to exercise the rate of diffusion of oxygen into the cells accelerates and helps to maintain a good supply of oxygen to the working tissues.

7.9 Control of breathing

Two factors are involved in the control of breathing:
- neural control and
- chemical control.

7.9.1 Neural control

The respiratory centre in the medulla of the brain controls breathing. This centre is made up of two main areas.

- The *inspiratory centre* is responsible for the rhythmic cycle of inspiration and expiration.
- The *expiratory centre* is inactive during quiet ventilation. When the rate and depth of ventilation increases (detected by stretch receptors in the lungs) the expiratory centre inhibits the inspiratory centre and stimulates expiratory muscles.

Neural control of breathing is summarised in Figure 7.10. In most circumstances the nervous regulation of breathing is involuntary. The

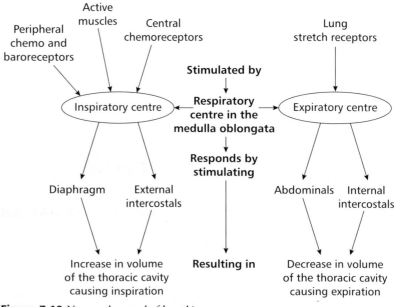

Figure 7.10 *Neuronal control of breathing*

respiratory centre sends out nerve impulses via the phrenic and intercostal nerves to the respiratory muscles. The muscles are stimulated for a short period, causing inspiration. Then, when the stimulus stops, expiration occurs.

The respiratory centre responds mainly to changes in the chemistry and temperature of the blood. The most significant factor is an increase in hydrogen ions in the blood (lowering of blood pH), which occurs when the amount of carbon dioxide being produced by the cells increases. This increase is detected by the respiratory centre and results in an increase in the rate and depth of breathing. A rise in body temperature will cause an increase in the rate of breathing but does not affect the depth of breathing.

Other factors influencing neural control of breathing include

- A large drop in oxygen tension. This is monitored by the chemoreceptors in the aorta and carotid arteries and results in an increase in the rate and depth of breathing.
- A rise in blood pressure, monitored by the baroreceptors in the aorta and carotid arteries, results in a decrease in ventilation rate.
- Proprioceptors in the muscles responding to movement stimulate the respiratory centre, increasing the rate and depth of breathing.
- The respiratory centre can also be affected by higher centres in the brain, for example emotional influences.

The lungs have a safety mechanism to make sure that they are never over-inflated. Stretch receptors located in the walls of the bronchi and bronchioles respond during excessive respiration by sending messages to the respiratory centre to inhibit inspiration. This is known as the *Hering–Breuer* reflex.

The response of the respiratory system to exercise should never really be considered in isolation – if a change occurs in the respiratory system then similar changes usually occur in the cardiac and vascular systems. For example, an increase in blood temperature will cause an increase in heart rate, an increase in ventilation and dilation of the vessels supplying the skin and working muscles. The response of all three systems is coordinated to ensure efficient delivery of oxygen and removal of carbon dioxide and other waste products.

Key revision points

The amount of air required by the body varies considerably, depending on the amount of oxygen used by the cells. This is why we have a 'working' volume of air (tidal volume) plus a reserve volume available (inspiratory and expiratory reserve volumes). The respiratory control centre works in conjunction with the cardiac control centre and the vasomotor control centre to ensure a coordinated response to oxygen demand and delivery.

KEY TERMS

You should now understand the following terms. If you do not, go back through the chapter and find out.

Alveoli
Bohr effect
Diffusion gradient
Expiratory reserve volume
External respiration
Inspiratory reserve volume
Internal respiration
Minute ventilation
Partial pressure
Pleural membrane
Pulmonary ventilation
Respiratory centre
Tidal volume
Vital capacity

PROGRESS CHECK

1 Define respiration.
2 List the respiratory structures that air passes through from the nose to the alveoli.
3 How is air filtered?
4 Define pulmonary ventilation.
5 What is the relationship between minute ventilation, respiratory frequency and tidal volume?
6 What happens to minute ventilation during exercise?
7 Draw a graph to show the response of the respiratory system to ten minutes of submaximal exercise followed by a five-minute recovery period.
8 How does the movement of the ribs and diaphragm affect the volume of the thoracic cavity?
9 Which inspiratory muscles are used only during laboured breathing?
10 Describe the pressure changes that cause air to move into and out of the lungs.
11 What is meant by the term partial pressure?
12 List the ways that oxygen and carbon dioxide are transported in the blood.
13 What factors influence the oxygen saturation of haemoglobin?
14 Explain what is meant by the Bohr effect and describe what effect it has on the transport of oxygen during exercise.
15 How is respiration regulated during exercise?
16 Define tidal volume, inspiratory reserve volume and expiratory reserve volume.
17 What effect does exercise have on these three volumes?
18 Complete the following equation:
Tidal volume + Inspiratory volume + Expiratory reserve = ?
19 Why might an athlete take sodium bicarbonate?
20 Identify the changes that occur to the lung volumes after a period of endurance training.

Further reading

Glen F. Bastian. *An Illustrated Review of Anatomy and Physiology*. 1: The Skeletal and Muscular Systems. 2: The Cardiovascular System. 3: The Respiratory System. Harper Collins College Publishers, 1994.

C. Clegg. *Exercise Physiology and Functional Anatomy*. Feltham Press 1995.

R.J. Davis, C.R. Bull, J.V. Roscoe and D.A. Roscoe. *Physical Education and the Study of Sport*. Wolfe Medical Publishers, 1991.

D. Davis, T. Kimmet and M. Auty. *Physical Education: Theory and Practice*. Macmillan, Australia, 1986.

E. Fox, R. Bowen and M. Foss. *The Physiological Basis for Exercise and Sport*. Brown and Benchmark, 1989.

W. Kapit and L.M. Elson. *The Anatomy Colouring Book*. Harper Collins College Publishers, 1993.

H.G.Q. Rowett. *Basic Anatomy and Physiology*. John Murray, 1975.

R.R. Seeley, T.D. Stephens and P. Tate. *Essentials of Anatomy and Physiology*. Mosby Year Book Publishers, 1995.

Clem W. Thompson. *Manual of Structural Kinesiology*. Times Mirror/Mosby College Publishing, 1989.

Peter Walder. *Mechanics and Sport Performance*. Feltham Press, 1994.

J. H. Wilmore and D.L. Costill. *Physiology of Sport and Exercise* 2nd edition. Human Kinetics, 1999.

R. Wirhed. *Athletic Ability and the Anatomy of Motion*. Wolfe Medical Publishers, 1989.

Part **2**

Skill acquisition

This part of the book contains:

Chapter 8   Skill and its characteristics

Chapter 9   Theories related to the learning of skills

Chapter 10   Theories related to the teaching of skills

In this part of the book we will investigate how we learn movement skills associated with physical education and sport. The process of motor learning can only be understood by studying the nature of skill and its characteristics. The more we know about a particular skill, the better we are placed to devise teaching strategies to teach that skill. The importance of fundamental motor skills is stressed because these are the building blocks of future skill learning. We will also look in detail at theories related to the learning of skills. There are no 'watertight' theories about learning because the human brain is such a complex organ, but this part highlights the relevant theories widely accepted by sports psychologists. Finally, this part deals with theories related to the teaching of skills. Effective teaching is dependent on a number of factors, including the personality, level of knowledge and ability of the teacher. To optimise the learning environment the teacher or coach must consider the research underpinning good practice – including the structure of training sessions, the type of guidance given and the possible teaching styles that can be adopted.

Skill and its characteristics

Are skilful people born that way or do they learn their skills? It seems that the answer is probably a mixture of both. We all have abilities that are thought to be predetermined genetically and these dictate our potential to be skilful. The acquisition of fundamental motor skills is probably undervalued in a child's early development. It is crucial that we are aware of what we actually mean by skill and whether we can affect future performance. The classification of skill is not an exact science but for us to teach and learn skills we must analyse the task to be performed so that we fully understand how to put movements into action. There may for instance be common actions needed for a range of different skills. If this is the case, then once we have identified these common actions, we can teach them or learn them so that we can transfer them between skills and activities.

8.1 The concept and nature of skill

ACTIVITY

Study the photograph. We would probably all agree that this performer is skilled. Before you read on, write a list of words and phrases which you feel would describe a skilled performer.

For the activity, you probably thought of *fluent*, *coordinated* and *controlled* and phrases like '*seems effortless*', '*looks good*' and '*good technique*'.

We often comment that an experienced sportsperson is 'skilful', but what do we actually mean by the word 'skill'? We use it to describe a task such as kicking a ball, but often we use it to describe the overall actions of someone who is good at what they do. There are two main ways of using the word 'skill':

- to see skill as a specific task to be performed
- to view skill as describing the quality of a particular action, which might include how consistent the performance is and how prepared the performer is to carry out the task.

When we see top-class sportsmen and sportswomen we are often struck by the seemingly effortless way that they perform, and it is not until we try to perform ourselves that we realise just how difficult it really is! We know that these performers are very fit but they don't seem to exert themselves and we are aware that whatever the skill – whether it is a somersault in gymnastics or a perfectly timed rugby tackle – the end product looks good and is aesthetically pleasing. A skilled performer knows what he or she is trying to achieve and more often than not is successful, which is annoying if you are their opponent! A beginner, or novice, will seem clumsy and slow and will lack control. The novice will also tire quickly and expend more energy than is necessary.

When an accomplished hockey player, for instance, performs a skilful pass, he or she shows a technically good movement. This movement is called the *motor skill*.

> **Definition**
> ## MOTOR SKILL
> *An action or task that has a goal and that requires voluntary body and/or limb movement to achieve the goal.*

> **Definition**
> ## FUNDAMENTAL MOTOR SKILLS
> *Skills such as throwing a ball or jumping or kicking a ball. We learn these skills at a young age, usually through play, and if they are learned thoroughly, a child can move on to the more sophisticated actions that are required in sport.*

A skilled hockey player needs both motor skills and perceptual skills

8.1.1 Fundamental motor skills

Fundamental motor skills are skills such as throwing, catching and running. These skills are important because they provide the basis for other skills. Without acquiring the fundamental motor skills, it is unlikely that a person would be able to excel in a sports activity. These skills provide the platform on which we can build the more advanced skills demanded in our sports. Acquisition of these essential skills also helps us to follow a lifestyle that is healthy. As we get older, we may draw on many fundamental motor skills to follow lifetime sports, such as golf. Acquiring fundamental motor skills can help children build their self-esteem and make them more accepted in group 'play' situations.

We learn fundamental motor skills at a young age

IN PRACTICE

If a tennis player often serves 'aces' in a match, we would label that player as skilled. If we watched him over a number of matches and he continued to serve aces, we would be more justified in labelling him as skilled. A squash player whom we might regard as skilled would anticipate where the ball is going to land and would put herself in a position to receive the ball early so that she could hit it early, thus putting her opponent at a disadvantage.

Definition

PERCEPTION

A complex concept that involves interpretation of stimuli. Not all stimuli are perceived and what is perceived depends on past experience and attention ability. For a detailed explanation of perception see the section on Information Processing on page 95.

Definition

COGNITIVE SKILLS

Skills that involve the intellectual ability of the performer. These skills affect the perceptual process and help us to make sense of what is required in any given situation. They are essential if the performer is to make correct and effective decisions.

IN PRACTICE

The abilities of balance, strength and flexibility are necessary before you can perform a headstand. A Frisbee catch needs the underlying abilities of hand–eye coordination and perceptual awareness.

The player also has to assess the position of the opponents and the players on the same team and will have to decide where to pass the ball and how hard to pass it. This interpretation of information or stimuli is called *perception* and the skill required is called *perceptual skill*.

For skill acquisition to take place the person also needs *cognitive skills*. These skills are intellectually based and are linked to working out or solving problems; they underpin verbal reasoning. These skills are often seen as innate, although there is considerable debate among psychologists as to how intelligence is acquired and whether there is only one or many ways that people can show intelligence. For instance, is a football player showing intelligence when he selects a particular skill to be used in a particular situation?

When we talk of skill, we usually mean a combination of perceptual, cognitive and motor skills.

Skilled performers are not born with most motor skills already programmed in their minds – they have to learn them in a number of different ways. The ways in which we learn skills are investigated in Chapter 9.

'Skill' has been defined in the following way:

A skilled movement is one in which a predetermined objective is accomplished with maximum efficiency with a minimum outlay of energy.

Key revision points

The main characteristics of skilled movement: learned, goal directed, pre-determined goals, consistent achievement, economy of movement, efficiency, coordinated, precise, aesthetically pleasing, fluent, controlled. Motor skills involve fundamental movement patterns and perceptual and cognitive skills.

ACTIVITY

Your own sport will require fundamental motor skills, more advanced motor skills and perceptual skills. Highlight a few examples of both.

8.2 Ability

We often talk about improving our own abilities and those of other people, but we probably usually mean 'skills' rather than 'abilities'. Skills are, as we now know, learned and involve often pre-planned movements that are goal directed. To carry out skills, we need certain underlying factors such as strength and hand–eye coordination. These factors are known as *abilities*.

Our abilities are largely determined genetically – they are *natural* or *innate* – and they tend to be enduring characteristics. This is bad news for some of us who would like to get to the top of our sport but who don't

Certain skills require specific abilities

ACTIVITY

List the abilities required for the following sports: tennis, rugby, snooker, golf, netball.

Definition

PSYCHOMOTOR ABILITY

Our ability to process information regarding movement and then to put our decisions into action. Psychomotor abilities include reaction time and limb coordination.

GROSS MOTOR ABILITY

Ability involving actual movement – strength, flexibility, speed.

Definition

KINESTHESIS

This is the information we hold within ourselves about our body's position. The information comes from receptors found in the muscles, tendons and joints. The term proprioception is often used in the same way.

---

have the natural ability to do so because, no matter how hard we try, we may never reach those giddy heights. We simply may not have the necessary innate qualities. However, research has revealed that some abilities can be enhanced to a certain extent, especially in early childhood.

In the activity you may have listed hand–eye coordination for tennis, strength for rugby, fine motor control for snooker, flexibility for golf and speed for netball. All of these abilities are found in most sports but their importance to the execution of skills and techniques varies with the particular sport. It would be nice to suppose that there is a general 'sporting ability' which underpins most sports, but research to date does not support this. Several specific abilities help form the foundation for certain sporting skills – two of the most important are *psychomotor* and *gross motor* abilities.

Certain skills require specific abilities or sets of abilities but most motor skills involve the abilities of strength, speed and coordination.

8.2.1 The general and specific views of abilities

Top sportspeople are popularly thought to possess an overall single ability to perform well. Many researchers believe in many different specific motor abilities but if these abilities were very closely related then a 'general' motor ability could exist. Some individuals seem to be very good at many different sports, which seems to back the idea of a general motor ability. The presence of a general motor ability could be explained by viewing the performer as having a high degree of prowess in *groups* of abilities. For example, a good all-round sports person may have good balance, speed and hand–eye coordination. It would therefore follow that this person is likely to be good at a wide range of sports involving these abilities. However, there is no firm evidence to support the notion that there is such a thing as general motor ability.

Some researchers have looked into ways of predicting athletic prowess after an individual's abilities have been identified. Tests have been performed on young people to find out their abilities and then to link these abilities to certain sports. This has not been very successful, because different abilities are needed at different stages of skill learning. For instance, good vision and the ability to process information rapidly are important when beginning to learn a complex task, but kinesthesis is more important in the later stages. Ability tests cannot, therefore, be used to accurately predict sporting prowess.

8.3 Classification of skill

In order to understand fully the nature of a particular skill, we need to analyse it. The traditional way of doing this is by classification but this can be very unsatisfactory and inaccurate because skills have many characteristics, which can change in different situations. For example, catching a Frisbee involves large and small muscle movements and involves the catcher adjusting their movements according to the varied flight of the Frisbee. It is very difficult to classify skills neatly, but to make teaching and learning more effective it is essential that we fully understand skills.

8.3.1 Analysis of skills

If we accept that skills cannot be neatly labelled the best means of analysis is to use a scale or continuum which will illustrate that skills have different characteristics to a greater or lesser extent. The skill in a tennis serve, for instance, has elements of fine muscle movements and gross muscle movements but we would probably agree that it involves more gross muscle movements. We might place the skill of the tennis serve at X on a continuum like that in Figure 8.1.

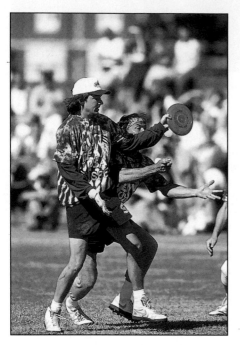

Catching a Frisbee involves large and small muscle movements

Gross ················· X ··· Fine

Figure 8.1 *Skills should be assessed on a continuum*

Most skill classification systems are based on the view that motor skills are affected by three factors:
1 how precise a movement is
2 whether the movement has a definite beginning and end
3 whether the environment affects the performance of the skill.

The following words and phrases are often used in the classification of skills. Always remember to classify skills according to a continuum because this reflects the true, although complex, nature of skill.

The gross–fine continuum

This is concerned with the precision of movement.

Gross skills involve large muscle movements. These skills are not very precise and include many of the fundamental movement patterns such as walking and jumping. An example of a skill which is predominantly gross is the shot putt.

Fine skills involve more intricate movements using small muscle groups. These skills tend to be precise in nature and generally involve a high degree of hand–eye coordination. An example of a fine motor skill is a snooker shot.

The open–closed continuum

This continuum is concerned with the effects of the environment on skills.

Open skills are affected by the environment and are, therefore, predominantly perceptual. Movements have to be adapted to the environment and the skill is mostly externally paced – for example, a pass in football.

Closed skills are not affected by the environment and are predominantly habitual. Movements follow a set pattern and have a definite beginning and end. These skills tend to be self-paced. An example of a closed skill is a free throw in basketball.

ACTIVITY

Choose a skill from either soccer or netball and attempt to classify it. Remember to use a continuum. Now analyse the skill or task more closely. Identify the sub-routines and the underlying abilities which are needed for effective execution of the skill.

The 'pacing' continuum

This is often used in conjunction with the open–closed continuum and refers to the timing of movements.

Self-paced skills. The performer controls the rate at which the skill is executed. Self-pacing involves proaction by the performer. Self-paced skills are usually closed skills – an example is a javelin throw.

Externally paced skills. The environment, which may include your opponent, controls the rate of performing the skill. This type of skill involves reaction and is usually an open skill such as receiving a serve in badminton.

The discrete–serial–continuous continuum

This is concerned with how well defined the beginning and end of the skill are.

Discrete skills have a clear beginning and a clear end. The skill can be repeated but the performer must start again from the beginning. It is a single, specific skill. A penalty flick in hockey is an example of such a skill.

Serial skills have several discrete elements which are put together to make an integrated movement or sequence of movements – for example the sequence of skills in a triple jump.

Continuous skills have no obvious beginning or end – the end of one cycle of movement is the beginning of the next. The skill is repeated as a set pattern, for example cycling.

ACTIVITY

Draw an open–closed continuum and place the following skills on it: long jump, netball catch, hockey penalty flick, pistol shooting, basketball dribble, receiving a serve in badminton, a vault in gymnastics.

8.3.2 Individual, coactive and interactive skills

Another method of describing groups of skills is to group them according to whether the skill is performed without reference to another player, whether there are others involved (called coactors) or whether the skill is dependent upon interaction with the environment. For example, throwing the javelin is an individual skill, blocking in volleyball is a coactive skill and many skills associated with sailing could be seen as interactive with the environment. However, with any system of classification, it is very difficult to put skills into particular boxes. Skills can be seen as partly individual, partly coactive and partly interactive. The process of analysing is important because it gives us clues to how we should be practising a skill.

ACTIVITY

Group the following according to whether they are individual, coactive or interactive: bowling in cricket, mountain biking, front row scrummaging in rugby, stopping the ball in hockey, road racing in cycling, turning in snowboarding, forming a defensive wall in football.

8.4 Task analysis

> *Definition*
> ### SUB-ROUTINES
> *The elements, or separate movements, that make up a particular skill. For example striking a ball in hockey involves grip, stance, backlift, forward swing, strike and follow through.*

This involves the teacher of skills understanding what needs to be taught in a detailed way so that a plan of what needs to be taught, when and where can be formulated. The information can be gathered by analysing the skill or task by using the classification systems already described. The analysis should reveal the specific abilities required for a particular skill. These abilities can then be used to develop the *sub-routines* that make up the skill. All this information can enable coaches and teachers to identify why a particular movement is not being skilfully executed. Once the cause of the problem is isolated then a strategy of eliminating the problem can be put into action.

IN PRACTICE

A hockey coach wishes to find out why a particular player cannot flick the ball effectively: she gets no height or speed on the ball and consequently any penalty flick that she may be asked to execute is a hopeless failure! The coach analyses the task, which is the hockey flick. She identifies the sub-routines and the abilities that underpin them and finds out that much of the power needed comes from the transfer of power or momentum from the leg muscles. She plans a training programme to develop strength and power in the player's leg muscles in the hope that this will eventually increase the player's skill in flicking the ball.

The server uses a pattern of movement but can also perceive the movement of his opponent

> *Definition*
> ### ATTENTIONAL WASTAGE
> *The performer's concentration can be misdirected to irrelevant cues. This can damage the effectiveness of their performance, and will particularly affect the way a novice learns.*

8.4.1 Using our knowledge of skill classification

The coach or teacher and the performer must be able to identify the important aspects of skills. A better understanding of the nature of the task is essential if the task is to be completed skilfully. A knowledge of which stimuli to attend to and which to ignore will help the performer ignore irrelevant information. The coach can also guide the performer towards making the right decisions.

Knowing how to classify skills can help to decide on the type of teaching/learning strategies that will optimise performance – it might be appropriate to split a skill up into its component parts (its sub-routines) if it is serial in nature, or to build strength of large muscles if the skill is predominantly gross in nature. Knowledge of the perceptual requirements of a skill will also help the performer to take in the correct amount and type of information so that there is no *attentional wastage*.

The importance of knowing all there is to know about the skill to be attempted cannot be overstated. It is particularly important at the top level of performance, where only a small difference in technique or tactics can mean the all-important advantage over your opponent.

Coaches who work with performers with disabilities can make important differences to physical performance using their knowledge of skill composition to ensure effective instruction (see Chapter 10).

Knowledge of skill will help to optimise performance

Key revision points

Skills are classified on a continuum. Knowledge of the task/skills gives good insight into movement requirements and teaching strategies. For example, receiving a pass in lacrosse is predominantly perceptual and therefore more of an open skill. A coach would adopt the strategy of giving a player experience in a variety of different situations (see section on schema, page 105).

KEY TERMS

You should now understand the following terms. If you do not, go back through the chapter and find out.

Ability
Attentional wastage
Cognitive skill
Continuum
Discrete, continuous and serial skills
Fundamental motor skills
Gross and fine skills
Gross motor ability
Kinesthesis
Motor skill
Open and closed skills
Perception
Perceptual skill
Psychomotor ability
Self-paced and externally paced skills
Stimuli
Sub routines
Task analysis

PROGRESS CHECK

1 What are the main characteristics of a skilled performer?
2 What is meant by a motor skill?
3 What is a perceptual skill?
4 Give the main differences between skill and ability.
5 Why is there no such thing as general sporting ability?
6 What is meant by the term psychomotor ability?
7 What is meant by the term gross motor ability?
8 Why are ability tests unable to predict sporting prowess?
9 Define kinesthesis.
10 How could early childhood experiences influence abilities?
11 Why can't we classify skills accurately?
12 What does the term 'continuum' mean in skill classification?
13 What is the gross/fine continuum?
14 Why are open skills predominantly perceptual?
15 If discrete is at one end of a continuum, what should be at the other?
16 Why is a triple jump a serial skill?
17 What is meant by an externally paced skill?
18 How can a skill be a closed skill in an open situation?
19 Why would a teacher or coach split a skill up into sub-routines?
20 How can knowledge related to skill classification help a coach of a disabled athlete?

Theories related to the learning of skills

Learning objectives

- To understand the associative and cognitive theories of learning.
- To understand the theory of information processing, including the role of memory.
- To understand the concepts of motor programmes and schema.
- To investigate different types of feedback.
- To understand the role of mental practice in the learning and performance of motor skills.

The human brain is an enormously complex organ and the way in which it receives information, processes it, retains it and then sends messages to our body to move can be explained using a number of different theories and ideas. None of these theories and ideas are watertight but they help to explain in easy terms how our brain operates, particularly when we learn. When we acquire skills we must be motivated to learn and see some benefit in it. In this chapter we will explore the well established theories of conditioning. We will then investigate why and how we are motivated to learn and how our brains receive and sort information. An important component for learning is our memory. We investigate in simple terms how we remember things and why we forget. As well as practising physically it is important to think about what we are doing and to make sense of our environment. We will be looking into how we mentally rehearse skills and the benefits of such mental practice.

9.1 The associationist or connectionist view of conditioning

The term *associationist* is given to a group of theories related to connecting *stimulus* and *response*. These theories are often referred to as *S–R theories*. An individual is conditioned by stimuli which are 'connected' or 'bonded' to appropriate responses.

A sprinter driving off the blocks is a response which is closely 'bonded' to the stimulus of the gun

9.1.1 Classical conditioning

In classical conditioning an existing S–R connection is replaced by a new bonding. The most famous example of classical conditioning was carried out by Pavlov. Pavlov's experiments with dogs show that pairing an unconditioned stimulus with a conditioned stimulus can eventually result in a conditioned response. Pavlov gave food to his dogs (this is the unconditioned or natural stimulus) and the dogs' natural response (the unconditioned response) was to salivate. Pavlov then rang a bell at the same time as presenting the food. The dogs salivated because of the food, but were unknowingly connecting the arrival of food with the sound of the bell. When the bell was rung again later the dogs still salivated even if no food was presented. The dogs' natural behaviour had now been changed through manipulation of the stimulus – their response became conditioned.

This process is also known as a *conditioned reflex*.

IN PRACTICE

A coach shouts 'now' to a performer when it is time to open out from a somersault. The performer learns to connect the word 'now' with the kinesthetic 'feel' of the movement at that exact time. Eventually, the word 'now' becomes redundant because the performer has been conditioned by associating the unconditioned stimulus (kinesthesis) with the conditioned stimulus ('now') to get the conditioned response (opening out at the right time). In the teaching of motor skills the practice of motor drills, where movements become almost habitual and bad habits are kept to a minimum, is common.

A coach shouts 'now' when it is time for a performer to open out from a somersault

Key revision points

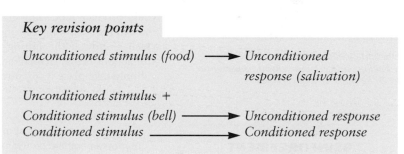

Unconditioned stimulus (food) ⟶ Unconditioned response (salivation)

Unconditioned stimulus +
Conditioned stimulus (bell) ⟶ Unconditioned response
Conditioned stimulus ⟶ Conditioned response

Conditioning is important in the natural environment – for instance, animals learn to recognise other dangerous animals by certain characteristics such as skin colour and avoid coming into contact with them. Conditioning usually allows modification of behaviour to ensure maximum rewards and to avoid punishment. In human behaviour phobias are often the result of conditioning in childhood, including the concept of learned helplessness in sport. By punishing their children parents could cause conditioned fear. It has been suggested that when this fear cannot be overcome aggression may result, becoming displaced and directed towards other targets. This may explain aggression in sports performers and some spectators. It is difficult to relate classical conditioning with sports performance, but there are times when a stimulus is manipulated to get a desired response.

ACTIVITY

Try to think of another example in the teaching of motor skills of a response that has been conditioned using another stimulus. What are the drawbacks of this type of teaching?

The main problem with the 'drill' style of teaching motor skills is that the performer can't gain a real understanding of why he or she is doing something. This lack of understanding can have a detrimental effect on future development of skills.

IN PRACTICE

If you wished to teach the long high serve in badminton, you could draw a large chalk circle at the back of the opposing service box and ask the performer to try to serve into the circle. After several trials (and eventual success) you would make the circle smaller and ask the performer to serve into this smaller circle. Once they are successful at this, wipe out the circle altogether. The performer should have been conditioned to serve long to the back of their opponent's service box. This is the operant method of conditioning: the performer's behaviour had been shaped by targets which became progressively more realistic to the game situation and the correct actions reinforced by praise. The actions were also reinforced through the player's perceived success in hitting the target. How would you go about teaching the same performer to serve high as well as long, using the operant method of conditioning?

9.1.2 Operant conditioning

Work undertaken by Skinner in 1964 revealed that conditioning was more effective through manipulation of behaviour towards a stimulus than through modification of the stimulus. Skinner used a box with a rat inside it. If the rat hit a lever inside the box a food pellet would be released. Through trial and error the rat eventually learned that hitting the lever would produce food. This has become known as *operant conditioning* or *trial and error learning*. Hitting the lever gave food and therefore a reward, which *reinforced* the hitting action. Operant conditioning is concerned with actions being 'shaped' and then reinforced. Conditioning of this type will only take place if reinforcement is present.

Operant conditioning, a process of shaping behaviour using reinforcement, is useful for teaching skills such as serving

---

> ### Definition
> ## REINFORCEMENT
> *The process that increases the probability of a behaviour occurring. Reinforcement strengthens the S–R bond.*

> ### Definition
> ## POSITIVE REINFORCEMENT
> *A stimulus which increases the probability of a desired response occurring.*
> ## NEGATIVE REINFORCEMENT
> *The stimulus is withdrawn when the desired response occurs.*
> ## PUNISHMENT
> *Giving a stimulus to prevent a response occurring. Not to be confused with negative reinforcement.*

ACTIVITY

Give examples in sport of positive reinforcement, negative reinforcement and punishment.

An example of operant conditioning may be a parent who gives a child a sweet to stop it crying. This reinforces the behaviour and the child cries to get another sweet.

Learning is faster if a reward is given on every occasion – this is known as *complete reinforcement*. Research shows that if a reward is given after a number of correct responses learning takes longer but lasts longer – this is known as *partial reinforcement*. Operant conditioning is commonly used in teaching motor skills.

Rewards are used extensively in skills teaching because they reinforce the type of behaviour required, but there are problems associated with the use of rewards.

> ### Key revision points
>
> *Operant conditioning/trial and error learning is a process which involves modification of behaviour. Behaviour is shaped and then reinforced. For conditioning to take place, reinforcement must be present but partial reinforcement is more effective in the long term than complete reinforcement.*

IN PRACTICE

A hockey player who has been drilled to perform a particular penalty flick may become predictable and demotivated by inhibition. Practice should be stopped for a while – perhaps new strategies should be discussed and practised later. New targets should be set and the practice resumed.

ACTIVITY

Choose a sport and, using Thorndike's laws, state how you would teach a specific closed skill.

 To find out more about drive theory, turn to page 95.

 To find out more about drive reduction, turn to page 113.

Definition

INTERVENING VARIABLES

Mental processes occurring between the stimulus being received and the response.

Definition

INSIGHT LEARNING

Problem solving involving memory. Previous experiences are used to help solve new problems.

Definition

GESTALTISTS

A group of German scientists (including Wertheimer, Kohler and Koffka) who established many principles or laws of perception. They extended these laws to provide accounts of learning and problem solving.

9.1.3 Thorndike's 'laws'

Thorndike developed a theory based on strengthening the S–R bond. He developed some 'laws' which he thought should be taken into consideration when trying to match a response to a particular stimulus.

Law of exercise

Repeating or rehearsing the S–R connections is more likely to strengthen them. If the desired response occurs, reinforcement is necessary.

Law of effect

If the response is followed by a 'satisfier', then the S–R bond is strengthened. If the response is followed by an 'annoyer', then the S–R bond is weakened. This means that pleasant outcomes are likely to motivate the performer to repeat the action.

Law of readiness

The performer must be physically and mentally able to complete the task effectively.

9.1.4 Hull's drive theory

Hull pioneered the 'drive theory'. He stated that if the S–R bond is to be strong a performer must be motivated to do well. He warned against too much repetition of practice, because he thought that it could lead to 'inhibition', which would demotivate the performer and weaken the S–R bond. The inhibition, or drive reduction, can be overcome after a rest interval or when new and more motivating goals are determined.

9.2 Cognitive theories of learning

The cognitive theories go beyond the associative or S–R theories. Many psychologists feel that there are *intervening variables*.

Cognitive theories are concerned with thinking and understanding rather than connecting certain stimuli to certain responses. Trial and error has no place in cognitive theory. It is sometimes known as *insight learning*.

Kohler used chimpanzees to illustrate this concept. The chimpanzee was placed in a cage with a box and a banana was hung from the roof of the cage. The chimp could reach the banana only by putting the box underneath the banana and standing on it. Only one in seven chimpanzees was able to solve this problem without help. Problem solving of this kind involves memory, because chimpanzees who had previous experiences of boxes seemed to be able to solve the problem quicker.

According to cognitive theorists, we are continually receiving information from our surroundings and we work out what has happened using our memories and by our previous knowledge and general understanding (or perception). This cognitive view is often known as *Gestaltist* theory. The word 'gestalt' means 'entirety' or 'wholeness of form'. The Gestaltists think that we perceive objects as a whole, rather than a collection of parts.

IN PRACTICE

A cricketer who learns to swing the ball when bowling by understanding the basic mechanics of this movement is using cognitive theory, although she might not know it. A basketball player who has the benefits of the zone defence explained to him and therefore understands when it is necessary to play this tactic is another example.

A wide variety of experience in childhood can have enormous benefits in future skill learning

The cognitive view lends support to 'whole practice' teaching, rather than part practice – playing the game, so that the participants understand what is required, is more effective than simply learning skills separately, according to the cognitive approach. Giving young children lots of sporting experiences may also help with their future learning and motor development because the child can draw from these experiences to understand a problem and then solve it – gaining insight into the learning process.

ACTIVITY

To illustrate that you understand the differences between the S–R (associative) approach and the cognitive approach, create two different training practices for teaching the front crawl in swimming. Try to integrate both approaches by creating a third training session.

Key revision points

The Gestaltists formed the cognitive theory of learning, which involves understanding a problem to give insight into learning. Insight is facilitated by past experiences. This is the 'highest' form of learning, and needs mental reasoning and intelligence. Practical applications of this theory include using a whole approach to skill learning, rather than to split a skill into parts, and giving many different sports experiences to children, which allows the learner to develop problem-solving and decision-making skills. Cognitive theory could be used as an argument against didactic, command approaches to skills teaching.

9.2.1 Social learning theory

Many examples of human behaviour have been copied from others. As children we were all aware of our elders and their actions, habits and attitudes. Those we view as being high status to us, or 'significant others', are much more likely to be copied than those who we regard as relatively unimportant.

Definition

SIGNIFICANT OTHERS

People who are highly significant to us. Even if we may not agree with their behaviour, we have a tendency to copy them. Their behaviour represents what we should ourselves be doing and therefore we copy and imitate.

Human beings like to be accepted by others

Human beings like to be accepted by others and part of a group. We observe and copy behaviour because it helps us to be part of a group and be more socially acceptable. This process is called *social learning*. We can relate this type of learning to the acquisition of motor skills. We copy the skills performed by others because we are motivated to achieve success and because of our drive to be accepted by others. The coach or teacher could be viewed as a 'significant other', and therefore as a role model he or she is copied.

9.3 Motivation

Motivation is extremely important because without it there is no reason for anyone to want to acquire motor skills. There needs to be a drive to learn and achieve success. The study of motivation has been wide, and it could take a whole book to cover each aspect of motivational research in any detail.

Sage (1974) stated that motivation is 'The internal mechanisms and external stimuli which arouse and direct our behaviour'. This definition has three key points.

1 Motivation involves our *inner drives* towards achieving a goal.
2 Motivation depends on *external pressures* and rewards that we perceive in our environment.
3 Motivation concerns the *intensity* (often referred to as our *arousal level*) and the *direction* of our behaviour.

9.3.1 Intrinsic motivation

Intrinsic motivation is a term used for the internal drives to participate or to perform well. Such drives or emotional feelings include fun, enjoyment in participating and the satisfaction that can be felt through playing a particular game. Personal accomplishment and a sense of pride are also intrinsic factors, as well as the physical feeling of well-being when exercising (sometimes referred to as *muscular sensuousness*). The motivation to participate and to perform well in sport can come from internal drives or from external pressures

Intrinsic motivation involves enjoyment of the activity

ACTIVITY

Choose a sports activity or hobby that you are involved in and write down all the reasons why you participate. Next to each write either 'external' or 'internal', depending on whether you feel that the reason is a result of inner drives or external pressures. You will see that it is not a clear-cut exercise – some external pressures lead to inner drives and vice versa.

IN PRACTICE

A child who learns to swim and who enjoys swimming can be motivated to swim further by giving them swimming badges. After a time, when the child has achieved the full range of badges, he could lose interest in swimming because he may feel that there are no more rewards to be had. This is an example of rewards assuming too much importance. The intrinsic motives of the swimmer have mainly been lost because there is no longer a sufficient reason to continue. A similar example could also enhance intrinsic motives. The young swimmer may experience more enjoyment in swimming because of the inner drive to achieve something worthwhile (a badge), which may give a lifelong love of swimming.

Extrinsic motivation often comes from external rewards

IN PRACTICE

Instructors who wish to optimise the effects of intrinsic and extrinsic motivation should involve performers in goal-setting and decision-making. An athlete who shares in planning a training programme will view success with a sense of personal achievement.

i To find out more about reinforcement, turn to page 90.

9.3.2 Extrinsic motivation

External factors can be extremely powerful in determining whether we want to learn a particular skill and whether we want to perfect it. External factors often come in the form of rewards such as medals, badges and prizes. The pressures from other people can also be extrinsic motivators – some young people participate in a particular activity to please their parents, for instance, or you may continue to play for a team once you have lost interest, simply to not let the team down.

As we know, reinforcement from others can ensure that an action is repeated. This is relevant to extrinsic motivation – rewards act as the reinforcers.

9.3.3 Relationship between intrinsic and extrinsic motivation

There has been much debate among sports psychologists about whether external rewards undermine or enhance intrinsic motives.

The need to win could be seen as both intrinsically and extrinsically motivating. The performer could be striving for success to gain a sense of satisfaction or to achieve recognition. In nearly all cases motivation is a mixture of both. Weinberg (1984) makes the key point that 'Rewards do not inherently undermine intrinsic motivation.' Many people feel that it is not the presence of extrinsic rewards that motivates but rather the way the performer perceives the reward. In other words, performers should put rewards into the proper perspective and the people that have influence over the performer (coaches, teachers or parents) must be aware that the performer's perspective can be influenced greatly by their own. If there is too much emphasis on winning the performer will concentrate only on that goal and will not think about the pleasure of taking part.

9.3.4 Theories related to arousal levels

Motivation is related to the intensity and direction of behaviour. *Arousal* represents the intensity aspect of motivation. The effects of arousal can be positive or negative. The physiological effects of arousal, which occur along with the psychological reactions, include an increase in heart rate, breathing and production of sweat. In this chapter we are concerned with the psychological reactions. High arousal can cause us to worry and become anxious, which is a negative aspect if it is not controlled. Raising arousal level can also cause a state of 'readiness' to perform – this is largely a positive aspect and can enhance performance.

As a performer's arousal level increases (often referred to as getting 'psyched up') the state of readiness and expectation increases, but if the level of arousal gets too high a performer can lose concentration and feel over-aroused, which we may refer to as being 'stressed out'. This relationship between arousal and performance is often explained through the *drive theory*, the *inverted U theory* and the *catastrophe theory*.

Drive theory

This was first developed by Hull in 1943. The drive theory, represented in Figure 9.1, sees the relationship between arousal and performance as linear: performance increases in proportion to arousal. A very high arousal level would result in a high performance level. Hull saw that performance depends on how a dominant learned response is intensified. Learned behaviour, according to Hull, is more likely to occur as the intensity of the competition increases. The formula often used to explain this theory is

$$P = f(H \times D)$$

where P represents performance, f the function, H habit and D drive.

If the dominant learned response is correct then the performance will be enhanced. The dominant response for a beginner, however, may be an incorrect action and if this was intensified performance levels would actually decrease.

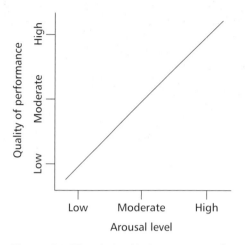

Figure 9.1 *The relationship between arousal and performance: drive theory*

Inverted U theory

This theory is more popular among sports psychologists, although it does have drawbacks because of its simplicity. It was first put forward by Yerkes and Dodson (1908) and has since been applied to sports situations. According to this theory, as arousal level increases so does the level of performance – but only to an optimum point, which occurs usually at moderate arousal level. Once past a moderate arousal level, performance decreases. Participants in sport can become anxious if they are over-aroused and their performance usually suffers. This theory fits many observations of sports performers, although it needs modification to apply it to different types of activities, skill levels and personalities.

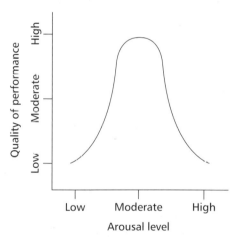

Figure 9.2 *The relationship between arousal and performance: inverted U theory*

IN PRACTICE

A novice is best taught basic skills in a low arousal environment. It is better if no-one else is watching and if competition is not applied in the early stages of learning.

Types of activities

If the activity to be performed involves many fine controlled movements, then the arousal level of the performer needs to be fairly low for optimum performance. Pistol shooters and archers, for example, go to great lengths to control their emotional arousal levels. If the activity is much more gross, such as weightlifting, arousal levels need to be fairly high to expend so much dynamic strength. Rugby forwards have often been seen 'psyching themselves up' before a match.

Skill levels

If the performer is highly skilled, many movements are controlled by motor programmes. Many of their actions need little conscious attention and therefore they can cope with higher levels of arousal. A performer who has

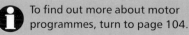

To find out more about motor programmes, turn to page 104.

low skill levels will need to attend to many details related to movement and consequently will need to consciously process much more information. If the arousal level is even moderate, a novice may lose concentration or become anxious, and so a low level of arousal is likely to produce optimum performance.

Personality

Personality types who enjoy high levels of excitement and are generally more extrovert can cope in a high arousal situation. People who are more introverted are generally more likely to perform well under low arousal conditions. This is backed up by the link between the reticular activating system and personality.

Catastrophe theory

There is much anecdotal evidence to support the view that as arousal increases there is a sudden and dramatic drop in performance. We see many top sports people 'go to pieces' in the big events. The inverted U hypothesis shows only a steady decline in performance when arousal is raised above the moderate level. Catastrophe theory shows a much more dramatic decline in performance – hence its name. The theory takes into account that our anxiety can be of two types: *somatic anxiety* (anxiety experienced physiologically, such as sweating) and *cognitive anxiety* (anxiety experienced by the mind – for example, worry about failing). These two types of anxiety interact with each other, with cognitive anxiety being the most crucial in determining the performer's reactions to high levels of stress. The catastrophe theory is a complex multidimensional theory.

9.3.5 Peak flow experience

'Peak flow experience' is a phrase that has been used about sportsmen and women who achieve optimum performance levels and associate this with a particular emotional response. Many top athletes describe their feelings when almost nothing can go wrong. They relate that they are 'in the zone', where all that matters is the performance – all else is insignificant. Peak flow experience can be explained by the arousal theories. All the theories related to arousal show that performance is related to the amount of inner drive and self-motivation. There are mental strategies which can help performers achieve this experience, to motivate them to want to repeat it and drive them to achieve their very best.

We see many top sportsmen and women 'go to pieces'

The 'in-zone'

> ### Definition
>
> ## RETICULAR ACTIVATING SYSTEM (RAS)
>
> *This is located in the central core of the brainstem and maintains our levels of arousal. It can enhance or inhibit incoming sensory stimuli. According to the theories linked to the biological basis of personality, extroverts tend to inhibit the intensity of stimuli and introverts tend to increase the intensity. According to Eysenck (1970), introverts dislike high arousal conditions because their RAS is already stimulated. Extroverts seek high arousal levels because their RAS lacks stimulation.*

IN PRACTICE

Adapted from Sugarman, 1998.

Achieving the 'In Zone' for top performers:

1   Be relaxed. As a top sports performer you do not need very high levels of arousal. You need a balance between wanting to achieve the very best and yet you are relaxed and in control.
2   Be confident. You will have an overall belief that you have great ability. A lapse in performance will not undermine this belief. You will not show fear and you exude pride and confidence. You expect success rather than hope for it.
3   Be completely focused. You will be completely absorbed by your performance. You will not dwell on what has happened before and what may happen in the future.
4   Activity is effortless. You can accomplish often complex and difficult tasks with very little effort. Body and mind are working almost perfectly together.
5   Movements are automatic. This can be related to the motor programme theory visited later in this chapter. There is no real thought that goes into your movement. You move instinctively and there seems to be little conscious thought.
6   Fun. When you are experiencing the flow, the enjoyment is immense. You experience satisfaction and fulfilment. Without this fun feeling you are unlikely to achieve the peak flow experience.
7   In control. You have command over your body and your emotions. You are in charge and you dictate your own destiny.

9.4 Information processing

In this theory the brain is viewed as working like a computer. Stimuli entering the brain are known as *information* or *input*, which is then processed, decisions are made and a response (known as *output*) takes place:

Input → Decision-making process → Output

A more detailed model than this would help us to understand the cognitive processes involved and therefore give us valuable clues to make skill learning more effective. This can be seen in Figure 9.3.

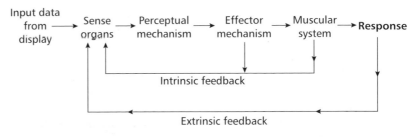

Figure 9.3 *Information processing*

IN PRACTICE

When practising a serve in table tennis, a player would use their short-term memory to store the last shot so that they could compare it with the next to help improvement. The coach may give information to the player, but only a small amount because of the limited capacity of the short-term memory.

The display represents the environment surrounding the performer

Models that set out to explain human behaviour are meant only to be illustrative and should not be taken as a factual representation of what actually happens. The environment is constantly changing, as is the nervous system controlling the body's actions. The model of information processing must be taken as dynamic.

To understand what happens at each stage of information processing, we will look at each part of the model from the environment, before information is processed, right through to the feedback immediately after the response.

- The *display* represents the environment surrounding the performer. For instance a basketball player's display might be her opponents, the ball, the basketball, the crowd, the noise and the score board.
- *Sensory input* is the way information is taken in – vision, audition, proprioception, smell, etc.
- The *sense organs* are receptors which pick up the information and transport it to the brain.
- In the *perceptual process* the relevant information is selected, interpreted and then used to make a decision. Memory is also used in the perceptual process.
- *Decision-making process* or *translatory mechanism*. Once information has been interpreted a motor plan is formed for movement to take place.
- Using the *effector mechanism* the decisions that have been made are put into action and impulses are sent to the muscles for a response to be made. This plan of action may well be in the form of a '*motor programme*'.
- *Feedback* may be extrinsic via knowledge of results or intrinsic, which arises via proprioception.

Definition

MOTOR PROGRAMME

Sometimes called an executive programme, this is a generalised series of movements stored in the long-term memory that can be retrieved by making one decision

 To find out more about feedback, turn to page 106.

9.4.1 Stages of information processing

The whole process of information processing is complex but one way of understanding the process is to divide it into three stages:

1 stimulus identification stage
2 response selection stage
3 response programming stage.

Stage 1: stimulus identification

In this part of the process the sense organs pick up information from the environment and recognise them for what they are. There are aspects of parallel processing which take place in this stage.

Stage 2: response selection

This stage involves making a decision about how to respond to the information that has just been received.

Stage 3: response programming

When the decision to move has been made, the appropriate response is selected. At this stage a motor programme may be used to initiate muscle movement. Some aspects of serial processing occur in this stage.

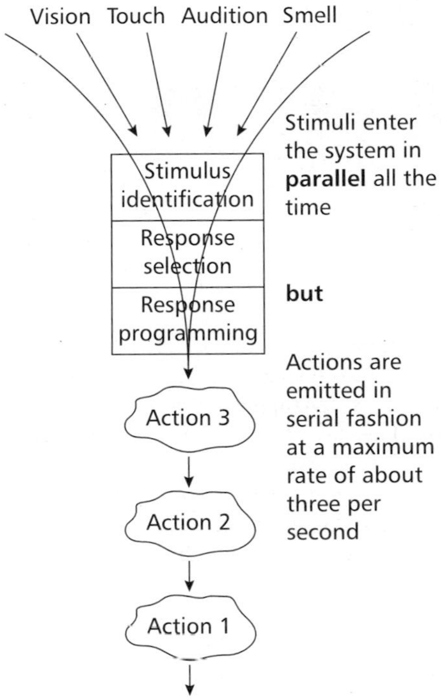

IN PRACTICE

Stimulus identification: A netball player who is about to catch the ball detects the movement of the ball, including its speed and direction.

Response selection: The netball player now decides to change direction to get into line with the ball and catch it.

9.4.2 Serial and parallel processing

Some of the processes within the information-processing model involve decisions that are *sequential* – one decision follows on from another and affects the next one. Some decisions, however, are simultaneous or *parallel* in nature – in other words, processes are occurring independently from one another. It is generally recognised that if information processing is to be applied to the learning of motor skills there is a mixture of both serial and parallel processing.

Figure 9.4 shows parallel and serial processing.

IN PRACTICE

In cricket, a batsman may take into account two or more pieces of information – e.g. the flight of the ball and the movement of the players in the field. This can be seen as an example of parallel processing because he has processed the different types of information separately.

In gymnastics a girl performs a handstand to forward roll. She decides to move sequentially into the handstand and then into the forward roll. This can be seen as serial processing in the response programming stage.

9.4.3 Attentional control

We explored the debilitating effects of attentional wastage in Chapter 8. Attentional control involves concentration, which is crucial if motivation is to be sustained and skill learning is to be effective. Attention needs to be focused on relevant cues or items of information that are important for the execution of a particular skill. To enable a performer to reach and stay in the peak flow experience, attentional control is necessary. Nedeffer (1976), who is a sports psychologist, stated that there are two types of 'attentional focus':

1   *Broad/narrow focus*. It is broad focus if the player's attention takes into account a lot of information at the same time. A basketball player may well take into account the position of the basket, the position of opponents and the position of his own players. The focus is narrow if the player is concentrating on only one or two important pieces of information or cues.

Figure 9.4 *Information processing involves parallel and serial processes*

Definition

SERIAL PROCESSING

A type of information processing in which each stage is arranged sequentially, with one stage affecting the next, and so on.

PARALLEL PROCESSING

A type of information processing when two or more processes occur at the same time and one does not necessarily affect the other.

ACTIVITY

Choose a particular sport and imagine you are playing in a particular position. Identify examples of your broad focus, your narrow focus, your external focus and finally your internal focus.

Definition

COGNITIVE OVERLOAD

A netball player may have just missed a shot at goal. She will have heard the coach shouting instructions at her; she is aware of her own feelings of disappointment; she will be aware of team mates' disappointment and shouts of encouragement. She may well lose concentration because she is overloaded with information. This is often caused by the player being over-aroused.

---

2   *External/internal focus.* If the focus is external then the player is attending to stimuli originating from the environment. The basketball player would be focusing on the position of a player on the other team. If the focus is internal then the player would focus on his own feelings – for example, how anxious he is at that particular moment.

The control a performer has over the type of attention that is used affects arousal levels and therefore motivation levels. It is important that the performer learns how to control his or her attention. If there is too much information available then the performer is said to have *cognitive overload.*

'Cognitive overload' – mistakes can occur if there is too much information

9.4.4 Reactions

The speed with which we process information is known as *reaction time.* The process of attending to relevant stimuli, making a decision and responding involves all three of the stages outlined above.

Several factors affect response time:

- whether the reaction involves making a choice
- your age
- your sex
- whether you were expecting the stimulus or not
- previous experience
- how quickly one stimulus follows another
- whether you can anticipate what is going to happen.

Let us look at each of these in more detail.

Definition

REACTION TIME

The time between first presentation of a stimulus to the very start of the movement in response to it.

MOVEMENT TIME

The time between starting and finishing a movement.

RESPONSE TIME

The time between first presentation of the stimulus to completion of the movement (reaction time plus movement time).

IN PRACTICE

An example of stimulus–response compatibility could occur in squash, when the position of your opponent's feet indicates that he is going to make a drive down the wall, but he then executes a boast on the side wall. Your reactions may well be slower because the response required is different from the one you were expecting to make.

Quick reactions are often crucial if a skill is to be successful

IN PRACTICE

Think of situations in your own sport
where reactions are important.
Identify the stimulus or stimuli which
trigger your information processing
system into action. When does the
response finish?

9.4.5 Hick's law – simple or choice reactions

A performer will take a lot less time to react to only one stimulus or to a
stimulus that requires a simple response than to more than one stimulus or
if more than one response is possible. According to *Hick's law*, the more
responses that are possible, the longer the reaction time will be.

Age

Your reaction time gets quicker, up to an optimum age and then deterio-
rates.

Sex

Males have generally quicker reactions than females but the reaction times
of females deteriorate less quickly than those of males.

Stimulus–response compatibility

If the response demanded by a stimulus is the one you were expecting, you
are likely to react more quickly than if the response demanded is not what
you expected.

IN PRACTICE

An activity involving simple reaction time is the start of a sprint race. The
sound of the gun is the only stimulus which needs attention. An example
of choice reaction time is waiting to receive a tennis serve – there are
several possible responses that could be made to the stimulus of the ball.

Previous experiences

If you have had to react to the same stimulus, or a similar one, in the past
your reactions may be quicker, particularly if choice reaction time is
involved. Motor programmes may be formed and can be 'run' automatically, cutting down the decision-making requirements.

Psychological refractory period

If a second stimulus follows quite closely behind the first, reaction time is
slowed because of the increased information processing time needed. The
single-channel hypothesis underpins this phenomenon.

Anticipation can save valuable time in reaction to a situation

Anticipation

As we discussed earlier, a skilled performer seems to have more time available to complete the actions necessary. This is because he or she has drawn on past experience to anticipate what is about to happen, and has processed information before the event actually happened, which saves them time. Anticipation can set a pattern of movement in advance, which can then be used when it is required – this is called *spatial* anticipation. Using anticipation to predict what is about to happen is called *temporal* anticipation.

IN PRACTICE

A basketball player might be able to predict that an opponent is about to make a shot and jumps to block the shot (spatial anticipation). He or she may also use clues given by particular movements of the opponent to predict that a shot is about to be taken (temporal anticipation).

However, anticipation *can* be wrong and could lengthen reaction time instead of shortening it. The delay could be caused by the psychological refractory period coming into play because the first decision was the wrong one. For example, the basketball player who is perceived to be going for a shot could well be 'faking' the movement.

IN PRACTICE

'Selling a dummy' is a typical way of delaying an opponent's tackle. The opponent has to clear the initial decision to tackle before dealing with the realisation that a 'dummy' has taken place. This can give a player valuable time to change direction or make an unexpected pass.

ACTIVITY

Imagine that you are about to receive a tennis serve. List the cues that you could take notice of to anticipate effectively and cut down your reaction time. Identify the spatial anticipation and temporal anticipation processes.

Other factors affecting reactions

Other factors, such as the intensity of the stimulus, the presence of warning cues and the type of stimulus/stimuli may also affect the speed of information processing.

Key revision points

Information processing is only one of many different ways of understanding how we learn skills. The basic model involves input, decision-making and output. According to Schmidt, there are three stages in processing stimuli: stimulus identification, response selection and response programming. A short reaction time is essential in many sporting activities. There are two types of reaction time: simple and choice. Many factors affect reaction time and the key to shortening reaction time is to optimise the positive effects of these factors.

9.5 Memory

The memory is very important in processing information. Our previous experiences affect how we judge and interpret information and the course of action we take.

The memory process is very complex and, although there has been much research in this area, it is still not fully understood. It is useful to try to simplify the process by using the information processing approach discussed above. The model in Figure 9.5 seeks to explain the components of memory.

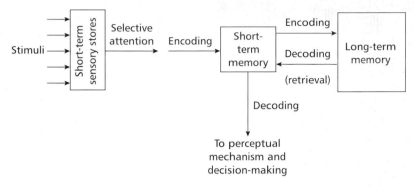

Figure 9.5 *Model representing the memory process*

Selective attention involves concentration

9.5.1 Short-term sensory stores

Information in the form of stimuli enters the brain from the environment. Each store has a large capacity but information is only stored for between a quarter and one second before it is *filtered*. This filtering takes place in the stimulus identification stage. *Selective attention* takes place in the short-term sensory stores.

9.5.2 Short-term memory

This has been named the 'workspace' or the 'working memory' because this is where the information is used to decide what needs to be done. Only a limited amount of information can be stored in the short-term memory (research is ambiguous but points to about 7 pieces of information) and is only held for a short time (about 30 seconds). To extend the time that the information is stored in the short-term memory, the performer would have to rehearse the information, through imagery or sub-verbal repetition (by talking to yourself). Information can also be held in short-term memory through a process called *chunking*.

If information is considered important enough and is rehearsed it can be passed into the long-term memory. This process is called *encoding* the information. Information that is not considered important, or is not rehearsed, is usually lost because it does not go into the long-term memory.

9.5.3 Long-term memory

This store of information has almost limitless capacity and holds information for long periods of time. The information which is stored has been encoded (see above). Information is stored in the long-term memory, possibly by associating it with other information or with meaning. Meaningless items are usually not stored for long periods of time. Motor programmes are stored in the long-term memory because they have been rehearsed many times. The process of continued rehearsal leads to a skill being almost automatic and the process of learning by rehearsal is often referred to as 'overlearning'. If you are regularly using particular motor skills you are more likely to remember them – for example, once you have learned to swim you are unlikely to forget.

ACTIVITY

If you were about to receive a serve in badminton, how would selective attention help you? List the items of information that you would use your short-term memory to process and those you would use your long-term memory for.

Key revision points

The memory process is still largely a mystery but simplified models have been developed to try to explain the process. The basic model describes memory as essentially a three-stage process: short-term sensory store → short-term memory → long-term memory. All information that is selected passes through the short-term memory. The process of chunking (organisation of information) can help a performer deal with larger amounts of information. Items of information need to be rehearsed before they can be stored in the long-term memory.

9.5.4 Motor programmes

Open loop control

Motor programmes are generalised series of movements stored in the long-term memory and each is retrieved by a single decision. They usefully explain how we perform very quick actions in sport, especially closed skills. Some almost automatic movements do not seem to be under conscious control – if a decision had to be made about every single muscle action to catch a ball the information processing would take far too long. This kind of control over our actions is known as *open loop control*, and a model of open loop control is shown in Figure 9.6.

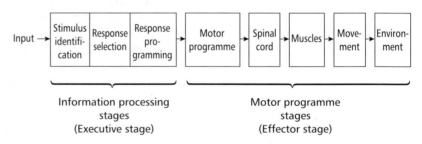

Figure 9.6 *Model of open loop control*

There is no feedback involved with open loop control. If the environment remains constant and predictable then a motor programme can be used or 'run' effectively.

The more a performer practices a series of movements, the more likely it is that a motor programme will be formed. Most movements that we make in sport are a mixture of open loop control and closed loop control.

Closed loop control

This involves the process of feedback. The feedback for this type of control is internal – information is received from the proprioceptors which detect and correct errors in movement. A model of closed loop control is shown in Figure 9.7.

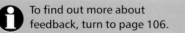 To find out more about feedback, turn to page 106.

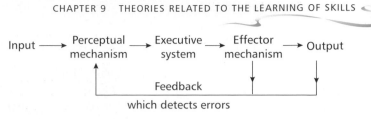

Figure 9.7 *Model to show closed loop control*

9.5.5 Schema theory

Some people feel that the open loop and closed loop theories do not fully explain how we perform so many actions in sport with relatively little conscious control – there simply cannot be enough storage space for so many motor programmes. Under the schema theory a motor programme is seen as only a generalised series of movements that can be modified by taking in information as a skill is performed. The theory usefully explains how we can immediately learn a new skill, and also solves the storage problem. When a movement takes place we perceive information about where we are (knowledge of the environment), what we have to do to perform successfully (response specifications), what the movement feels like (sensory consequences) and what happens when we respond (response outcomes). These items of information, called 'schema', are then stored and used to update the motor programme when we next want to use it.

An experienced basketball player has probably developed a motor programme for the shot

Recall schema

Recall schema are the information stored about the production of movement – the environment and the response specifications. The recall schema starts the appropriate movement.

Recognition schema

These include information stored about evaluating the response – the sensory consequences and the response outcomes. The recognition schema control the movement.

Teachers and coaches who want their students to be successful in a variety of situations must bear the schema theory in mind. If information about many different situations is to be stored, the performer must be exposed in training to as many of these different situations as possible and must be aware of both recall and recognition schema.

IN PRACTICE

An experienced basketball player probably has developed a motor programme for making a shot at the basket, but will not have a programme for shooting from every possible position on the court or for dealing with every possible position of a blocking opponent. However, she will have had many different experiences from which to draw. These will have become schemas stored in the long-term memory which she can use to modify her shooting programme.

IN PRACTICE

A teacher or coach *must* give feedback to the performer – he or she may not be able to detect errors on their own because of limited kinesthetic awareness. For example, a novice gymnast might not be aware of what a good handstand feels like and therefore feedback related to the end result would help him or her detect errors. The coach could use a video of the performance to show the novice how he performed.

ACTIVITY

Think of a practical example for each of the types of feedback listed here, using one of the sports that you are involved with.

IN PRACTICE

The coach of a trampolinist should use simple verbal feedback, and playing a video of the performance in slow motion is a good teaching aid. Once the major errors have been corrected the feedback would become less frequent. Any feedback given must be as accurate as possible and should not contain too much information. The trampolinist needs to develop her own awareness of what movement is good and what movement is poor.

9.6 Feedback

Feedback involves using the information that is available to the performer during the performance of a skill or after the response to alter the performance. There are several forms of feedback:

- *Continuous* feedback – feedback during the performance, in the form of kinesthesis or proprioception.
- *Terminal* feedback – feedback after the response has been completed.
- *Knowledge of results* – this is a type of terminal feedback that gives the performer information about the end result of the response.
- *Knowledge of performance* – this is information about how well the movement is being executed, rather than the end result.
- *Internal/intrinsic* feedback – this is a type of continuous feedback that comes from the proprioceptors.
- *External/extrinsic/augmented* feedback – feedback that comes from external sources, for example from sound or vision.
- *Positive* feedback – reinforces skill learning and gives information about a successful outcome.
- *Negative* feedback – information about an unsuccessful outcome, which can be used to build more successful strategies.

Two of these types of feedback are more important than the others in sports performance: knowledge of results and knowledge of performance.

9.6.1 Knowledge of results

This feedback is external, and can come from the performer seeing the result of their response or from another person, usually a coach or teacher. It is extremely important for the performer to know what the result of their action has been. There can be very little learning without this type of feedback, especially in the early stages of skill acquisition.

9.6.2 Knowledge of performance

This is feedback about the pattern of movement that has taken, or is taking, place. It is normally associated with external feedback but can be gained through kinesthetic awareness, especially if the performer is highly skilled and knows what a good performance feels like.

Both knowledge of results and knowledge of performance can help with the motivation of a performer but if used incorrectly they can also demotivate. Reinforcement, as we discovered earlier in this chapter, is essential for effective skill learning and feedback serves as a good reinforcer. If the movement and/or the result is good then the performer will feel satisfaction, and the S–R bond is strengthened. Knowing that the movement and results are good will help the performer form a picture of what is correct and associate future performance with that picture, image or model.

A gymnast can gain knowledge of performance through kinesthetic awareness or external feedback

To find out more about kinesthetics, turn to page 83.

External feedback should be used with care because the performer may come to depend too heavily upon it and will not develop internal feedback. The type of feedback that should be given depends on the ability of the performer, the type of activity being undertaken and the personality of the performer – different performers respond differently to different types of feedback.

9.6.3 Feedback and setting goals

There is an important link between feedback and setting goals and future motivation and performance. In research carried out by Bandura and Cervone in 1983, 20 cyclists were given performance goals, 20 cyclists received performance feedback but were not set goals, 20 were set goals and received feedback and a further 20 acted as a control group (they were given no feedback and were not set goals). The results of this experiment are set out in Figure 9.8 and clearly show that the effects of feedback are enhanced by goal setting.

When performance is measured and is given to performers as feedback, their motivation can be enhanced and their performance improved. Sports performers often set themselves targets from their previous performances but teachers and coaches can help by constructing performance/goal charts that the performer updates as necessary. These charts serve as feedback on current performance and set clear and progressive targets. This is another useful way of strengthening the all-important S–R bond.

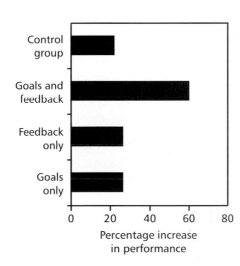

Figure 9.8 *The relationship between performance, feedback and goal-setting*

Key revision points

Feedback occurs both during and after movement. The two main types of feedback are knowledge of results and knowledge of performance. Feedback can help to reinforce effective movements and to detect and correct errors. When intrinsic feedback is involved in the detection and correction process, it is known as closed loop control. In order to motivate a performer it is very important to give the appropriate feedback and to set relevant goals

ACTIVITY

Give examples of performance feedback. Choose a sport and identify the goals that you might set a novice. How would you link goal setting with performance?

Mental rehearsal can help the performer concentrate

Figure 9.9 *The effects of mental practice on performance*

9.7 Mental rehearsal

This is sometimes called *mental practice* and is a strategy adopted by many sportsmen and women. By mentally rehearsing you form a mental image of the skill or event that you are about to perform. No physical movements are involved in mental rehearsal. Some performers find mental rehearsal easier than others but the ability can be improved with practice. Mental rehearsal is used either to learn a new skill or to improve existing skills. It is important in the cognitive stage of skill learning.

IN PRACTICE

Before performing the serial skill of a floor routine a gymnast will go through the routine in his mind by creating a mental image of each stage of the routine. Before taking a penalty kick a soccer player may visualise the kick and the desired result. A demonstration will help the novice tennis player to form a mental picture of a serve before actually serving.

9.7.1 Mental rehearsal and skill learning

The cognitive stage of skill learning (identified by Fitts in 1967) involves the performer understanding what is required to perform the skill. This understanding is associated with building a mental image. Mental rehearsal is thought to involve going through possible movements and mentally experiencing the possible outcomes. This process can help to eradicate unnecessary and energy-consuming movements.

For the novice, mental rehearsal may well improve confidence and help to control arousal levels. Research has shown that if a performer concentrates on successful movements rather than unsuccessful ones, a degree of optimism is experienced.

Figure 9.9 clearly shows the positive effects of mental practice on the performance of a fine motor skill.

By combining physical and mental practice all performers, especially ones who are already skilled, will be able to improve their performance.

IN PRACTICE

To maximise the effects of mental rehearsal, teachers and coaches should encourage the performer to mentally rehearse successful movements away from the heat of competition. Mental rehearsal should include as much fine detail as possible. The performer should also be encouraged to mentally rehearse during rest periods between practice sessions.

9.7.2 Mental practice versus physical practice

Many researchers have concluded that mental rehearsal which is combined with physical practice can lead to high performance levels. Physical practice alone has been shown to be less worth while than the combination with mental rehearsal. If the skill to be performed is serial in nature (see Chapter 8), then metal rehearsal is particularly important to ensure that the right sequence of movements takes place. Mental practice can help to visualise faults and the correction of those faults, can help with controlling arousal levels and can activate the body to respond to particular cues.

An experiment by McBride and Rothstein (1979) investigated how mental practice affected the learning of a closed and an open skill. All subjects were told to hit a golf ball with a table tennis bat at a 6 foot target that was 10 feet away as a control. The closed skill was also attempted by all the

IN PRACTICE

Coaches and teachers should not underestimate the positive effects of mental practice. Fewer physical practices can in fact be better, as long as there is enough good mental rehearsal and preparation.

subjects, where they had to hit the ball off a 3-foot-high tee. In the open skill condition the subjects had to hit the ball that came at them every 10 seconds from a ball feeding apparatus. The subjects were divided up into groups:

- Physical practice group – performed the tasks 40 times.
- Mental practice group – were given a demonstration, had three practice trials and then performed the task mentally 40 times.
- The physical/mental group, who alternated physical and mental trials.

For both the open and the closed skills the group that combined mental and physical tasks performed better than the other groups, even though the combined group actually performed fewer physical trials than the physical practice group.

KEY TERMS

You should now understand the following terms. If you do not, go back through the chapter and find out.

Arousal level
Associationist/connectionist
Classical conditioning
Closed loop control
Cognitive theory
Drive reduction theory
Feedback
Hick's law
Information processing
Insight learning
Long-term memory
Mental practice
Motivation
Motor programme
Open loop control
Operant conditioning
Peak flow experience
Psychological refractory period
Reaction time
Reinforcement
Schema
Selective attention
Serial and parallel processing
Short-term memory
Short-term sensory store
Social learning

PROGRESS CHECK

1. What is the S–R bond?
2. Why is operant conditioning different from classical conditioning?
3. What is meant by the term reinforcement?
4. What is the difference between negative reinforcement and punishment?
5. Give a practical example, other than the one cited in this chapter, to show operant conditioning in action.
6. What are Thorndike's three laws which help to strengthen the S–R bond?
7. According to Hull, what is wrong with too much repetition in practice situations?
8. What did the Gestaltists say about the learning process? Give a practical example of the cognitive theory in action.
9. Define motivation and give examples of intrinsic and extrinsic motivation.
10. Explain the positive and negative aspects of the relationship between intrinsic and extrinsic motication.
11. Draw a graph to show the drive and inverted U theories.
12. Why is the inverted U theory so much more popular than the drive theory?
13. Draw a detailed information processing model.
14. What are the three stages in information processing?
15. Define reaction time.
16. Choose an example in sport when the time to respond needs to be short. Write down as many factors affecting the performer's response time as you can.
17. Draw a simple model of the memory process.
18. What is meant by the term selective attention?
19. How can a teacher ensure that information is stored in the performer's long-term memory?
20. What is meant by a motor programme?
21. How does schema theory help with the problems of the programme theory?
22. What are the two most important types of feedback and how can they help in future performances?
23. What is mental rehearsal?
24. What are the main effects of mental practice on skill learning?

Chapter 10

Theories related to the teaching of skills

Learning objectives

- To recognise the different stages in the learning process.
- To understand the concept of transfer.
- To be able to investigate the most effective ways of structuring practices.
- To be able to apply different types of guidance to practical situations.
- To be able to identify different teaching styles, along with their advantages and disadvantages.
- To understand the need to adopt different teaching styles in different situations.

The theories related to skill acquisition have been investigated in the last two chapters. In this chapter we apply these theories directly to the teaching process. Effective skills teaching is dependent on the recognition and understanding of the stages that are passed through by the learner. What to include in skills practices is also crucial. It is important for the coach or teacher to include only those skills practices that will benefit rather than hinder the acquisition of motor skills, and this is where the concept of transfer comes in. The personality of the teacher or coach will dictate to a certain extent the way in which they teach skills. There are, however, proven strategies that teachers and coaches can use to optimise the learning process.

10.1 Stages or phases of learning

Fitts and Posner identified several different stages in the learning process, although it must be remembered that learning is a complex process and the stages, or *phases* as they were labelled, are not clear cut. However, it is useful to try to identify the different levels of understanding that each phase represents because we are then better able to create successful teaching strategies throughout the learning process.

10.1.1 Phase 1: the cognitive phase

The cognitive phase is the earliest phase of learning, when the performer understands what needs to be done. There is quite a lot of trial and error in this phase, the beginner trying out certain movements which may be successful or may fail. The successful strategies can be *reinforced* by the performer experiencing success or being told by their teacher that the move has been successful. Unsuccessful strategies should not be dismissed because all experiences can be worth while. The performer should understand why failure occurred in order to avoid the same experience in the future. To establish understanding teachers may use demonstrations or other methods of guidance (these are discussed later in this chapter). It is important that relevant cues are highlighted by the teacher and recognised by the performer.

10.1.2 Phase 2: the associative phase

In the associative or motor phase of learning the performer practises, and compares or associates the movements produced with the mental image.

There are stages that a learner of a skill has to go through

IN PRACTICE

If a novice badminton player is in the cognitive phase of learning and needs to understand the serve, her teacher could demonstrate the correct technique and highlight important points (this is called *cueing*) so that the player builds up a mental picture of what needs to be done. This 'visualisation' of the movement is more effective if the teaching is simple, clear and concise.

This is the stage at which feedback occurs and the learner gradually becomes more aware of increasingly subtle and complex cues. During this stage a vast improvement in performance usually occurs. Motor programmes are said to be formed in this phase of learning, although skills have probably not been 'grooved' automatically yet.

IN PRACTICE

The novice badminton player who is now aware of what needs to be done for the serve has tried various strategies and is now entering the associative phase. Her service is now more consistent and most serves fall into the service box. The performer is concentrating on getting the service lower and into different areas of the service box and the teacher is giving feedback. The performer is starting to detect and correct errors, even without her teacher's help.

10.1.3 Phase 3: the autonomous phase

This is the final phase of the skill learning process. Movements are becoming almost automatic, with very little conscious thought. Any distractions are largely ignored and the performer is able to concentrate on more peripheral strategies and tactics. It is said that during this stage motor programmes are completely formed in the long-term memory and reaction time is short. Some performers may never reach this stage or may reach it with only the basic movement patterns. For performers to stay in this phase they must continuously refer back to the associative phase, where practice ensures that motor programmes are reinforced.

IN PRACTICE

The performer of the badminton serve is now confident and able to consistently perform an accurate serve with the minimum amount of thought. The performer can use more sophisticated strategies such as disguising the nature of her serve, putting her opponent at a disadvantage. She can now also take into consideration more peripheral cues such as her opponent's position on court and, in doubles, the position of the other opposing player.

The skilled performer who is in the autonomous phase can disguise intentions more effectively

Key revision points

Three phases of learning have been identified. In the cognitive phase the learner understands the requirements of the task. There is some trial and error learning in this phase. The associative phase is the practice phase in which the learner receives feedback and starts to build motor programmes. In the final, or autonomous, phase execution of the skill is almost automatic. There is apparently little conscious control and the skill is speedily executed. The performer can now concentrate on more complex responses.

Definition

PERFORMANCE

Performance is only a temporary measurement, which can alter from time to time. It differs from learning in that learning is relatively more permanent.

10.1.4 Learning curves

You will often hear coaches or performers mention 'being on a learning curve'. This refers to the relationship between practice trials and levels of performance. Strictly speaking, this relationship could be seen as a curve

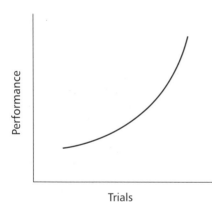

Figure 10.1 *The relationship between trials and performance*

of performance but the overall picture gives us a rough idea of how much learning has taken place, hence the label – curves of learning.

So curves of learning show an individual's range of performances at particular moments in particular situations. If you were to plot a graph showing your own performances while learning a new skill, you would find that your performances vary quite a lot and that the learning curve would not be very smooth. However, if you took out all the extremes in performances, you would probably find that a curve of sorts is visible. Obviously, the more trials you record the better indication you will get of the learning that is taking place.

ACTIVITY

Carry out a simple experiment with a partner. You become the experimenter, your partner becomes the performer. The performer has 20 trials of performing a novel, gross, simple task. Choose a task that can be measured easily after each performance (e.g. throwing a dart with your non-preferred hand at a target, with the greater scores at the centre of the target). Record the scores after each trial, construct a table to show your results. Draw a graph using the axes shown in Figure 10.1

Figure 10.2 *A positive acceleration curve*

Figure 10.3 shows a typical curve of learning. Looking at the S-shaped curve you can see that there is an initial period when there is no learning. The performer may fail completely in the early stages of learning a motor skill. At position A you can see a slow rate of improvement over the early trials, when the performer is starting to learn the skill. The curve at A is called a *positive acceleration curve*.

At point B we see a sharp increase in performance levels over a relatively small period of time, indicated by the number of trials. The performer seems to be learning quickly now and consequently the performances are rapidly getting better. This part of the overall picture is called a *linear curve of learning*, which is not a curve at all; rather a straight line showing a short period of proportional improvement.

At point C you can see that there is a slowing down in improvements in performance. This may be because the performer has reached his or her optimum or best possible performance, or could be due to fatigue or lack of motivation to do better. This curve is called a *negative curve of learning*.

The performer then enters into a period, shown at point D, where there is no improvement or a decrease in performance, which is called the *plateau effect*.

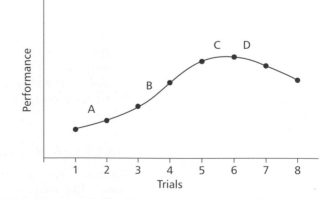

Figure 10.3 *The amount of learning over a given time period*

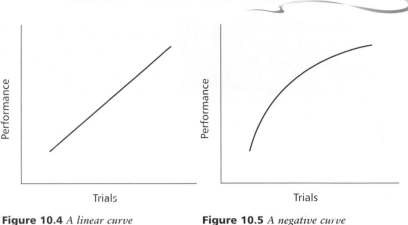

Figure 10.4 *A linear curve*   **Figure 10.5** *A negative curve*

> **Definition**
>
> ## NEGATIVE CURVE OF LEARNING
>
> *This is when an individual has greater gains in terms of performances earlier but later there are fewer gains. This is the opposite of the positive curve of learning.*

> **Definition**
>
> ## PLATEAU
>
> *There may well be differences or fluctuations from trial to trial but overall there is little or no change in the measured performance. Performances neither increase nor decrease.*

> **Definition**
>
> ## DRIVE REDUCTION
>
> *An individual may be motivated to complete a task, which can be seen as a 'drive'. When that drive is perceived as being fulfilled, then the drive is reduced. If the individual feels that he or she is performing to the best of their ability, the performance may well become habitual and the performer sees no reason to be motivated or 'driven' to do better. Problems can occur if the performer thinks that there is no need to drive to improve, even though there may well be room for much improvement.*
>
> ## REACTIVE INHIBITION
>
> *This is a phrase that arises from the work of Hull and his drive theory (1948). A performer of a motor skill may think that they have done their best and reached their goal (e.g. high percentage of effective serves in volleyball), and this causes them to stop trying so hard or 'inhibits' their effort. This can lead to a decrease in performance.*

The motivation or drive to do well may well have been fulfilled if the performer feels that he or she has made their best possible performance. This is known as drive reduction. This is an aspect of drive theory (dealt with in Chapter 9). This reduction in drive can inhibit the performer to improve and this is referred to as *reactive inhibition*. The concept of drive reduction and the resultant reactive inhibition illustrates well that performance curves are not true reflections of learning.

Reasons for a plateau occurring:

- Lack of motivation by the individual performer. For instance, the practices may lack variety and be boring.
- Physical and/or mental fatigue.
- Perception by the performer that he or she has achieved the goals.
- Lack of rewards, either intrinsic or extrinsic and therefore loss of interest.
- The performer is not receiving the right information on how to improve.
- The learner feels that the goals are too high for them and therefore becomes demotivated.

Strategies to combat the plateau effect:

- Regular rest intervals.
- New and stimulating rewards.
- Praise and encouragement by the coach or teacher.
- Selective attention employed. Concentration on relevant cues.
- Employment of a positive attitude to improve an individual's skill level.
- Physical and mental training to prepare the performer and to offset the effects of fatigue.
- Setting realistic but challenging goals. For instance, skills could be split up into parts to enable success before going on to more complex movements.
- Being aware of the plateau effect and therefore being prepared to combat it.

IN PRACTICE

When coaching or teaching a novice the tennis serve for instance, be aware that there may be times when improvements could slow – and performance could even get worse. After 20 trials the novice may be getting fewer serves in the serving box than after 10 trials. Give the novice a rest and reassess the goals. Go back to technique and give the novice success again to improve confidence. Make the novice aware of the plateau effect and reassure and encourage. Give plenty of praise when it is earned.

Teach basic skills first and then build up to more complex actions

A skill which is highly organised is best practised as a whole but with the support of mechanical or manual aids – like these stabilisers

10.2 The concept of transfer

Transfer in skill acquisition is the influence of the learning and/or performance of one skill on the learning and/or performance of another. If this influences a skill yet to be learned or performed it is called *proactive* transfer, if it influences the performance of a previously learned skill it is called *retroactive* transfer.

One skill can help in the learning or performance of another, in which case it is known as *positive* transfer, or may hinder the learning or performance of another skill, when it is called *negative* transfer.

It is important that teachers of skills maximise the effects of positive transfer and minimise the negative aspects. Throughout this chapter we will be investigating the best ways of presenting and teaching skills, always bearing in mind the important concept of transfer. In order to do this we must first understand this complex concept.

ACTIVITY

Identify whether the following situations are examples of proactive or retroactive transfer, and whether positive or negative transfer are involved.

1 Practising overarm throwing of a ball, then learning the basic cricket bowling action.
2 A novice badminton player spends a day playing tennis, then returns to badminton and finds that many of his shots lack control.

10.2.1 Basic to complex

In all areas of education it is common practice to teach basic skills first and then to build upon these skills to achieve more sophisticated skills. In physical education in primary schools, basic throwing and catching, kicking and striking activities are encouraged so that these basic skills can be transferred to more complex activities such as passing in football and netball or the serve in tennis. Skill teaching is therefore progressive and involves a step-by-step approach from basic 'foundation' actions to more finely tuned complex skills.

IN PRACTICE

To teach a straddle vault in gymnastics, the coach may well use the following sequence of activities:

1 star-jumps with legs wide and straight
2 running with 'two feet take-offs'
3 straddle vault over a partner
4 straddle jump onto a low vault, with support
5 make the vault higher and gradually reduce support.

This encourages transfer of skills in a logical fashion, increases confidence, ensures safety and gives kinesthetic awareness.

10.2.2 Situational influences

Positive transfer is likely to occur only if practice conditions are as realistic as possible. If the response to a training stimulus is not consistent with the response demanded in the real situation, negative transfer could take place and bad habits could be encouraged. For instance, a teacher may use traffic cones to coach dribbling skills in hockey, but the method used to go around the cones is very different from the way a player will go around a real opponent – you don't meet many traffic cones on a hockey pitch! Land drills are often used in the coaching of swimming because it is assumed that positive transfer will take place from the 'dry' situation to the water. However, use of land drills may involve some negative transfer because the different situations have different kinesthetic experiences. The real situation should be used as much as possible to maximise the transfer effects.

10.2.3 Positive transfer

To ensure that any transfers are helpful, the coach must bear in mind that positive transfer will take place only if the structure and context in which the skills are performed are similar to those used in teaching. Positive transfer is also more likely if the information processing requirements in practice are similar to the ones of the actual skill.

For example, an overarm throw and the tennis serve are both similar skills and therefore positive transfer is likely if the throw is used to learn the serve (the context is not similar but cannot be confused). The information processing requirements are different in some ways – in the tennis serve, for instance, the position of the receiver must be taken into account – but this difference is unlikely to interfere with successful execution of either skill. The 'identical elements theory' (developed by Thorndike in 1914) suggests that the greater the number of components of practice that are relevant to the 'real' situation, the more likely positive transfer is to take place and future responses to be correct. The term 'transfer-appropriate processing' is given to the idea that a new skill might be different from any skill performed before, but if the cognitive, information processing requirements are similar then positive transfer could occur.

It is important to remember that the amount of positive transfer that takes place often depends on how well previously performed skills have been learned. If a skill is broken down and taught in parts, each part must be learned thoroughly before positive transfer can be maximised.

ACTIVITY

Using your own sport, give examples of skills which could be used to positively influence the learning of new skills. Identify any movement or motor elements which may be useful and also identify similar information processing requirements.

10.2.4 Negative transfer

Fortunately negative transfer is rare, and mostly temporary. It is more often than not associated with the performer misunderstanding the movement requirements rather than having problems with movement control. Negative transfer must be minimised, and coaches must understand the strategies to avoid it occurring. Negative transfer often occurs when a familiar stimulus requires a new response, particularly if the demands of the new response are so similar to the old demands that the player becomes confused. For example, a tennis player may misjudge her shots when playing indoors because the techniques needed are subtly different from those required in outdoor play. Such problems are usually short lived and, once the performer gets used to the new requirements, normally disappear. If the coach understands that initial performance may be hindered because of negative transfer and draws the performer's attention to the problem, negative transfer can be eliminated.

Key revision points

Transfer in skill acquisition involves one skill influencing the learning and performance of another. Transfer that helps to learn and perform other skills is known as positive transfer. If it hinders other skills it is known as negative transfer. Factors affecting transfer include the structure of practice sessions, situational influences and awareness of possible negative effects. Other types of transfer are listed below:

Bilateral transfer – transfer between one limb and another.
Intertask transfer – the influence of one skill on a new skill.
Intratask transfer – the way different conditions in practice can influence the learning of a skill.
Near transfer – when the tasks given in training are very similar to the 'real game' situation.
Far transfer – the training tasks are very different from the 'real game' tasks but give general experiences which could be used in a variety of situations.

10.3 The structure and presentation of practices

To optimise skill learning teachers and coaches must create the best possible practice conditions. Using what we learnt of Schmidt's schema theory in Chapter 9, we know that variety in training is very important – not just to build up schema in the long-term memory but also to increase motivation.

IN PRACTICE

In hockey the reverse stick tackle is a complex skill. The information which needs to be processed includes the position and speed of the opponent, the tackler's position, the position of the ball, and an awareness of other players. This skill may be best taught using a slow demonstration, followed by practice at walking pace. The pace of both players may then be increased and then put into a small game situation before coaching within the full game.

For practice to be meaningful and relevant the following factors need to be taken into consideration:
1   The nature of the skills involved – are they open or closed for instance?
2   The amount of technical knowledge needed.
3   The amount of information the performer needs to process.
4   Environmental factors.
5   The previous experience of the performer.
6   The performer's personality and how well they are motivated.

The teacher or coach should analyse carefully the nature of the task involved. A *complex* task involves skills which require a lot of information processing. The perceptual requirements are therefore quite high and the decision-making process depends on feedback and previous experience. The performer needs to fully understand the task and therefore careful explanation is needed. The task may be broken down into easier subunits and as the performer improves is made more complex, until the complete

The highly organised skill of cycling would have to be taught as a whole movement, because of the difficulty of splitting it into sub-routines. The use of stabilisers is common; these enable the novice to experience the action safely and effectively. The novice will eventually be able to cycle without the stabilisers, first with manual support and then without any help. The low organisation of the tennis serve is best practised by splitting the skill up into its constituent parts. The throwing action of the arm could be practised first, followed by throwing the ball up, hitting it and following through. Eventually the separate actions could be brought together.

task can be performed. This technique is most effective in learning open skills, which need high levels of information processing.

The organisation level of the task must also be taken into consideration. A *highly organised task* involves skills that are difficult to split into sub-routines – it is often a continuous skill, such as cycling. A skill which has *low organisation* is easily broken down into its constituent parts – for example the tennis serve involves preparation, throwing up the ball, striking it and finally following through.

The actual structure of the practice session is important when considering the most effective way of teaching skills

10.3.1 Teaching skills using the 'whole' method

In the 'whole' method a skill is taught without breaking it down into sub-routines or parts. If possible this method should be employed more than any other because the player experiences the true 'feel' (or kinesthetic sense) for the skill and transfer from practice to the real situation is likely to be positive. The player is also likely to execute the skill fluently and can appreciate the relationships between each part of the movement. If a task is rapid or ballistic in action, the 'whole' method of teaching is best because the components of the skill interact closely with one another.

The golf swing is a good example of this. For the swing to be effective, the action as a whole must be practised because each part of the swing interacts closely with the next. If a motor programme, like a golf swing, is to be built up, then again it is better to practise the movement as a whole.

10.3.2 Teaching skills using the 'part' method

A gymnast will benefit from concentrating on one element of a floor routine at a time but must remember that one part of the routine interacts with another. For instance, the way in which he finishes the 'round-off' will affect the start of the back somersault in a sequence.

The 'part' method is often used when the skill is low in organisation and can be split up into sub-routines. If the skill is complex this method is useful because it allows the performer to make sense of the skill and to achieve initial success with basic movements before progressing to the more complex movements. Part practice can also be useful in learning a dangerous skill.

The performer can gain confidence by learning each element of the skill separately and then, when the separate parts are brought together, the performer will have a better idea of the technique involved and be more confident of success. This practice technique is particularly useful when trying to teach serial skills.

10.3.3 Progressive-part method

This is often referred to as 'chaining' in the teaching of skills. The skill, usually serial in nature, is broken down into sub-routines which are thought of as the links of a chain. The performer learns one link at a time, then adds on a second link. She practises the two links together, then adds on a third link – and so on, until the links can be practised together as a whole. This process is sometimes referred to as the 'gradual metamorphosis' process.

Many skills are best practised using a mixture of part and whole methods. For instance, a performer may well benefit from trying out the skill as a whole, to get the idea of the complete movement and to understand the interrelationships between the various components. Each component could be practised separately and the skill then brought together and performed as a whole. This mixture of methods highlights weak areas, which can be isolated for more intensive practice.

10.3.4 The operant method

This method was described in Chapter 9. It involves 'shaping' behaviour using trial and error followed by reinforcement. The operant method is particularly effective in teaching complex skills. The performer will be able to understand the interrelationships between the components of the skill and also to build strategies for avoiding errors in the future.

10.3.5 Variable practice

Practice needs to be varied so that the performer can come into contact with a range of experiences (in line with Schmidt's schema theory, discussed in Chapter 9). Relevant experiences are stored in the long-term memory and can be used to modify motor programmes in the future. With closed skills it is important that practice conditions closely resemble the 'true life' situation. Stimuli that are irrelevant to the closed skill should be varied but those that *are* relevant should *not* be varied.

With open skills, each situation will be different from the last – the conditions, unlike those in closed skills, are not constant. It is essential, therefore, that practice involves many different situations so that the performer can draw from the strategies in long-term memory that he or she has learned in previous practice.

10.3.6 Massed and distributed practice methods

The structure of the practice session is important when considering the most effective way of teaching skills. There are many different definitions of what is meant by 'massed' and 'distributed' practice, but we will take 'massed' practice to mean practice that involves very short, or no, rest intervals within the practice session. Massed practice, then, is a continuous practice period. 'Distributed' practice involves relatively long rests between trials. The 'rest' intervals could involve tasks that are unrelated to the main practice activity: for example, between basketball drills players could go and play table tennis. It is important to remember the theory of transfer – these rest periods should not involve activities which could lead to negative transfer. Many performers, particularly the experienced ones, use the intervals between activities to practice mental rehearsal, the effects of which have already been discussed.

Research has shown that distributed practice is generally best because massed practice can lead to poor performance and hinder the learning process because of fatigue and demotivation. Massed practice may help learning of discrete skills which are relatively short in duration but distributed practice is best for learning continuous skills because the player rapidly becomes tired. With tasks that are potentially dangerous, distributed practice is also best because it ensures that physical and mental fatigue does not negatively affect performance and put the performer in danger.

10.3.7 Overlearning

The word 'overlearning' suggests that this is a negative concept but it is usually positive, although in some situations it can be detrimental to skill acquisition. Overlearning is extremely helpful in retention and retrieval of the information needed to perform motor skills.

ACTIVITY

Construct two training sessions using your knowledge of whole and part practice and massed and distributed practice conditions, along with the concept of overlearning.

Session 1 – A 1-hour session teaching a novice a skill such as a tennis serve, a basketball shot or a gymnastic sequence.

Session 2 – A 1-hour session with an advanced-level performer – in an athletic field event, an advanced swimmer or an advanced badminton player for instance.

The definition that is often used for overlearning is 'the practice time spent beyond the amount of practice time needed to achieve success'. This 'extra' practice time can help to strengthen motor programmes and schema. If a skill has been learned so well that it is almost automatic, a performer can concentrate on other variables – for instance, a basketball player may have learned to dribble so well that he or she can direct attention to other aspects of the game, such as the position of colleagues and opponents.

There is, however, an optimal level of practice – too much practice could result in demotivation and fatigue. The teacher or coach must ensure that good performers stay in the autonomous phase of learning by rehearsing skills, but must also be aware of the plateau effect and the costs of doing too much.

Key revision points

Practice sessions must be well planned, taking into consideration the skill to be learned, the performer and the environment. If the skill is complex, with many items of information to process, the skill should be split up into sub-routines and each part taught separately. If the skill is highly organised, and the sub-routines closely interrelated, then it is better to teach as a whole. If the skill is serial in nature, then the progressive-part method may be appropriate. Using this method each section is taught and linked or 'chained' to the next. The operant method of teaching allows learning by trial and error and reinforcement of appropriate responses. Variable practice is important to build up schema in the long-term memory. Massed practice is generally not as effective as distributed practice and involves a practice session with no or very few rest intervals. Massed practice is better for more able performers and can help with overlearning. Distributed practice involves relatively long rest periods. It can help with motivation and delays fatigue. Mental rehearsal is facilitated through this approach. Overlearning generally helps the performer to retain information in the long-term memory. Overlearning helps to ensure that the performer reaches and stays in the autonomous phase of learning.

10.4 Types of guidance in the teaching of motor skills

When a teacher or coach presents a new skill to a student or seeks to develop the skills of an experienced performer he or she needs to decide the best way to transmit the knowledge necessary for effective performance. There are four main types of guidance:

- visual
- verbal
- manual
- mechanical.

The type or combination of types chosen depends on the personality, motivation and ability of the performer, the situation in which learning or development of skills is taking place and the nature of the skill being taught or developed.

10.4.1 Visual guidance

Visual guidance is widely used when teaching motor skills. During the cognitive phase of skill learning visual guidance (often a demonstration by the instructor of another competent performer) helps the learner develop a mental image of what needs to be done. Some instructors use videos, charts or other visual aids to build up the 'ideal' picture of what is required to successfully perform a new skill. The demonstration must be accurate so that there is no possibility of the learner building up an incorrect picture. To avoid confusing the learner and overloading him or her with information in the early stages of learning, it is important to concentrate on only a few aspects of the skill. The teacher may therefore only 'cue' the performer onto one or two aspects of the whole movement. One way of ensuring that the learner cues on to the right stimuli is to change the 'display'. The instructor may highlight certain features of the display to help the learner to concentrate on relevant and important information.

During the cognitive phase of skill learning visual guidance is important for the learner to develop a mental image of what needs to be done

IN PRACTICE

The following points should be considered before using visual guidance.

- Demonstrations must be accurate and should hold the performer's attention.
- Demonstrations must be repeated but should not be too time consuming.
- Videos can be useful, especially if they have a slow motion facility, but the student must be able to copy the model presented.
- For a learner to gain maximum benefit, their position during training should be considered. For example, the demonstration of a swimming stroke is best viewed from above on the poolside.
- During the cognitive phase of skill learning visual guidance is important for the learner to develop a mental image of what needs to be done

ACTIVITY

Choose a skill from any sport. How would you teach this skill with visual guidance only? Include any ideas about modifying the display.

10.4.2 Verbal guidance

This is often associated with visual guidance, being used to describe the action and explain how to perform the activity. Verbal guidance has limitations if used on its own – motor skills are very difficult to describe without a demonstration of some kind. Remember that the instructor is trying to create an image in the learner's mind of what needs to be done. Verbal guidance of the more advanced performer is effective when the more perceptual information, such as tactics or positional play, needs to be conveyed.

IN PRACTICE

When using verbal guidance the teacher/coach needs to be aware of the following points.

- Do not speak for too long – sports performers have notoriously short attention spans!
- Some movements simply cannot be explained – stick to visual guidance in these cases.
- Direct (or didactic) verbal guidance is better in the early stages to ensure that the learner has a clear idea of what needs to be done.
- Questioning techniques can encourage personal development and develop confidence if handled in the right way – especially for the more advanced performers. Feedback from the performers will also test understanding.

10.4.3 Manual and mechanical guidance

This involves two factors:

1 Physical support for the performer by another person or a mechanical device. This is commonly known as 'physical restriction'. An example of this is supporting a gymnast over a vault or the use of a twisting belt in trampolining.

2 The response of the performer being directed physically by another person. This is commonly known as 'forced response'. Holding the arms of a golfer and forcing his or her arms through the movement of a drive is an example of forced response.

Manual/mechanical guidance can reduce fear in dangerous situations – e.g. arm bands in swimming

IN PRACTICE

The following points should be considered before using manual or mechanical guidance.

- Manual/mechanical guidance can reduce fear in dangerous situations. For instance, wearing arm bands will help in learning how to swim.
- This method of guidance can give some idea of kinesthetic awareness of the motion.
- However, it could give unrealistic 'feeling' kinesthesis of the motion. For example, it is advisable to remove the arm bands as soon as possible to be able to teach stroke technique in swimming.
- The intrinsic feedback received could be incorrect and may instil bad habits or negative transfer.
- There is a reduction in the learner's participation, which could negatively effect motivation.

Key revision points

Visual guidance is used in early stages of teaching a skill. Demonstrations are the most common form. Important cues must be highlighted through this guidance.

Verbal guidance is not very effective if used on its own, except with very able performers, but with visual guidance it can be very effective, especially to help identify important cues.

Manual and mechanical guidance is important in the early stages of learning. It can help a performer cope with fear and can help with safety. This type of guidance helps to give kinesthetic awareness but should not be overused.

Is coaching like acting on a stage?

10.5 Teaching styles related to the acquisition of motor skills

There are many different styles that can be adopted by teachers and coaches. Each instructor has his or her own way of presenting information and the style each chooses depends on several variables.

- The teacher's personality and abilities.
- The type of activity to be taught.
- The ability of those being taught.
- The level of motivation of those being taught.
- The age range of the students.
- Environmental factors.

ACTIVITY

Think of some of your instructors. Write down the characteristics they display – are they humorous in their approach? Are they strict? Do they let you have a say in what happens?

An effective style takes into account all of these variables. Some teachers are far more extrovert in their approach than others and may adopt a style which is far more open and sociable. Teachers who are more introverted may adopt a style which ensures they don't get into situations where they feel uncomfortable. Teachers who are very able physically may adopt a style to use their physical prowess for demonstration purposes. Some teachers are naturally more charismatic than others and so they tend to use a more teacher-centred approach. Coaches need to be aware of their own personality characteristics and abilities before they decide on the approach they will take. Some feel that teaching is an act and that a 'performance' is required – they create an artificial 'persona', masking their own personality and abilities. Others believe that if they act out a role, their pupils will eventually find out and the learning that has been achieved will be devalued. Both arguments are valid, and each individual must decide on the style they will adopt.

The type of activity being taught also has an influence over the style the teacher adopts. For instance, if the activity is dangerous the coach is more likely to adopt a strict, authoritarian style. If the activity is complex and the perceptual demands are high, a more explanatory style will be appropriate. We have already looked at how to analyse and classify motor tasks. Once the instructor has analysed and classified the motor tasks involved, he or she will be in a position to choose an appropriate style of delivery.

The characteristics of the group or individuals being taught is another important element to take into account.

Experience – a novice may need a more direct style to begin with so that he or she gains a clear understanding of what needs to be done. If the individual is experienced, a more consultative or democratic style will allow the individual to give some valuable contributions and share in the decision-making process.

Motivation – if the performers are highly motivated the coach can concentrate on the task rather than attempting to increase motivation. If motivation is low, the teaching style adopted should be more enthusing and reward based.

Age – with very young children a non-threatening style should be adopted, with the emphasis on fun. As the performers get older the emphasis could be more democratic and more responsibility could be shifted onto them. There is nothing worse than the teacher or coach treating responsible adults like children and not valuing their input. Similarly, too much responsibility should not be placed on young people. A key to successful teaching is to know the characteristics of those who are trying to learn and then to adopt a suitable approach.

ACTIVITY

Think of some teaching/coaching situations where the teacher needs to 'act out' a role, rather than be themselves. Give reasons for your choices. Think of some situations when it is better for the teacher to be truthful about their own thoughts and feelings.

Environment – Teaching approaches may be affected by the situation. For instance, the weather may dictate the style adopted: a consultative, democratic approach is the last thing that is needed on a cold, wet day! In a dangerous, hostile environment a more task-oriented approach could be called for. Instructors should assess each environmental situation as it arises and adopt the appropriate approach.

Environmental situations need to be taken into account when adopting a teaching style!

10.5.1 Mosston's spectrum of teaching styles

In 1986 Mosston and Ashworth identified a range of styles, which are characterised by the amount of decisions that the teacher and learner make in the teaching/learning process. This is shown in Figure 10.6.

When more decisions are made by the teacher, the style is said to be more 'command'. When the learner makes nearly all the decisions the style is said to be 'discovery'. The spectrum includes many styles between these two extremes. At about C or D the style is said to be more 'reciprocal' – this style is characterised by the learners becoming 'teachers' themselves and teaching their peers. This style involves both the instructor and the pupils making decisions. The 'discovery' method is essentially pupil centred; the performers are largely self-motivated and have the experience and creative ability to work largely without help and guidance.

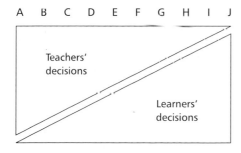

Figure 10.6 *The spectrum of teaching styles*

ACTIVITY

The command, reciprocal and discovery styles are all relevant to the teaching of motor skills. List the advantages and disadvantages of each of these styles.

Successful teachers and coaches are able to adopt a range of styles, depending on the variables identified above. It is important to ensure an enjoyable and productive atmosphere, and motivation can be enhanced if personal achievements are recognised. The teacher should analyse the variables in each situation so that performance and motivation can be optimised.

The teacher or coach must know what teaching technique motivates each individual in the team if performance is to be optimised

The best style to use if the teacher has good discipline and the group is large, or if the situation is dangerous, is the command style. This style does not allow social interaction or individual involvement in learning. The learner can simply end up being a clone of the teacher, which may be useful up to a point but does not allow development of new ideas and is not a dynamic process. The reciprocal style of teaching allows more social interaction and encourages a sense of responsibility. Group members must be mature enough to handle the responsibility and have reasonable communication skills. This style is not recommended for complete beginners. The discovery style allows individual creativity but the performer must be well motivated. The instructor must be prepared to step in and guide if the performer runs out of strategies or is beginning to develop bad habits. It can be difficult to 'unlearn' incorrect practices, and the learning process could be severely delayed.

Key revision points

There is a range of teaching styles possible. Teachers or coaches should adapt their approach to the type of activity, the age, ability and motivation level of the performer, environmental factors and their own personality and capability. Mosston's spectrum of teaching styles takes into consideration the proportion of decisions made by the learner and the teacher in the learning process. The more decisions that are made by the teacher, the more authoritarian the style. Each style in the spectrum has its advantages and disadvantages and should be chosen, bearing in mind the factors just mentioned. Successful teachers use a wide range of styles, and know how to adapt to changing environmental circumstances and the different needs of performers.

KEY TERMS

You should now understand the following terms. If you do not, go back through the chapter and find out.

- Associative phase
- Autonomous phase
- Cognitive phase
- Distributed practice
- Identical elements theory
- Learning curves
- Manual and mechanical guidance
- Massed practice
- Negative transfer
- Organisation of a task
- Overlearning
- Part method
- Performance curves
- Positive transfer
- Proactive transfer
- Progressive part method
- Retroactive transfer
- Spectrum of teaching styles
- Variable practice
- Verbal guidance
- Visual guidance
- Whole method

PROGRESS CHECK

1 Name the three main stages or phases of learning that were identified by Fitts and Posner.
2 What are the characteristics of each of these phases?
3 Why is it important to know what happens in each phase of the learning process?
4 Define what is meant by the term transfer in skill acquisition.
5 Give a practical example of how negative transfer can inhibit effective skill performance.
6 How can a teacher or coach ensure that only positive transfer takes place?
7 What factors must be taken into consideration when structuring a practice session?
8 What is meant by a complex task? Give a practical example.
9 When is it best to use the 'whole' method of teaching a skill?
10 Give a practical example of using the 'part' method of teaching a skill.
11 Why is the 'variable practice' method so important for building up schema?
12 Why is distributed practice usually better than massed practice?
13 What is meant by 'overlearning'?
14 Identify the four main types of guidance.
15 Choose any skill and describe how you would teach it, selecting only one type of guidance.
16 What variables should be taken into consideration when adopting a particular teaching style?
17 Choose one of these variables and justify the 'discovery' approach of teaching it.
18 What could be the problems of adopting a reciprocal approach to teaching?
19 What did Mosston take into account when he developed his spectrum of teaching styles?
20 Give as many advantages and disadvantages as you can for the 'command' style of teaching.

Further reading

D. Davis, T. Kimmet and M. Auty. *Physical Education: Theory and Practice.* Macmillan, 1986.

P.M. Fitts. *Human Performance.* Brooks/Cole, 1967.

C.L. Hull. *Principles of Behaviour.* Appleton-Century-Crofts, 1943.

R.A. Magill. *Motor Learning, Concepts and Applications.* Brown and Benchmark, 1993.

M. Mosston and S. Ashworth. *Teaching Physical Education.* Merrill, 1986.

M. Robb. *The Dynamics of Skill Acquisition.* Prentice Hall, 1972.

R.A. Schmidt. *Motor Learning and Performance.* Human Kinetics, 1991.

R. Sharp. *Acquiring Skill in Sport.* Sports Dynamics, 1992.

B.F. Skinner. *Science and Human Behaviour.* Macmillan, 1953.

K. Sugarman. Peak performance. *Winning the Mental Way.* Step Up, 1998.

E.L. Thorndike. *Educational Psychology: Briefer Course.* Columbia University Press, 1914.

Part 3

Sociocultural aspects of physical education and sport

This part of the book contains:

This part of the book investigates how society can affect the sports performer and how society can be influenced by physical education and sport. In order to understand what is happening today, it is useful to look back at what has happened before and this part deals with historical factors. The terms we use when describing the activities related to sport differ, which can lead to confusion. We encourage readers to analyse these different terms to develop a better understanding of why people get involved in physical education and sport at different levels and the factors which influence and restrict their choices. This part compares physical education and sport in the UK with that of other countries so that we can learn from the experiences of other cultures. Many social issues surround physical education and sport and this section of the book takes an in-depth look at the main issues affecting the performer. It is hoped that the reader will base any future decisions and attitudes on careful consideration of the facts surrounding a particular issue, not on hearsay or stereotypes. Discrimination of all forms is unfortunately a feature of our society, in sport as in other aspects. We must strive for equality of opportunity and we hope that this part of the book will help all of us consider the issues surrounding physical education and sport intelligently and without prejudice.

Chapter 11 · *The origins and study of sport*

Learning objectives

- To develop knowledge of the history of sport.
- To be able to discuss the role of the study of sport.
- To be able to define the concepts involved in the study of sport.
- To understand the role that concepts such as outdoor recreation play in society.
- To know the factors that affect sport and recreation in Britain.

Sports are developmental – they develop from *conquest* or from *social hierarchy*.

For example, rugby was introduced by the upper classes at Rugby public school in the early 1800s and then spread with the British Empire around the world. The game was taken to Western Samoa from New Zealand by plantation farmers and merchants at the beginning of the twentieth century. The Western Samoans play the game by the same rules as everyone else, but to them rugby is a *war game* – this is very evident in the ferocity of their tackling. The New Zealand Maoris (and even the national team) play the modern game but have incorporated parts of their own culture into it with the ritual Haka, performed before the game.

Definition

HAKA

A ritual war dance performed by several southern-hemisphere nations before rugby internationals.

In human activity, the invention of the ball may be said to rank with the invention of the wheel

11.1 The origins of sport

The oldest sports were probably gymnastic displays. One of the earliest recorded forms of sport is evident in Minoan Crete – this is bull leaping, in which slaves leapt over the horns of a bull. Records of bull leaping give us a glimpse of the function of this ancient form of sport, mainly as a spectacle with some ritualistic or religious element. To the Minoans the bull symbolised God because it was the biggest, most ferocious and strongest animal known to them and by challenging the bull they honoured the God. However, bull leaping was also a *test of physique and temperament* – which is the essence of sport. The Minoans did not actually perform the bull leaping themselves – they used servants to represent them. This leads us on to another important element of sport, that of *spectacle*.

In the Haka, the Maoris are really saying 'today we get our own back!'

The modern game of lacrosse originated in a game that the Iroquois Indians of North America played, called Baggataway, in which they threw a bag containing the head of an enemy or rival to each other. The South American civilisations had a similar bloody use for the heads of their enemies – ritual games of football, which they played in purpose-built stadiums that can still be seen today. It has been suggested that the great British game of football has its origins in a game called 'Daneshead', played by men who had defeated Scandinavian raiders.

Wrestling originated in Graeco-Roman times. Wrestling was considered as the 'ultimate' sport because it was (and still is) one-on-one and could end in the death of one participant.

These examples point to another characteristic of sport – you often put your life on the line: *there is no sport without risk*.

11.1.1 Historical links of various sports

The many sports played today derive from five main historical areas:
- invasion games
- target games
- court games
- field sports
- religious rituals.

Invasion games

These games, such as rugby and football, are warlike games, where the object is to invade the opponent's territory. The origin of these games lies in mob games in which one part of a community played against another part, usually to defend or steal something.

Target games

These games involve use of marksmanship and include sports such as archery, with its clear link to war/defence and also sports such as golf and bowls. The urge to aim and hit targets is almost innate in humans. Think about how you put a piece of scrap paper into the wastebasket – no doubt you screw it into a ball and 'fire' it at the bin.

Court games

Court games originally reflected culture – sophisticated games were thought to represent sophisticated culture. Such games include real tennis, fives, rackets, squash and lawn tennis. The sports are non-contact because the opponents are on opposite sides of a net. Because of the sophistication and expense these games were often confined to the upper classes.

Field sports

Sports such as hunting, shooting and fishing are associated with finding food and survival but also the enjoyment of the chase. The fox is thought to represent man, master of the environment and so a challenge. These sports have also been associated with the upper classes, although the working classes found a similar satisfaction in 'coarse fishing' and in animal baiting.

Games involving ritual

These games included baiting animals such as bears and bulls with dogs. The bull was seen as 'bad', man showed his supremacy over the animal, and everybody could own a dog. Baiting the bull before slaughter was often a legal requirement. This is another example of sport reflecting the society in which it exists – but this sport shows an uncivilised society limited in its development.

In bull baiting the bull is tethered and attacked by dogs

11.1.2 A brief overview of the historical development of modern sport

Modern sport may be seen to have passed through four stages of development.

1 Popular recreation (before 1790)
2 Public school athleticism (1800–1860)
3 Rationalisation of sport (1860–1919)
4 Twentieth century of sport (1920 onwards)

The transition between the phases represents not only development in sport but also major developments in society.

Popular recreation

In pre-industrial Britain, sports clearly reflected the society. In the main sports were of two types:

- the sports of the aristocracy – complex and refined, such as real tennis and fencing
- the sports of the peasants – the so-called 'mob' games.

The mob games and other 'people's' sports were closely associated to the church calendar of holy days and wakes and to the farming year of spring and harvest. These sports were a chance for the people to meet as a community and 'let off steam'. They were not really sport in the modern sense – there were very few (if any) rules, the game being a kind of free-for-all. They were also not played often – sometimes only once a year (for example the annual Ashbourne Football game was played once a year on Shrove Tuesday).

Sports involving animals were also popular. Hunting was mostly the domain of the upper classes, and at this time there was still a great deal of 'quarry' available. The royal deer forests are a good example of the exclusivity of this 'sport' – these forests were protected for the sport of the king and those to whom he was pleased to grant a similar privilege. Rigorous Game Laws were enforced in every county, keeping the common people from catching animals on these lands.

For the lower classes this hunting drive was satisfied by the bloody spectacle of animal baiting. Cock-fighting was a huge gambling sport and bulls, bears and even horses were trained to fight dogs. Special arenas were built to house these events.

Definition

MOB GAMES

Peasant sports involving large numbers, and few rules, played during the popular recreation phase of sports development – often associated with football type games.

Mob football in the Middle Ages

Public school athleticism

At the beginning of the nineteenth century, public schools began to appear for the upper classes. Very quickly these became an essential element of training to be a gentleman – they were also to play a very important role in the development of modern sport.

Initially the boys took the rural sports into the schools and with some adaptation carried on the sporting traditions of an upper-class gentleman. The games of hare and hounds or cross-country running became substitutes for hunting, but games and sports were increasingly used for educational purposes. Football is the most popular example of this transformation. With its roots in the mob festivals of the populace, football was transformed by public schools into an organised regular game with rules and played an essential role in the education of a gentleman whose destiny was to lead and develop the Empire.

Sport was used as social control in the reformation of the public schools, which led to concept of 'muscular Christianity' – the idea that moral understanding could be developed through athletics.

Rugby School – the birthplace of rugby football

131

The public schools were the first bodies to codify sport – to give it rules. This process extended sports and ultimately gave us the concept of sport as we know it today.

Rationalisation of sport

From 1860 onwards the development of sport began to spiral. We can chart the development, codification and administration of all the major sports from this time on. Important changes occurred in society that would determine the image modern sport would portray. It is important that you know a little about the impact of industrialisation and the effect that this had on the people, their work, homes and leisure.

Most people now lived and worked in urban areas and the influence of the rural elements in sport declined – modern sport is also urban sport.

As boys left their public schools they played an important role in developing sport at the universities of Oxford and Cambridge. They began to unify the various strands and develop national sports, wrote rules and set up governing bodies to oversee these unified sports. These young men then spread their love of games around the world.

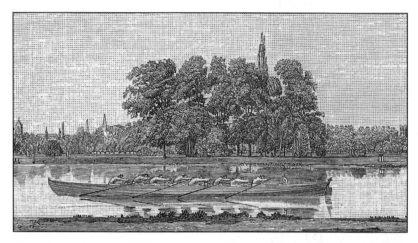

The university boat race, 1829

Sport in the twentieth century

Several factors have affected the development of sport through the twentieth century. There was a steady move away from participation in sport to the phenomenon of watching sport, initially through spectatorism but increasingly through the media. Spectatorism generated money, which led to professionalism in virtually all sports. Many sports performers are now full-time paid entertainers.

Sport has become a mass consumer spectacle unavoidably linked to commercialism, a point which is discussed further in Chapter 16.

11.2 An introduction to the study of sport

The rest of this chapter involves sociocultural study of the environment in which sports take place. This area is concerned with a family of activities:

- sport
- leisure
- physical recreation
- play
- outdoor recreation
- physical education.

We will take each of these separately and discuss them in their correct contexts. In this chapter we will consider only sport.

11.2.1 A brief history of sport

In the middle of the nineteenth century the word 'sport' referred to the 'field' sports of hunting, shooting and fishing which the upper classes enjoyed. Gradually it became more widely applied to all games played in the open air.

Sports (plural) was the name given to a series of athletic contests, often held at rural festivals or gatherings. The Scottish Highland Games and the Basque Games in southern France are good examples of events of this type which still take place.

The modern meaning of sport was born during the industrial revolution at the public schools such as Rugby. Gradually these games were passed on to the lower classes and new pastimes of playing, watching and reading about sport developed. The number of activities that come under the name of 'sport' is ever increasing. Some of the latest additions to this list are speed climbing and mountain biking.

11.2.2 What is sport?

We can identify certain characteristics that are shared by all sports.

ACTIVITY

Look at the following list of sports and make a list of the characteristics they have in common.

Hockey, rugby, cricket, cycle pursuit, orienteering, netball.

From your answers to the activity above, you will have probably discovered the following points:

- they all contain an element of *chance*
- they all involve *competition* between *distinct sides*
- *physically strenuous activity* is involved
- the *clear outcome* has *winners* and *losers*
- games are *spontaneous* and *enjoyable*
- *special equipment* is usually needed to play.

From this list we may develop the hypothesis that all sports must have the features in this list.

Definition

SPORT

According to the dictionary 'to sport' means 'to play, or frolic'. A more appropriate definition for this book is 'Institutionalised contests, using physical exertion between human beings or teams of human beings'.

Competitive mountain biking is an example of a modern sport

The essence of sport?

ACTIVITY

Would you consider the following activities sports?

1   Darts
2   TV's *Gladiators*
3   Jogging
4   Competition ballroom dancing

To check the effectiveness of this hypothesis let us study a particular activity – recreational swimming, for example. Although this activity certainly involves physical exercise and some (very basic) equipment, there is no real competition in swimming a few lengths of a pool. We could argue that there is an element of competition against self, but there are no clear winners and losers, nor any distinct 'sides'. Consequently we may conclude that recreational swimming is not a sport, according to our hypothesis.

Therefore, for a theoretical approach to the study of physical activity, sport can best be defined as an activity that involves competition, which is physically strenuous and enjoyable.

11.2.3 Why study sport?

In Britain, sport holds a special place in education and culture. According to Winston Churchill, 'sport was the first of all the British public amusements'. We have a long tradition of sport in Britain. Several sporting events have become national pastimes – Derby Day, the Boat Race, the FA Cup, the Grand National, Wimbledon.

Sport and education

Education has long been associated with sport. Through sport you can learn a lot of life's moral issues and experiences – it also has the advantage of making you healthy!

Sport and social control

Definition

SOCIAL CONTROL

Where sport is used to control the masses

Sport has been used to control the masses – a concept called *social control*. If people are playing or watching sport they are not getting themselves into trouble. Social historians have often said that Britain never had a social revolution because its people were too busy playing games!

Britain has a unique position in the history of world sport. Most of the modern games played throughout the world were invented and developed here, and then taken to the extremes of the British Empire.

Sport and international relations

Sport can be used to keep up morale in times of war. For example, the Kuwaiti soccer team toured Britain during the Gulf War. It can also be used to promote trade and cement allegiances or offer an olive branch to nations that are in conflict with each other. For example, England and Argentina played rugby and soccer internationals soon after the Falklands conflict as a means of peace making.

Sport and the media

Perhaps the best illustration of the importance sport plays in our culture is the amount of time and space the media devote to it. The BBC alone devotes at least 20 hours each week, and most national newspapers donate 10–20% of their space to reporting sport.

The armchair sports enthusiast

Key revision points

Sport is a complex concept, the true meaning of which has been distorted by its use in the media. Sport is best seen as any physical activity that includes competition with a clear winner, which is strenuous and enjoyable. As Samuel Johnson concluded in 1756, above all, sport is 'Tumultuous merriment'.

Ancient sports had the following characteristics: ritual/symbolism, function and spectacle. These elements are still visible in many modern sports. Popular recreation took place in pre-industrial Britain, the games being played having close links to the social background of the players. Sport in public schools was based on the concept of athleticism. Schoolboys adapted the popular games at these schools. Later, schools used sports to develop character ('muscular Christianity') and as a means of social control. A great deal of development and codification of modern sports occurred at universities in the late nineteenth century, which was also a period of great change in society. By the end of the nineteenth century the games ethic was being carried all around the world. In the twentieth century spectatorism, professionalisation and the media have had great influence on sport

KEY TERMS

You should now understand the following terms. If you do not, go back through the chapter and find out.

Athleticism
Court games
Field sports
Haka
Invasion games
Mob games
Popular recreation
Rationalisation
Social control
Sport
Target games

PROGRESS CHECK

1 Taking Minoan bull leaping as an example, what were the functional aspects of primitive sport?
2 Invasion games have played an important role in Britain's sporting tradition. Suggest reasons for this importance.
3 Why were court games limited to the upper classes in the early years of their development?
4 What are the main characteristics of a sport?
5 What does the New Zealand Haka symbolise?
6 What were 'baiting' sports?
7 Give three examples of activities classified as 'field' sports.
8 Give a historical time scale for our study of popular recreation.
9 In the popular recreation era what were the two main divisions of sporting activity?
10 List the main characteristics of a mob game.
11 How was hunting divided along social lines during the popular recreation era?
12 What role did the public schools play in the development of sport during the nineteenth century?
13 Comment on the origins of 'Hare and Hounds', a game played in public schools during the nineteenth century.
14 Give a historical time scale for our study of the rational phase of sports development.
15 What are the main factors that affected the development of sport in the first part of the twentieth century?

12

Leisure, recreation and play

Learning objectives

- To develop an understanding of the concept of leisure.
- To be able to discuss the historical development of leisure
- To be develop an understanding of the concept of recreation.
- To differentiate between and discuss the use of physical recreation and outdoor recreation.
- To develop an understanding of the concept of play.

Many other terms are used when discussing issues relating to sport and physical education. We will concentrate on the following in this part of the book: *leisure*, *recreation* and *play*. All can be related to physical activity and it is very probable that you have experienced all three. You need to appreciate that an activity can be classified as *any* of these concepts, depending on the context in which it occurs. In terms of preparation for your exam it is important that you can characterise the key points for each of these concepts.

12.1 Leisure

If we listed all the particular things we do in a day, we would probably end up with a very long list. However, most of our activities could be categorised under the following headings:

- work
- bodily needs
- duties
- leisure.

We need to *work* to earn a living. Work consumes a large amount of our time. This definition of work includes related activities such as housework, school and college work, travel to work. Our *bodily needs* include sleeping and eating. *Duties* include the tasks we must perform in relation to family, pets and the home. If we exclude from our day the time required for these three activities we are left with *free time* – this is the time we have available for *leisure*. The average split of a person's daily activities may be represented in a pie chart, as shown in Figure 12.1.

ACTIVITY

Make a record of your time over the next few days, put the activities into the categories described above and produce your own pie chart.

The key to leisure time is that you perform the activities that you *choose* to do. Figure 12.2 shows how the various activities involve choice.

12.1.1 What exactly is leisure?

We use the word leisure in two ways:

1. as the period of free time which is left after work.
2. to describe an activity or something we do. A leisure activity is freely chosen.

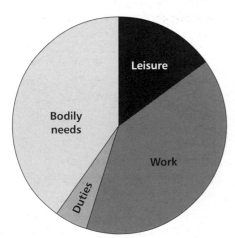

Figure 12.1 *Average split of a person's daily activities*

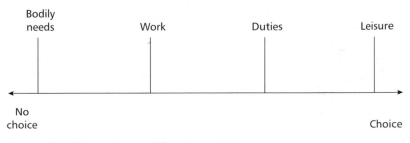

Figure 12.2 *The continuum of choice in activities*

Definition

LEISURE

'Time in which there is an opportunity for choice.' (Arnold, 1978). 'An activity, apart from the obligations of work, family and society, to which the individual turns at will, for either relaxation, diversion, or broadening experiences and his spontaneous social participation, their free exercise of his creative capacities.'
(Dumazedier, 1967).

Definition

WAKE

Initially derived from the ceremony honouring the dedication of the local parish church, extended into first a one-day holiday after the all-night vigil and then in the industrial northern towns to an annual weekly holiday based on the Saint's day of the parish church.

ACTIVITY

Is housework a leisure activity?
To help you answer the question look at the definitions above and the key words we have identified.

A great many definitions of leisure are available. Perhaps the best suited to our study are given in the definition box on this page.

Any attempt to fully answer the question 'What is leisure?' reveals it to be a frustrating and elusive concept whose definition changes depending on the context in which it is used. However, leisure does have positive connotations of enjoyment, freedom of choice, self-fulfilment and self-actualisation. These keywords are our criteria for a definition of leisure.

12.1.2 Is leisure a new concept?

We often hear talk of increasing leisure time and we are said to be living in a leisured society. Increasing automation and development of labour-saving devices, along with the general decline of manufacturing, have meant that most people have more spare time than they used to. However, there has always been leisure time – Roman Britain had 156 'Holy' days (equivalent to our bank holidays), then there were wakes and fairs, half days on Saturdays and other days (e.g. shopkeepers and their half days on Wednesdays). In Sheffield the shop owners formed a sports club so that they could play cricket and football on Wednesday afternoons. They called their club Sheffield Wednesday – a name that is retained by today's Premier League soccer team.

Leisure has historically been compensation for work done, an escape from drudgery. Clearly the most simple definition of leisure is time away from work. This of course raises the question of what is work – and it is wrong to consider work as only a job one is paid for. Over half of the population are not in paid employment and therefore are not included in the conceptual boundaries of such a definition.

The essence of leisure is that it is not so much the activity but whether it is freely chosen that counts. For example, a person may hate cutting the lawn and will therefore look at it as a duty. However, if she spends hours feeding the grass, talking to it and cutting it so that it resembles the pitch at Wembley, this is obviously a freely chosen leisure activity.

Other problems arise when we look at high sport – sport undertaken by top performers. To these people, amateurs and professionals alike, sport is not simply time away from work (it takes up most of their time). Their chance for spontaneous participation in a range of leisure interests is also severely limited. A professional footballer may well be under contract not to take part in any other contact sports or activities such as ice skating because they involve too high a risk of injury.

Key revision points

Key words for leisure: free time, choice, not work. Definitions of leisure tend to infer that it is time not at work, but work can include many things. Although there has always been some form of leisure throughout history, we all have more leisure time and can choose from a far greater list of activities than people in the past.

RECREATION

According to Lumpkin, 'Recreation, refreshes or renews one's strength and spirit after toil.'

Kaplan defines recreation as '. . . activity voluntarily engaged in during leisure and motivated by the personal satisfactions which result from it . . . a tool for mental and physical therapy.'

Parker says about recreation: 'In its literal sense of re-creation, it may be seen as one of the functions of leisure: that of renewing the self or preparation for work.'

12.2 Recreation

The word recreation stems from the Latin word *recratio*, which means 'to restore health'. Recreation is an active aspect of leisure, something useful, not simply a time left over after work, duties and so on.

Keywords that are appropriate for recreation include:

- *relaxation* – a chance to escape
- *recuperation* – recovering from stress
- *re-creation* – to be creative.

These are often referred to as recreation's 'three rs'

In modern life, stress is one of the greatest dangers to health. Worry about work or unemployment, difficulties at the home or in the family can make people ill. Recreation does not usually solve any of these problems but it will enable the individual to relax and get 'away from it all' for a while.

ACTIVITY

Make a list of your own recreational activities. What do you do to relax? To recuperate?

12.2.1 The history of physical recreation

The term physical recreation is closely linked with middle-class culture. Its modern usage has been shaped by the public schools and industrial philanthropists of the nineteenth century. In that century people in the middle and upper classes were very concerned about the moral well-being of the working masses – mainly about how the working classes amused themselves in their increasing leisure time. Recreation was considered as positive use of leisure time and the middle classes promoted parks, fresh air, recreation grounds and 'muscular sports' to combat the appeal of the gin palaces and ale houses. Religious movements were also quick to seize on the idea that recreation could be used as a form of social control (keeping the masses in check). This was highlighted by the expansion of church soccer teams, YMCA clubs and organisations such as the Boys' Brigade at the end of the nineteenth century. Holt reports how the Boys' Brigade lured the youth of Glasgow off the corrupting streets by the prospect of 'banging drums, blowing whistles and kicking balls!'

12.2.2 Physical recreation and outdoor recreation

Traditionally, *physical recreation* has been used to describe physical activities within the concept of leisure. The term is now better known as 'Sport for All', which describes physical performance opportunities for all members of the community, and places emphasis on participation rather than performance standards.

Outdoor recreation is associated with tradition and the romantic movement. Outdoor recreation usually involves an individual undertaking a challenging activity in the natural environment. Again, many such activities are available.

12.2.3 Physical recreation now

Playing for the sake of playing, or playing sport for intrinsic rather than any extrinsic rewards, is the key to understanding the true meaning of physical recreation.

However, this also accounts for the low status which sport often achieves in our society – if an activity has no external value it serves little function. This is certainly the view of sport that many politicians and leaders adhere to.

SPORT FOR ALL

Physical performance opportunities for all members of the community, with emphasis on participation rather than performance standards.

ACTIVITY

List the possible rewards that may arise from taking part in a physical recreation under the headings of intrinsic or extrinsic rewards.

Jogging, step aerobics, a knock-up in tennis and visiting a water 'splash' theme pool are all recreational activities. They all involve physical exercise and the participants gain something from doing them. However, they are not sport as we have defined it, because there is no definite outcome, extrinsic reward or stringent organisation.

A new range of activities is developing, associated with this idea of taking part in sporting activities for fun – the 'life-time sports'. Activities such as badminton and walking can be carried on throughout life, and all generations are being encouraged to get involved. It is hoped that this will break the myth that sport is only for the young – you are not really a veteran at 35, as is currently the rule in sports such as hockey and rugby.

Definition
LIFE-TIME SPORTS
Sports that can be played throughout life, generally ones that can be self-paced or can be adapted.

> ## Key revision points
>
> *Physical recreation is physical activity of a relaxing nature, with limited outcome and organisation. It is a positive use of leisure time, involving an activity worth doing. Physical recreation has a strong link with middle-class moral guidance of the nineteenth century. Intrinsic rewards dominate in physical recreation.*

12.3 Outdoor recreation

In the last section we defined and discussed the term recreation, and in particular physical recreation. We also identified another term: *outdoor recreation*. This is associated with challenge in the natural environment, but due to the popularity of such activities and the importance the 'great outdoors' plays in our culture the term deserves more detailed investigation.

The simplest and most straightforward definition of outdoor recreation is simply the participation in any enjoyable, *holistic activity* in the outdoors, where the term outdoors refers to the natural, or at least rural, environment.

Definition
HOLISTIC ACTIVITY
Participation involves immersing your whole body in the activity, a complete commitment to the activity.

12.3.1 A brief history of outdoor recreation

The term really developed from two movements that occurred as Britain became an imperial nation and the leading industrial centre of the world in the nineteenth century:

- The Naturalist movement
- The Romantic movement.

Both these middle-class cults saw England as 'God's own country' and believed that every Englishman had the right to go out and breathe the fresh air of the country.

Rambling and fishing are our most popular outdoor recreations, and both retain a link with our rural past and the seemingly inherent need to seek out rural roots. The oldest of outdoor recreations, the so-called 'field sports' (a collection of various forms of hunting and other rural pursuits) have in the main been available only to the upper classes.

Rambling, the most popular of modern outdoor recreations, is a much more open activity. It is free and the general development in transport has increasingly opened up the countryside to all. From about the 1850s onwards walking clubs were set up by a variety of organisations. Holt reports how the Manchester YMCA were 'truly muscular Christians', organising weekend rambles of up to 70 miles. Great emphasis was placed on this flight from the rigours of urban life into the more natural pacing of the countryside – a theme the French call *rustic simplicity*. The descendants of these Manchester walkers were no doubt among the working-class ramblers who in 1932 helped cement the status of outdoor recreation with

Fishing – Britain's most popular hobby

The challenge of the environment

their mass trespass on Kinder Scout – this led to the setting up of our National Parks and to other measures which helped open up the countryside to all.

Cycling followed rambling as a popular form of enjoying the outdoors and has continued to develop – the latest boom being in mountain biking.

Most people now have the use of a car – and this is the way that most of us now enjoy some 'fresh air'. Unfortunately, much of the benefits of outdoor recreation seem limited by the fact that few people move more than 200 yards from the car when we do get out into the natural environment.

ACTIVITY

William Wordsworth (an influential member of the Romantic movement) wrote that the Lake District of Cumbria was: '. . . a sort of national property in which every man has a right and would interest anyone who had an eye to perceive and a heart to enjoy.' Do you agree with Wordsworth's idea? What do you think are the advantages and disadvantages of developing outdoor recreation and tourism in such areas?

Some countries have used outdoor recreation as a central part of nation building and even as a political tool. This usually is concerned with fostering a love of the 'Mother country', as seen in the Soviet concept of tourism. The French actively promote 'Le Plein Air' in a country steeped in rural heritage, instilling a love of the outdoors in the young which lasts throughout life. The Americans quest the Frontier Spirit, a concept related to the history of the country and a counter-culture to the urban 'win at all costs' society.

12.3.2 The boom in outdoor recreation

In recent years there has been a boom in outdoor sports. Activities such as windsurfing and mountain biking have become extremely popular and part of 'fashion' culture. This expansion has been linked to the greater availability of transport, particularly ownership of cars, which has meant that more and more people can get out into the outdoors. Developments in technology and manufacturing have allowed the mass production of cheap equipment (mountain bikes for example), opening these sports up to more and more of the population.

Key revision points

Outdoor recreation involves challenging activities in the natural environment. Most people in Britain partake in some form of outdoor recreation frequently. For most people, the essential element is an escape from the urban environment. The most popular outdoor recreations are walking and fishing.

12.4 Play

One important concept we have not yet looked at and one which has an important part in our society is *play*.

Play is a term with a number of meanings:
- it is an issue in itself, as in *I Play*
- it is also part of the morality of sport, as in the phrase *Fair Play*.

Huizinga suggests that our ability to play has formed the basis for all human cultures and civilisation – humans have always played and it could

Definition

PLAY

According to Huizinga: 'Play is a quality of experience within an activity. It is fun.' Armitage says, 'Play is only true, if it is performed with free will, for fun, and only as long as the participant wants it to go on.'

INTRINSIC REWARDS

Merits such as enjoyment and self-satisfaction that come from an activity.

EXTRINSIC REWARDS

Material benefits, such as cups, medals and money that some sports performers receive for their activities.

be argued that all inventions and discoveries have been a product of play. Our children learn about life through play and adults use play to relax and escape from the 'seriousness' of everyday life.

Play is the base from which sport begins. All sports have their origins in play – as children we first play, then move on to more sophisticated games and eventually to sport.

12.4.1 What is play?

Play is considered to be a free activity, generally non-serious and outside the maintenance of life. There is certainly a large play element in sport – at the lower level sport is fun and we play to escape and relax. However, the higher you get the more competitive and serious the activity becomes. Sport is not play when there are extrinsic rewards such as money: it becomes too serious.

We can pick out the following keywords that characterise play activities:

- spontaneous
- childlike
- self-fulfilling
- intrinsic.

12.4.2 The concept of play

As we have seen above, play is not connected with material interest or profit – so do professional sportsmen *play*?

ACTIVITY

List in the terms of play the differences between an amateur and a professional sportsman, using the keywords to help you.

Play creates an order of its own and often symbolises overtly and covertly aspects of the real world. If we study children at play, it is easy to identify aspects such as competition, dominance and leadership. Gender differences are also obvious: often the boys' football games will dominate the play space, with the girls being confined to the edges.

As mentioned above, we play to learn about life and we usually associate the term with younger people but adults *do* play. Adults play to escape the rigours of work and the stresses of life – paintball or laser arcades are clearly older, if a little more sophisticated, forms of the shooting games that all children play.

12.4.3 The functions of play

What role do play activities have in our lives? It has been suggested that play has three functions:

Biological – play is an instinctual part of the learning process. It forms a crucial part in the development and refinement of many skills.

Psychological – play allows us to learn about ourselves; we direct it and it allows us to gain experience. We need to learn how to make decisions and control our emotions and arousal levels, which we usually develop through role plays and games when we are young.

Sociological – play enables children (and to some extent adults) to practise future social roles. We acquire a knowledge of how other people respond to us and how they react to us when we try different roles.

Play also helps to defuse conflict – because of its non-serious nature it can be used to dispel aggression and frustration.

KEY TERMS

You should now understand the following terms. If you do not, go back through the chapter and find out.

Bodily needs
Duties
Extrinsic rewards
Holistic activity
Intrinsic rewards
Leisure
Lifetime sport
Outdoor recreation
Play
Recreation
Re-creation
Recuperation
Relaxation
Sport for All
Wake

PROGRESS CHECK

1 Our daily activities can be listed under which four headings?
2 Why, for some people, is leisure not free from the obligations of work, family and society?
3 How has the development of labour-saving devices in the home had an effect on leisure?
4 What is the history behind Sheffield Wednesday FC's name?
5 What was a wake?
6 Why is ' time not at work' too simple a definition for leisure?
7 Explain how an activity may be leisure for one person but a duty for another.
8 Why, for professional sports performers, is a definition of leisure difficult?
9 Why is recreation said to be an active aspect of leisure?
10 What therapeutic qualities does recreation have?
11 Why did the upper classes try to promote physical recreation amongst the working classes during the later part of the nineteenth century?
12 How did organisations such as the YMCA and Boys' Brigade use sport?
13 What are intrinsic values in relation to sports activity?
14 Why is badminton a 'life-time' sport?
15 Why is outdoor recreation a holistic activity?
16 What factors have led to an increase in participation of outdoor sports?
17 Do professional footballers play?
18 Why do adults play? Give some examples of adult play.

13 Physical and outdoor education

Learning objectives

- To develop an understanding of the concept of physical education.
- To be give an overview of the historical development of physical education
- To be develop an understanding of the concept of outdoor education

In this chapter we will discuss the concepts of physical education and outdoor education. These both occur within the education system of the UK. Both have developed over the last century and we will trace this development and investigate the factors which have shaped these concepts today. We will also discuss recent initiatives that have been introduced in an attempt to promote physical activities in schools.

13.1 Physical education

In the UK, physical education takes place only in educational institutions (schools, colleges and universities). It always involves a 'teacher' passing on knowledge to a group of 'pupils' and is almost always concerned with bodily movement. However, it is a wide concept with many different interpretations. Even with the National Curriculum for physical education, no one school's programme is the same as another's. In recent years the academic study of physical education has grown greatly and it is now studied at many levels.

The values developed through physical education are twofold:
Practical skills, which will enable players to take part in a variety of sports.
Social skills such as leadership, discipline and cooperation, which will help a individual develop independence and at the same time produce a love of sport that will continue throughout life and reverse the *Post 16 gap*.

Physical education occurs within the school curriculum, although other physical activities may also take place in schools.

> ### Definition
> ### PHYSICAL EDUCATION
> *The formal inculcation of knowledge and values through physical activity/experience.*
>
> ### POST 16 GAP
> *It is estimated that after young people leave education over 60% of them will never take part in any physical activities.*

ACTIVITY

The following scenarios may occur in schools, but can you link the correct definition to the scenario?

Scenario	Definition
Impromptu game of football during dinner break	Sport
Playing for school team	Physical education
Attending aerobics club after school	Play
Year 9 football lesson	Recreation

The activities actually undertaken vary from school to school, but most of the time is spent on the traditional team games such as football, netball and hockey. Swimming and athletics are the main individual activities and now new innovations such as 'health-related fitness' and the 'life-time' sports such as badminton and table tennis are gaining in popularity.

13.1.1 A brief history of physical education

Physical education is a modern phenomenon, less than 100 years old. However, its origins go back further than this and it developed from many different strands. Two main pathways can be identified, which developed from the two traditions of education in England in the nineteenth century.

Public school sports education

In the public schools of the upper classes organised games began to appear, at first as spontaneous recreations played by the boys and for the most part disapproved of by the teachers. However, as they became more developed it was recognised that educational objectives could be passed on through participation in games.

Sports became an important feature of all public schools and were regarded as a powerful force in the education of the sons of the upper classes. Team games formed the central core, particularly football and cricket (and rowing at the schools situated near a river). These games were physically strenuous, demanding and relied on cooperation and leadership – all characteristics that a gentleman needed to acquire.

The term 'games cult' has been used to describe the influence of sport in these schools, as have the phrases 'athleticism' and 'muscular Christianity'.

Sports education outside public schools

Outside the public schools, a different type of physical education grew up, springing from several roots: military drill, callisthenics and gymnastics. From these grew the system of physical training, which at the end of the century was adopted in the Elementary schools of the lower classes.

From 1902, the government began producing and prescribing a National Syllabus in Physical Training. The 1902 Model Course was composed by the War Office in an attempt to rectify the poor levels of fitness of the lower classes, which had been identified from the performance of recruits during the Boer War (1899–1902). The emphasis of these *drill* exercises was on discipline and obedience – they were aimed at creating a fit, disciplined workforce and army. Drill exercises were compulsory for schoolchildren up to the age of 12 years, and were carried out in the schoolyard with instructions barked out by instructors. Many of the activities involved wooden staves in clear imitation of guns. The instructors were peripatetic, and non-commissioned officers were paid 6d a day by the school to drill the children. This military influence and view of children as 'young soldiers' persisted well into the 1920s.

The course was revised periodically and gradually became a little more educational. The Board of Education took control of the national syllabus and produced a new syllabus in 1904 with revisions in 1909, 1919 and 1933. With each revision the military influence was reduced and slowly 'physical education' grew into something that we would recognise today. However, in 1933 physical education lessons were very formal; instructions were given to teachers in a set of tables and very little variety was allowed. An example of the 1933 syllabus is shown in Table 13.1.

> **Definition**
> ### GAMES CULT
> *The use of team games such as football, rugby and cricket to develop character in public schools.*

> **Definition**
> ### ELEMENTARY SCHOOL
> *Free schools for the working classes that taught children an elementary education including reading, writing and arithmetic.*

> **Definition**
> ### DRILL
> *Exercises for working class-children that taught fitness, discipline and obedience.*
> ### MODEL COURSE
> *Set up by the government in 1902 as a response to the poor fitness of working-class soldiers during the Boer War.*

ACTIVITY

Your grandparents could well have experienced some of the above syllabuses. Ask one of them, or another older person you know, about their physical education. Compare this with the physical education lessons your parents experienced and your own physical education programmes.

Table 13.1 *Part of the 1933 syllabus for physical education*

Section 1

1. Here, There, Where. Leap-frog practice in three's.
2. 4 Astride jumps with rebound, 4 Skip jumps without rebound.
3. (*Astride*) **Trunk bending downward** with 2 taps forward, 2 backward, 2 pulls on ankles and **Trunk stretching forward** with hands on hips. (1–8). (Latter, with Arm bending upward and Arm stretching upward.)
4. **Upward jumps in three's.** Free Practice. Fig. 39.
5. i.   (*Arm Sideways*) **Arm bending and stretching** sideways alternately in one count and two counts.
    ii. ([*Astride*] *Arms Crossed*) **Rhythmical Arm swinging** mid-upward (Heels raising). Fig 40.
    iii. (*1 Arm Sideways supported at wall*) **Informal Leg circling**.
6. ([*Astride*] *1 Arm Mid-Upward Support*) **Trunk bending sideways** with outer arm raising sideways-upward to touch other hand. (Rhyth.) Figs. 41 and 42.
7. Move to team files, **hopping** with leg swinging forward.
8. (*Knees Full Bend*) **Jump** to "*Astride, Heels Raise*" position with arm bending upward or swinging mid-upward.
9. **Riders and Horses.**

Section 2

10. (*Kneel Sitting, Trunk Forward, Arms Upward Rest*) **Rhythmical Trunk pressing downward.** (Bench.) (.) Fig. 43.
11. (*Kneel Sitting, Trunk Downward, Forehead Rest*) **Trunk stretching forward** with Elbow swinging sideways. Fig. 44.
12. **Hand-standing,** in pairs, one supporting. (Benches.) Fig. 45.
13. Race round bench twice and mount in "Knee Raise, Upward end" position. leg stretching backward with arm stretching upward. Race round twice in opposite direction and repeat balance exercise standing on other leg. (Bench top.)
14. (*Astride High Sitting, 1 Arm Sideways Clenched*) **Trunk and Head turning** to side of raised arm. (Bench.)
15. (*Low Front Support*) **Head turning**. (Benches, 2 high) Fig 45.
16. Free March on toes, six counts; Knee springing with Knee forward, six counts.
17. (*Front Standing, Trunk Downward, Hands on bench*) **Bouncing up and down,** i.e. pushing off 2 feet and raising hips high. (Benches, 2 high.)
18. **Face vault** with bent knees. (Benches, 2 high.) See Fig 13, page 39.
19. **Running Thro. vault** to High Standing. (Benches, 2 high, and supporters.)

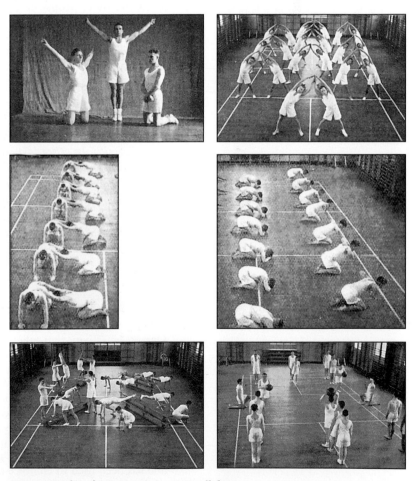

Some examples of exercises in the 1933 syllabus

Physical education in the last 50 years

After 1944, the move towards a free comprehensive education for all was reflected in the development of physical education. The two pathways began to come together, many of the state schools programming both games and physical education into their curriculum. Team games had been adapted by the Grammar schools and, with the widespread popularity of sports such as football, became central to all schools. Other activities such as swimming, cross-country and athletics are universally accepted in all physical education programmes.

In the last 30 years physical education has also become an all-graduate profession. Since the introduction of the non-commissioned officers as instructors in the early 1900s the profession has always had a low status in schools, but now the training and career paths of physical education teachers are on a par with those of other subjects. The other great step has been the development of physical education as an academic subject – courses are currently available at GCSE and 'A' level. This has again raised the status of the subject and greatly advanced the study of sports science. We also now have a National Curriculum for physical education, which has given the subject a little more formality and has attempted to bring uniformity to physical education across the country.

The National Curriculum identifies six sport activity areas: games, athletics, gymnastics, dance, swimming and adventure. Schools should offer pupils experience in at least five of the activity areas.

Extracurricular sport (sport outside the actual curriculum) still continues and in most schools is an important part of the school culture. In the main extracurricular sport involves teams representing the school in fixtures against other schools, but increasingly sports clubs are being used to involve more people in sport. The main problem is that most physical education teachers supervise extracurricular sport in their own time, and are not paid for the extra work. With the increasing demands on all teachers it is difficult to say how long many of them will continue this goodwill activity.

> ### Definition
> **NATIONAL CURRICULUM**
>
> *Issued by the government, this sets out what schools should teach pupils, including physical education.*

> ### Definition
> **EXTRACURRICULAR**
>
> *Activities undertaken in school but outside of normal lesson time – for example, playing for a school team after school.*

Key revision points

Physical education takes place only in schools, colleges and at university. In schools a variety of activities can take place – physical education is included within the curriculum and involves learning through practical activities. Modern physical education has developed from two differing systems – the games of the public schools and the drill of the elementary schools. Teaching physical education is now an all-graduate profession and academic courses in physical education are now available.

13.2 Outdoor education

One other activity that takes place in schools that can also involve some form of physical activity is outdoor education. We will briefly look at some of the main characteristics of this concept.

The National Association for Outdoor Education gives the following definition of outdoor education: 'A means of approaching educational objectives through guided direct experience in the environment using its resources as learning materials.' According to Passmore, 'Outdoor education is learning in and for the outdoors.'

Outdoor education is also a concept which has a number of meanings and has been used to embrace all educational activities that take place out of doors. Education out of doors includes many disciplines – geography,

> ### Definition
> **OUTDOOR EDUCATION**
>
> *All those activities concerned with living, moving and learning in the outdoors.*

biology, history and art as well as physical education. Where do outdoor pursuits fit in? These achieve particular educational objectives: overcoming challenges and the total emergence of one's self in the natural environment.

The definition of outdoor education given in the definition box on page 146 is probably the best one. It covers all the activities above and involves learning many skills, the learning environment is outside, and preferably the natural environment.

13.2.1 The aims of outdoor education

To heighten awareness of and foster respect for

Self – by giving yourself a challenge and overcoming that challenge. A good example of this is climbing a rock face.

Others – to gain group experiences, share decisions and work together as a team. Canadian canoeing demonstrates this well.

The natural environment – through direct contact with it.

In outdoor education the emphasis is on holistic experiences and relationships rather than specific skills.

Outdoor education forms some part of most school curricula and is now a stated aim of the National Curriculum. However, in most schools it is only an extracurricular activity. The problems are that outdoor pursuits are very expensive in terms of transport and equipment needed, and many safety precautions must be considered, especially in light of several recent tragedies. Time is another major problem – most schoolchildren have to travel some distance before they can experience the 'natural environment', which makes it very difficult to include such activities within a normal school day. In attempts to solve these problems 'trim trails' are being developed, schools setting up orienteering courses around their grounds and artificial climbing walls are being put up in sports halls and playgrounds.

A keyword for outdoor education is *adventure*. In 1984, Mortlock introduced the concept of the 'adventure alternative', believing that we have an instinct for seeking adventure and that outdoor education is one way of fulfilling this drive.

It can be argued that outdoor activities have an advantage over more conventional games in that the decisions that have to be made are much more real. These activities always contain an element of risk because the

---

ACTIVITY

We discussed earlier the development of both practical and social skills through physical activity. Identify four outdoor activities you have experienced and link them with the type of skills that you may have developed within them.

If you want to stay afloat and go in a straight line, teamwork is the key

unpredictability of the natural environment means that there are many uncontrollable (and sometimes life-threatening) factors that need to be taken into consideration.

Key revision points

Outdoor education is learning in the natural environment. The objectives of outdoor education are the development of the individual through scenarios and experiences that are very novel. Challenge is the essential element, and risk makes the experiences so novel.

KEY TERMS

You should now understand the following terms. If you do not, go back through the chapter and find out.

Drill
Elementary schools
Extracurricular
Games cult
Model course
National Curriculum
Outdoor education
Physical education
Post 16 gap

PROGRESS CHECK

1 Where does physical education take place?
2 What are the two types of skills that physical education helps to develop?
3 What type of activities tend to take most of physical education time in schools?
4 How might a school's physical education programme reverse the Post 16 gap?
5 Explain the two pathways that led the development of physical education in UK schools.
6 What led to the introduction of the Model Course in 1902?
7 What were the key characteristics which the 'games cult' developed in its pupils?
8 Why was drill an essential component of elementary schooling in the early part of the twentieth century?
9 Extracurricular sport tends to be elitist. What does this statement mean?
10 What advantages might outdoor education have over normal lessons in the inculcation of social skills?
11 What are the unpredictable parts of the natural environment?
12 In the concept of outdoor education, what does the term 'outdoor' refer to?
13 What are the aims of outdoor education?
14 Why does outdoor education tend to take place as an extracurricular activity in most schools?
15 What advantages do outdoor activities have over conventional games in terms of decision making?

The organisation of sport in the United Kingdom

Learning objectives

- To have an overview of the structure of sport in the UK.
- To know the key organisations in this structure.
- To understand the role of the government in the organisation of British sport.
- To be able to construct a brief historical analysis for the present structure of sport.
- To be able to compare the structure and organisation of sport in the UK with that in other countries.
- To understand the organisation of sport at the local level.

Definition

OPEN OLYMPICS

The modern Olympic Games were set up in 1896, and the International Olympic Committee stated that sports performers should not make a living or any form of profit from sport. The games were encased in the Olympic Ideal – the important thing was to take part, not win. However, the dramatic rise in performance and needs of the media have led to athletes needing to train all year round and so require money from sport. In the 1980s the Olympics became more open and the rules were altered so that both amateurs and professionals could take part, although the latter will soon dominate as more and more sports become professional.

The development of sport in the UK has not followed a regular pattern. Individuals, groups and clubs have always been free to develop their sport as they liked and the government has never really involved itself directly in the organisation of sport at either local or national level.

Today the *UK Sports Council* has overall responsibility for British sport, with four national Sports Councils overseeing sport in each of the four home countries. In England, *Sport England* has direct responsibility for sporting matters. However, the administration and affairs of each individual sport are controlled by a governing body; there are well over 200 such bodies in the UK.

These governing bodies are all members of the *Central Council of Physical Recreation* (CCPR), a body set up in 1935 to help coordinate sport. The CCPR was superseded (though not replaced) by the Sports Council. The CCPR now has the duty of telling the sports councils how the governing bodies as a group feel about the development of sport.

The governing bodies of sport, for example the Football Association and the Lawn Tennis Association, represent everyone who takes part in their sport and are members of international governing bodies – in these two cases FIFA and the International Tennis Federation. This membership allows British players to take part in international competition.

A governing body may also be affiliated to the British Olympic Association, allowing participation in the Olympic Games. In the past this affiliation was restricted to amateur sports but now the Olympics have become 'open' and many more sports are receiving Olympic status. In the 2000 Olympics surfing and ballroom dancing will be given trials.

An overview of the structure of sports organisation in the UK is shown in Figure 14.2.

14.1 History and background

The administrative structure of British sport has changed little, in general terms, since most of our modern sports and physical activities developed in the late nineteenth century.

To control and codify these increasingly popular activities a number of sporting organisations were established, often with strong ties to the upper classes but particularly to the emerging middle class that had begun to dominate industrial Britain. Elements of this social class hierarchy can still be seen in sport today. The upper classes, who had held power before the industrial revolution, jealously guarded their sporting interests by forming clubs and associations to control participation by more lowly members of society.

Figure 14.1 *Some of the key bodies that organise sport in the UK*

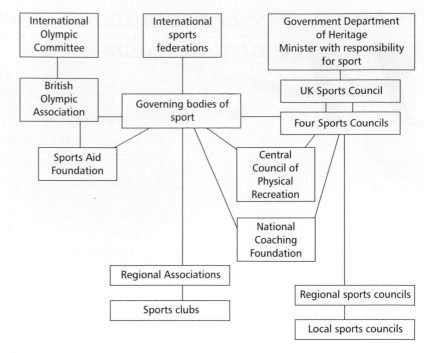

Figure 14.2 *The structure of sports organisation in the UK*

The Jockey Club and the Marylebone Cricket Club are good examples of these upper-class organisations still evident today. The MCC was set up in 1787 and remains an exclusive gentleman's club. Although its influence is in decline, the MCC is still credited with writing the rules of cricket, selecting England's teams and developing many of the game's traditions. The Jockey Club, set up in 1750, has been the governing body for racing for 240 years.

The industrial revolution led to the rise of the middle class – the factory owners and entrepreneurs. In the same way as they took over the control of commerce and industry, they also took over control of sport. The middle-class approach to sports administration was a little more democratic; however, they introduced the concept of amateurism into sport, which to a large extent still controls the opportunity to take part in sport. Good examples of governing bodies set up during this time are the Football Association (FA) in 1863 and the Amateur Athletics Association (AAA) in 1880. These national governing bodies appeared in response to the increased participation in sport throughout the country. Generally their task was to establish and maintain the rules of the sport and to organise national competitions.

One characteristic of the British system is that sports are very isolated. The clubs that joined these new governing bodies tended to be single-sport clubs and as a consequence so were the organising bodies. The result was a very decentralised organisation, with individual bodies showing little interest in the affairs of other sporting organisations.

In contrast, in the rest of Europe a more centralised approach developed and organised sport developed 15–20 years later than in the UK. Clubs in France and Germany tend to cater for a number of different sports. This approach encouraged the establishment of multisport federations to coordinate the aims of different sports – an example is the UNSS in France, which has responsibility for sport in all schools in France.

It is only relatively recently that an attempt was made to develop a coordinated approach to sport organisation in the UK. This has centred on the evolution of the CCPR and Sports Council and, more recently, Sports England. However, both of these organisations are concerned with encouraging participation and the provision of facilities rather than actually controlling sport.

IN PRACTICE

If you were given the task of reorganising British sport, what areas would you change? What have been the limiting factors in the development of sport in the UK? What have other countries done differently? Try to come up with five major changes, with explanations.

The individual sports retain their autonomy – this is the key to understanding the organisation of sport in the UK.

ACTIVITY

In 1980 many nations boycotted the Moscow Olympics in protest at the Soviet invasion of Afghanistan but the British government left the decision to compete to the individual governing bodies. How does this reflect the autonomy of British sport?

Key revision points

Sport in the UK does not follow a regular pattern and the British government has little control over sport. The UK Sports Council has overall responsibility for sport in the UK – aided by the CCPR. The governing bodies control the affairs of each particular sport – each sport is autonomous. These governing bodies have changed little since their inception 100 years ago.

14.2 The role of government in the administration of sport in the UK

Despite the popularisation of sport and introduction of universal physical education during the early 1900s, sport and physical recreation have never really been accepted as realms of government responsibility. Since the Second World War, the government has increased its involvement in sport, yet it openly accepted the justification of sport in its own right only during the 1960s.

At various times governments have become involved in control of some parts of the organisation of sport, but this has tended to be only in isolated areas and in response to a problem rather than any planning or development. At the beginning of the twentieth century the government intervened in sport for a while, in order to get the population fit for war (see Chapter 13 for more information on this). Back in 1541, laws were passed to ban all 'frivolous' sports such as football, golf and bowling to make sure that every man under the age of 60 spent his spare time practising archery – a skill needed to defend the country.

The Taylor Report (1990) into the Hillsborough Football disaster prompted government legislation concerning football stadiums in an attempt to stem football hooliganism. The Taylor Report recommended that all Football League grounds should become all-seaters by August 1999. Part of the money required to carry out this massive undertaking was provided through a levy that the government placed on the Football Pools in 1990, forming the Football Trust – however, most clubs will have to bear most of the cost of refurbishment themselves.

14.2.1 The role of Quangos in sports control

Most of the administration and organisation of sport in the public sector is carried out by the various Sports Council *Quangos* and local authorities, the latter being the biggest providers of facilities and funders of sport.

14.3 Structure of governmental control

Most of the government's coordination of sport is now undertaken by the *Department of Culture, Media and Sport*. However, sporting concerns do

Definition

QUANGO

Quasi-Autonomous National Governmental Organisations – agencies created by the government to carry out a variety of functions. Quangos have a limited amount of independence.

still filter through to other departments, principally the Department for Education and Employment.

14.3.1 The Department of Culture, Media and Sport

Although Britain has had a Minister for Sport since the early 1960s, this role has never really risen in status above that of a junior minister, who was a lower member of the Department of the Environment. The many calls for sport to be given Cabinet status were ignored. The Sports Council initially planned and campaigned for a Department of Sport and Tourism to be set up, but eventually a coalition with the existing Office of Arts and Libraries was seen as the most effective means of gaining a degree of power.

In 1992 The Department of Heritage was set up and had responsibility for sport and recreation. The new department took up the responsibilities that were previously shared by six government departments and has an extremely varied portfolio, including broadcasting, films, the press, national heritage, arts, sport and tourism. It has two ministers, a secretary of state and a deputy. Sport is further served by a sub-department, the *Sport and Recreation Division*. In 1997 the department was renamed the Department of Culture, Media and Sport.

The major concern of the Department after it was set up was the establishment and development of the National Lottery. The National Lottery was established by an Act of Parliament in 1993 and the first draw was made on 14 November 1994. It followed the pattern developed in many other countries as a means of raising funds for worthy causes, including sport. Five areas of 'good causes' benefit from the income generated by the National lottery:

- sport
- art
- heritage
- charities
- The Millennium Fund (now renamed the New Opportunities Fund).

Various bodies send bids for funds to the Sports Council, which scrutinises the bids and distributes the money allocated to sport. The amount of money to be distributed by Sport England each year is approximately £200 million.

ACTIVITY

Try to find out if any of your local sports bodies have received lottery funding. If any did, how much money did it receive and what was it used for? Information should be available from your local library, council or sports council.

In the summer of 1995 the Prime Minister and the Department of Heritage published a sports policy statement called *Sport – Raising the Game*. This set out the government's proposals for rebuilding the strength of British sport. The main emphasis of these proposals was to recognise the role that schools can play in the development of a sports culture. The publication goes on to outline what the government feels each sector of sport should be undertaking to promote the development of high standards of sport in the country. The other major proposal in the policy statement was that a British Academy of Sport should be set up, similar to the Australian National Institute, which will be a centre of excellence for British sporting talent.

In 1999 Sport England announced its new strategy for the new millennium, entitled 'More people more places, more medals'. This strategy introduced two new programmes: the Active Sports Programme, aimed at encouraging mass participation, and the World Class Programme, aimed at increasing the standard of England's elite performers. Sport England's

ACTIVITY

Your school, college or local library should have a copy of *Sport – Raising the Game*. Have a look at the proposals and see if they match your ideas on how British sport should be organised.

plan is to extend the concept of a national academy of sport in to a 'national network of 10 elite training centres around England', though they have a headquarters (known as the UK Sports Institute) which is based in London.

14.3.2 The Sports Council

This government-funded Quango was established in 1965, receiving its Royal Charter in 1972. It is an autonomous body under the Department of Culture, Media and Sport, with a brief to take overall responsibility for sport in the UK.

The Sports Council has four main aims:
1 To increase participation in sport.
2 To increase the quality and quantity of sports facilities.
3 To raise standards of performance.
4 To provide information for and about sport.

In 1994 it was announced that the Sports Council would be reshaped to create two new bodies: the *UK Sports Council* and the *English Sports Council*, rebranded as *Sport England* in 1999. This brings England in line with the other home countries in that it now has its own Sports Council. The UK Sports Council has a coordinating role, ensuring that all councils work in the same direction, and has responsibility for drugs testing and doping control in all UK sport.

Each council is split further into regional and local sports councils, enabling area-specific planning. Funding for the Council comes from the National Lottery Sports Fund and Sport England receives £200 million per year. This money is used to run the regional councils, fund campaigns and capital projects and provide information services, although most of it is redistributed to sports governing bodies and institutions as grants to be used for increasing sports participation, building new facilities and setting up recreation programmes.

ACTIVITY

Have a look at the sports facilities where you live and look for the Sports Council's emblem. Make an inventory of the facilities the Sports Council has helped to fund in your area.

14.3.3 The Countryside Commission

This Quango is an independent body which investigates matters relating to the conservation and enhancement of the natural environment, and the provision and development of facilities in the countryside for recreation. You have probably come across the *Country Code*, an initiative set up by the Countryside Commission to teach people how to use and respect the countryside. Its link with sport is to help develop access for outdoor sports and also to manage them so that the landscape is not destroyed.

Key revision points

The limited role of central government in sports organisation reinforces the decentralised nature of sport organisation in the UK. Most administration in the public sector is left to Quangos such as the Sports Council or local authorities. The Department of Culture, Media and Sport has taken charge of sport – its first major job was to develop the National Lottery to help fund sports and charities. The Sports Council has overall responsibility for sport in the UK.

14.4 The national sports agencies

14.4.1 An overview

We have already identified that most sports administration in the UK is carried out by individual governing bodies – these will be discussed in detail in the next section. However, a number of *national agencies* coordinate particular areas of sport, once again characterised by their autonomy and diversity.

Some of these agencies have specific tasks, for example the National Coaching Foundation develops coaching expertise and the British Olympic Association coordinates all Olympic matters. Others are more general in their approach, for instance SportsAid is a charitable organisation that helps to fund amateur sports performers, allowing them to compete at international level.

Most of these bodies are funded by the public sector or by voluntary donations – again there is much diversity. In general their role is to advise and provide information rather than administer and organise.

14.4.2 Central Council of Physical Recreation

This independent voluntary body was set up in 1935, and is the 'voice of the governing bodies' in that it represents the governing bodies of sport and after consultation passes on their views to the Sports Council and government.

Its greatest success was in establishing the National Sports Centres, specialist centres where our national teams and performers train. Management of these was transferred to the Sports Council and has now moved toward self-management.

When the Sports Council was developed in the early 1960s it gradually took over many of the roles of the CCPR. The idea was that the Sports Council would replace the CCPR but the governing bodies, fearing too much government intervention, decided to maintain some independence and the CCPR became a charitable trust. The Sports Council still has some control over the CCPR.

The CCPR now acts as a consultative body to the Sports Council, advising it of the views of the more than 240 individual governing bodies. Its other roles include commissioning reports on sports issues and running a number of sports leaders awards. It is funded by a grant from the Sports Council.

14.4.3 The British Olympic Association

This independent organisation is responsible for all Olympic matters in the UK, primarily entering competitors for the Olympic Games. Other functions include raising funds to enable British performers to compete at the games and for the transportation, clothing and other expenses involved in sending a British team (up to £4 million). A more general role is to develop interest in the Olympic movement in Britain. It also helps to coordinate any bids to host the games.

The fund-raising role of the British Olympic Association is unique to the UK. In most other countries, even the USA, central government helps to finance the Olympic team – but the British Olympic Association raises all the money itself. This has traditionally been achieved through schoolchildren's sponsored events and donations from the general public and business. Increasingly, more money is being raised through commercial sponsorship, specifically in the use of the Olympic logo (you have probably seen the five-ring logo on Mars Bars and cans of Coca Cola).

14.4.4 SportsAid (formerly The Sports Aid Foundation)

The Sports Aid Foundation was formed in 1976 by Dennis Howell, then Minister for Sport. This autonomous fund-raising body is managed by a

FOUNDATION FOR SPORT AND THE ARTS

A trust founded in 1991 by the companies organising the football pools. They donate up to £60 million a year, two-thirds of which is passed on to sport. Sports bodies apply for funds and after consultation with other bodies such as the Sports Council the trustees of the foundation issue grants.

board of governors and trustees and aims to raise and distribute funds to help the very best amateur sports men and women, though it is now mainly aimed at young sports performers.

The money issued through grants is used to cover the expenses of training, travelling and attending competitions. If performers are successful they often become self-supportive through sponsorship and prize money and so no longer need the assistance of the Sports Aid Foundation – examples are Torvill and Dean, Daley Thompson, Steve Backley and Nick Gillingham. However, participants in less commercial sports may need funding for their whole career.

The income required is generated through fund raising, voluntary donations, National Lottery contributions and commercial sponsorship. In the past international insurance brokers Minet have provided considerable support, although at the moment the biggest contributor is the Foundation for Sport and the Arts.

The Sports Aid Foundation was established to enable our top amateur competitors to train in the same way as many others throughout the world without worrying about finance. Their slogan reinforces this point: 'Giving Britons a Better Sporting Chance'.

To qualify for a national SportsAid grant you must be:
- aged between 12 and 18,
- in genuine need, not in receipt of a National Lottery World Class Performance Grant
- a member of a national squad.

Regional grants raised by SportsAid regions are also available to local competitors who are not in receipt of any kind of national grant and have a top six ranking in their sport or are a member of a national squad.

14.4.5 The National Coaching Foundation

Established by the Sports Council in 1983, with its headquarters in Leeds, the NCF is run by a small staff under the control of a director. The Foundation provides a wide range of opportunities for coaches to improve their knowledge and practice of sport. This function is carried out by regional coaching centres based at higher education institutions throughout the UK (eleven in England, two in Wales, two in Scotland and one in Northern Ireland).

The problem that the Foundation faces is the fact that the UK has such a complex sports structure, mainly due to the autonomy of each governing body (and consequently the coaches). Also most coaches work voluntarily and so don't have the time or the funds to obtain qualifications.

The NCF has two main aims to overcome these problems:
1. To promote education through its coaching courses and awards.
2. To increase knowledge through information centres, its monthly magazine *Supercoach*, videos and its subsidiary (Coachwise Ltd), which provides a service for coaches to purchase books and resources on coaching matters.

Recent major programmes have included *Champion Coaching* and *Coaching for Teachers*.

CHAMPION COACHING

Aimed at developing the performance of 11–14-year-old children through specialist coaching. (This will transfer into the World Class Start Programme over the next few years.)

COACHING FOR TEACHERS

Set up in 1996 in association with the Sports Councils, aimed at encouraging qualified and trainee teachers to take advantage of enhanced coaching opportunities.

AUTONOMOUS

A body is self-governing, makes decisions independently without interference from other bodies, including the government.

14.4.6 The British Sports Association for the Disabled

This was founded in 1961 with the aims of helping to develop sport and recreation for people with disabilities. It is a charitable organisation that raises its money through voluntary fund raising.

14.5 The national governing bodies of sport

ACTIVITY

See if you can find out the names of the national governing bodies for the following sports in the UK:

football, rugby union, athletics, tennis, hockey, badminton.

Try to find out the date each body was formed. Can you suggest why these dates are close together?

Most modern sports developed their present form within the last 150 years. As participation in sports began to increase at the end of nineteenth century and many activities became popular recreations, it became necessary for those taking part to agree to a common set of rules or laws. Until this time there had been many regional variations and it was very difficult for teams from different schools or areas to play against each other.

This need for *codification* led directly to the formation of a governing body within each sport. As Houlihan concludes, their 'main concern was to harmonise rules and develop a national pattern of organisation.'

It is for this reason that the rules and organisation of each individual sport in the UK lie in the hands of an autonomous national governing body.

14.5.1 Role of the governing bodies

These bodies are responsible for general administration of the sport and the conduct of competitions. They can be very large organisations – 43 000 football clubs are affiliated to the Football Association – or quite small organisations with the responsibility for minority sports, such as the British Water Ski Federation.

The foundation of the system is that clubs become affiliated to their particular governing body. Clubs pay a fee to become members of these bodies, which gives the club the right to vote on sports issues and to take part in sports competitions.

As participation in sport of all kinds has increased, the duties of the governing bodies have become more demanding and their workload has grown accordingly. Today, a number of governing bodies now require full-time administrators to look after their affairs but there is still an emphasis on voluntary work. This reflects the tradition in British sport – committee work and decision-making still tends to lie in the hands of unpaid volunteers.

At present there are over 300 national governing bodies in the UK. Their major concerns are:
1 To establish their own rules and regulations.
2 To organise competitions.
3 To develop coaching/leadership awards.
4 To have direct responsibility for sport at the local and national level, as well as representing the sport in international matters.
5 To select teams and competitors to represent the home countries or the UK at international events.

14.5.2 The structure of the governing bodies

Single sports clubs tend to be grouped into regional or member associations such as County Associations, whose representatives have an input to the national governing body. This is outlined in Figure 14.3.

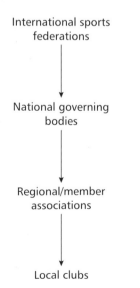

Figure 14.3 *Local clubs have an input at national and international level*

Nearly all of the national bodies are members of the international federations for their sport. The international federations decide the rules and regulations of international competition and are responsible for the organisation and administration of major international events and tournaments.

Many bodies in the UK are also linked through membership of the British Olympic Association, which allows a national governing body to enter its members in the Olympic Games.

14.5.3 Funding

The national governing bodies draw their income from a variety of sources.

Affiliation fees – membership fees from clubs, associations and individual members.

Sports Council grants – a number of bodies receive grant aid from the Sports Council.

Development grants – for special events/programmes from the Foundation for Sport and the Arts, the National Lottery sports fund, Millennium awards or New Opportunities Lottery Fund.

Sponsorship – from commercial companies.

Television rights – TV companies have to pay the governing bodies for the right to televise matches and tournaments.

14.5.4 Future roles

With the many changes affecting sport at the turn of the millennium, the national governing bodies are having to adapt and take on new roles.

Media and commercial interests are essential elements of modern sport and the governing bodies need to become more accountable and efficient in their work. Their structure is likely to become sophisticated and they will probably need to employ more full-time staff. Staff will also need a wider variety of skills – media relations and marketing will be essential roles in all sports governing bodies if they are to survive into the twenty-first century.

The other main issue facing many sports is the gap that is developing between elite performers and amateurs. This may result in the top elite breaking away, forming premier bodies and probably securing most of the funding and resources – this has already occurred in football and rugby league.

14.5.5 An example of the structure and responsibilities of a typical governing body: the Amateur Swimming Association

Affiliated to	International Federation of Amateur Swimming
Headquarters	Freehold offices in Loughborough, Leicestershire
Salaried permanent staff	20
Number of affiliated clubs	1784
Number of members	300 000
Number of registered competitive swimmers	53 000 (each paying an annual fee of £7.50)
Responsible for organisation of	Swimming
	Diving
	Water polo
	Synchronised swimming
Special schemes	ASA education programme for teachers/coaches
	ASA proficiency, life saving, survival awards
	ASA liaison with schools and leisure centres
	ASA contribution to health and safety guidelines
	ASA contribution to medical research
Income	ASA award scheme raises £90 000
	ASA education programme – books, videos, etc.
	ASA Enterprises Ltd – merchandising
	Television fees
	Sponsorship money
	Grant of £632 000 from the Sports Council

14.6 Sport at the local level

The Sports Council estimates that one in three people in the UK regularly participate in sports, mostly at the local level. Local authorities are the main providers of sports and recreational facilities, and are financed by the public sector.

However, most of the actual organisation falls within the voluntary sector, with the base level being small, single sport clubs. The role of some local clubs in British sport is shown in Table 14.1.

Table 14.1 *Examples of the role local clubs play in UK sport*

Activity/sport	Number of clubs	Total number of members
Athletics	19 000	110 000
Bowls (outdoors)	3 529	161 672
Football	42 000	1 250 000
Hockey	1 850	80 000
Golf	1 700	238 000
Netball	3 300	60 000
Swimming	1 784	300 000
Tennis	2 432	131 800

Sport at the local level consists of many small groups of people taking part quite independently. Clubs are small, the facilities basic and the organisation limited. There is no central organisation at this level to plan and coordinate sport development, again reflecting the autonomy of sport in the UK.

The Sports Council has attempted to tackle this issue by setting up *Local Advisory Sports Councils*. These are independent bodies, made up of local groupings of clubs and other interested bodies. They discuss issues that involve all sports at the local level and pass on their views to the local authorities. However, these bodies are not found in every area and their contribution to the administration of sport is often limited.

ACTIVITY

Sports clubs tend to be administered and organised by small voluntary committees. There are several key positions that all clubs require: Chairman, Secretary, Treasurer, Coach and Captain. Using a sports club you know, try to find out what each of these people actually does. Summarise the roles in a table.

14.6.1 Who provides local facilities?

Sports facilities at the local level are mostly provided by:
- local authorities
- schools
- private sector.

Local authority provision

Local authorities are the greatest providers of facilities. City, Borough and District Councils provide a vast range of sport and recreational facilities – parks, leisure centres and swimming pools, golf courses, community halls, for example. These centres cater for the needs of the local community, although pubic sector facilities can also be quite grand, as in Birmingham's National Indoor Arena and Elland Road, Leeds United stadium, which is owned by Leeds City Council.

There are about 1500 swimming pools and 2000 local leisure centres in the UK but the Sports Council states that the UK is under-resourced and has been campaigning to increase the provision of local sports facilities.

In the past much of the money needed to fund these facilities was drawn directly from central government grants and local taxes (Rates, Community Charge, Council Tax). The main objective of these facilities is to maximise participation in sport so prices are often subsidised, allowing lower admission charges and access to all sections of the community – with concessions for students, the unemployed and other low-income groups. However, local authority budgets have become a lot tighter because central government has been steadily reducing its grants. One of the first areas affected has been the sport and recreational facilities. Admission prices have had to rise and costs cut, which has led to the closure of some facilities.

Schools provision

A second major area of facility provision is the education system. Most schools in the UK have a good range of sports halls, pitches and pools. Increasingly these are also being used for public use. The policy of opening up facilities to the public is known as *dual use*. In the main schools allow their facilities to be used after school, clubs and organisations paying to use them.

Opportunities for developing dual use schemes will increase in the future with the recent changes in the financial responsibilities of schools. Local management gives a school's governing body more control over its budget and facilities, which may increase the amount of facilities available.

Private sector provision

This is made up of two main groups: commercial enterprises that provide facilities for the public in return for payment, and companies that provide facilities for their employees.

The role of the first group in providing leisure facilities is growing – the leisure 'boom' of the 1990s has increased demand and many people have seen this as an opportunity to cash in on the leisure trends. These leisure companies tend to cater for specific areas, such as fitness or water sports. Although the facilities provided are usually of a high standard the prices are also correspondingly high. The development of private sector facilities may encourage a move towards elitism, where only those on higher incomes will be able to afford to take part. The main aim of these companies is to make profit, and there is little emphasis on catering for the needs of the community.

Some companies and businesses provide sports facilities for the use of their employees and families. The company pays all the expenses involved in the upkeep of the buildings, pitches, courts and greens. Often a small membership fee is charged, though many companies provide the facilities free of charge. Companies see this as a way of encouraging people to work for them and of fostering the morale of the existing workforce. Recently many companies have put a lot of emphasis on reducing stress levels in their workforce – this can often be achieved through sporting activities.

Commercial fitness centre

ACTIVITY

Make a list of the sports facilities in a three-mile area near you. Find out where the money comes from to fund them and classify each facility as a public sector, private sector or voluntary sector facility.

Active Sports programme

As part of its millennium strategy, in 1999 Sport England introduced its new Active Sports programme. This programme aims to encourage mass participation amongst young people through funding and support schemes and by bringing together local providers – essentially schools, clubs and community groups.

In order to fulfil this, Sport England and local authorities are issuing lottery money to appoint Active Sports Managers in each local authority area. Their job will be to promote a coordinated approach to 'grass roots' sport.

Key revision points

Sport at the local level is carried on by small independent groups arranged in voluntary clubs. Three sectors are involved in the administration and funding of sport at the local level: voluntary, private and public. Local authorities provide most local sports facilities but increasingly private enterprises are providing high-quality facilities.

KEY TERMS

You should now understand the following terms. If you do not, go back through the chapter and find out.

Active Sports programme
Affiliation
Autonomy
British Olympic Association
Central Council for Physical Recreation
Champion coaching
Coaching for teachers
Codification
Decentralisation
Department of Culture, Media and Sport
Dual use
Elitism
Governing body
National Coaching Federation
Open sports
Private sector
Public sector
Quango
SportsAid
Sports councils
Voluntary sector
World Class Sports programme

PROGRESS CHECK

1. What problems in the development of sport in the late 1800s led to the formation of national governing bodies?
2. Describe the structure of the CCPR and the role it plays in coordinating sport in the UK.
3. Briefly describe the structure and function of the Sports Commission.
4. Why does a country as small as the UK need regional sports councils?
5. The Sports Council uses the term Target Group. What does this term mean?
6. What does the phrase 'autonomy of governing bodies' refer to in terms of the structure of British sport?
7. How is the National Coaching Federation aiding sport in the UK's general move towards raising standards in performance?
8. How has SportsAid helped Steve Backley to become an international champion?
9. What is the BOA? What specific role does it play in the organisation of elite sports in the UK?
10. Explain why British sports organisations may be unwilling to accept direct funding from the government.
11. How do the aims and objectives of a public sector facility differ from those of a private sector facility?
12. What are the possible disadvantages of a school developing a dual use policy with its sports hall?
13. What benefits may a company hope to develop by providing sports facilities for its employees?
14. 'Sport for All' is not yet a reality. What sociocultural constraints have hindered its development in the UK?
15. How might the National Lottery increase the opportunity to take part in sport?
16. The UK's decentralised system of sports administration leads to the limited funds being spread too thinly. What reforms could be introduced to get better value for money?

15

The organisation of European sport and global games

Learning objectives

- To look at how sport is organised on a European level and international level.
- To investigate the impact of sport on European life.
- To investigate how sport is used to promote politics and ideals of different countries through global games.
- To know about sports events that have world-wide importance.
- To learn about problems that have occurred in the Olympic Games.

Sport is a universal activity, played around the whole world. In this chapter we will discuss how countries have used sport to further political ideals and show how good *their* country is. This attitude has often affected the most important world sporting events such as the Olympic Games. The organisation of sport at European and international level follows that of the UK. With the rise of quicker travel times and increasing use of satellite broadcasting, sport is quickly becoming a global event. Champions' leagues and World Super Clubs cups appear to be the way that sport is moving forward as we enter a new millennium.

15.1 Sport around the world

Sport is played the world over. Many of the sports that were developed in the UK at the end of the nineteenth century spread around the world and many countries now play sports such as football, rugby and cricket, although some countries have changed such sports slightly and developed their own distinctive games. For example, Australian Rules Football and American Football are both based on rugby but they are very distinctive.

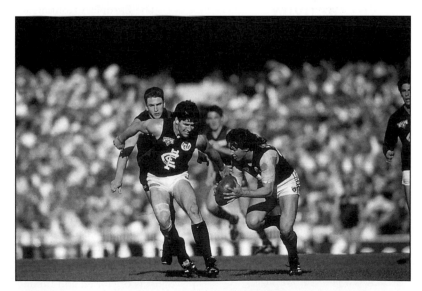

Australian Rules Football – a game found only in Australia

ACTIVITY

Which sports would you link to the following countries ? You may put down more than one answer.

USA, Ireland, India, New Zealand, Japan, Canada

To help you, here are some sports you could think about:
Ice hockey, Gaelic football, rugby, kabbadi, hockey, American football, sumo wrestling, baseball.

The sports and games played in a country can tell us a lot about that country. The way a sport is played is often a reflection of how people in a particular country live. Football is a good example of this. Although all countries play the same game to the same rules, it is amazing how different countries add their own unique style to the game. This is most evident in the World Cup when we see the skill and flair of the Brazilians, the tactical brilliance of the Germans and the fun and enjoyment the Cameroon team get out of playing.

15.2 The organisation of European sport

Sport at a European level follows the decentralised pattern developed in the UK, most individual sports having a European governing body that oversees competition at this level. However, as the European states move closer towards federation more influence comes from the European Commission.

In 1988 The European Commission identified sport as performing five functions throughout the European community:
- educational
- public health
- social
- cultural
- recreational.

European legislation is increasingly affecting sporting practices and activities at both professional and amateur levels, the biggest single impact being the *Bosman case*, which has changed the way professional sport is run throughout Europe.

The European Commission's main role is to consult with sports organisations across Europe to plan for sports development and to identify problems associated with sport. Only in extreme cases will the Commission produce legislation that directly affects sport. For example, sport will be affected by the Commission's decision to phase out from 2001 all forms of tobacco sponsorship and advertising, except on premises where cigarettes are sold.

In an attempt to try to unify European Sport the Commission now hosts an annual European Conference on Sport, which all sports Ministers from each country attend.

15.2.1 How European sport is organised

Over the last half century two different models of sport have developed in Europe:
- an Eastern European model
- a Western European model.

In the east of Europe sport has tended to be more ideologically orientated. Sport is organised and funded by the state government and has often been used for propaganda purposes.

Definition

BOSMAN CASE

The European Court of Justice recognised in the Bosman Case that there is no reason why professional sportspeople should not enjoy the benefits of the single market – and in particular the free movement of workers. This has resulted in national competitions now being open to any player from a European country. The new legislation also abolished transfer fees if a player is out of contract.

ACTIVITY

- Can you think of examples of how sport might reflect European identity?
- Does Europe exist as a team in any sports?
- Are there European competitions?
- Can you think of sports that reflect certain member states?

Definition

PROPAGANDA

Using a subject (in this case sport) to get across a political message.

In Western countries sport has developed as a mixed model, where sport is run by both governmental and non-governmental organisations. There is a further division to sport in the Western states – in northern states such as the UK and Germany the government does not regulate sport, whereas in southern states such as France and Spain the government does play a regulatory role.

15.2.2 The pyramid structure of European sport

In all member states sports are traditionally organised in a system of national *sporting federations*. Only the top federations (usually one per country) are linked together in European and international federations such as UEFA.

Basically, the structure resembles a pyramid with a hierarchy (Figure 15.1). The pyramid structure implies autonomy at each level, not only on the organisational side but also on the competitive side because competitions are organised at all levels.

Clubs – In all countries the sports club is the basic unit, in the main these are amateur and run within the voluntary system. There are about 545 000 sports clubs in Europe.

Regional federations form the next level. Clubs are members of these organisations. They are responsible for organising regional championships and coordinating sport on a regional level.

National federations, one for each sport, represent the next level. The regional federations are members of these organisations. These bodies regulate all general matters within their sport and represent their sport in European and international federations. They organise national competitions and act as regulatory bodies, dealing with rules and disciplinary matters. As there is only one national federation for each sport, they tend to have a monopolistic position. In each country, for example, there is only one national football federation.

European federations – The top of the pyramid is formed by European federations, which are organised along the same lines as the national federations. Every European federation allows only one national federation from each country to be a member. They organise European championships, administer rules and form the link to international federations such as FIFA.

15.3 The features of European sport

One of the main features of sport in Europe is that it is based on a *grass-roots* approach – the development of sport originates from the level of club. Sport in Europe has traditionally not been linked to state or business.

Sport in Europe is run mainly by non-professional and unpaid volunteers. For them sport is a pastime and a way of contributing to society. In this way European sport differs from that in, say, the USA, where sport is linked to business. In the USA sport is based on a more professional approach and is mainly run by full-time paid people.

15.4 Sport and national identity

The Amsterdam Declaration of 1988 stated that sport has an important social function in forging identity and bringing people together.

> Sport represents and strengthens national or regional identity by giving people a sense of belonging to a group, uniting players and spectators. Sport contributes towards social stability and is an emblem for culture and identity.

Although globalisation has affected European sport, it can still be seen as one of the last national passions. The EC is keen to promote sport as a

---

Definition

SPORTING FEDERATION

European equivalent of a UK national governing body of sport.

UEFA

Union Européenne de Football Association, the governing body of European football.

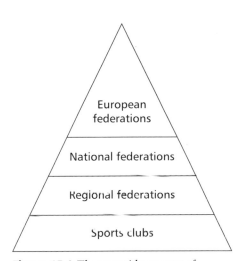

Figure 15.1 *The pyramid structure of European sport*

Definition

FIFA

Federation International de Football Association, the international governing body of football.

Definition

GRASS-ROOTS SPORT

Sport at the bottom of the pyramid.

ACTIVITY

Can you put your own sport into the European model?

Football – a game that all European countries share

means of safeguarding the cultural diversity of Europe (note the importance and support for European soccer championships). Again this differs from the USA, where there is no need for interstate competition.

15.5 The importance of sport in Europe

Traditionally the member states of the European Commission have hosted a significantly large percentage of world sports events:
- 54% of Summer Olympics
- 50% of Football's World Cups

This is mainly due to history; because Europe saw the start of the industrial revolution it was the first continent to see the development of modern sport. All the major global games have their origins in European initiatives, specifically the Olympic Games and Football World Cup.

ACTIVITY

Why has Europe been chosen as the host for most major world sporting events? Can you give sporting and cultural reasons?

15.6 Sport For All in Europe

The concept of *Sport For All* first emerged in the early 1960s in German and the Nordic countries. In 1968, the *Council of Europe* initiated the setting up of several projects aimed at encouraging mass participation. Their stated aim was to:

> Provide conditions to enable the widest possible range of the population to practice regularly either sport proper or various physical activities calling for an effort adapted to individual capacities.

Growing interest in sport and in the specific development of Sport For All by all European countries led to the adoption of the European Sport For All Charter in 1972. This asserted that 'Every individual has the right to participate in sport' and that 'It is the duty of every member state to support financially and organisationally this ideal'.

15.6.1 The implementation of Sport For All in Europe

The main organisation charged with implementing Sport For All has been the Committee for the Development of Sport (Comité Directeur pour le developpement du sport), known as the CDDS.

15.7 Politics in global games

As mentioned above, sport has long been used as a means of proving that one political system is better than another. Part of international sport is that different countries and systems are put in competition with each other.

The best example of this was the USA and the USSR during the 1960s, 1970s and 1980s, two countries that spent huge amounts of money trying to outdo each other in sport. A win at the Olympics, it was said, proved that one political system (capitalism or communism) was better that the other.

Each country also boycotted the Olympics, and they used their power and influence to persuade other countries not to take part in particular Olympics.

Human rights issues have also brought politics and sport together. Human rights are basic entitlements and opportunities all people should

---

Definition

EUROPEAN CHARTER OF SPORT FOR ALL

Set up in 1972, this aims to give every European individual the right to participate in sport.

Definition

BOYCOTT

Refusing to compete in an event, usually for political reasons.

Welcome back – South Africa win at the Rugby World Cup after their return to global sport

have. In some countries certain types of people are denied these rights – for example, Black people under the Apartheid system of South Africa (which was abolished in the 1990s). Sport is one area that other countries can use to show their feelings by boycotting sporting events in that country or persuading international sports organisations to ban the country from competition.

Many sportspeople state that politics and sports should not mix, but it is very difficult for them not to when so many governments actively support and fund the sports organisations in their country. The Olympic Games has been the major focus for these political problems and we will look at this in more detail below.

15.8 Sport on the world stage

Sport is very popular around the world and major events like the Olympic Games and the football World Cup are televised in every country. This is why such events have been the focus for political demonstration. Any person or country that wants to make a point is guaranteed maximum exposure at these events. We have already described how countries and governments manipulate sport and sporting success to their gain. Other, smaller, groups have also used the Olympics as a stage on which to make their point to the world. This has meant that the security and safety systems at the Games have to be very complex and are therefore very expensive.

The Olympics – a global event that attracts audiences around the world

165

Definition

IOC

The International Olympic Committee, the governing body of the Olympic movement.

Definition

OLYMPIC OATH

'We swear that we will take part in these Olympic games in the true spirit of sportsmanship and that we will abide by the rules that govern them, for the glory of sport and the honour of our country.'

FESTOON

The Olympic five-rings symbol, sold to the highest bidders amongst international companies.

15.9 The Olympic Games

The Olympic Games have their origins in Ancient Greece, where they were held every four years as part of a religious ceremony to the god Zeus. At the end of the last century Baron de Coubertin reintroduced the games (the first being held in Greece in 1896), and set up the International Olympic Committee (IOC) and the modern Olympic Games, which are held every four years in a different city.

There are actually two Olympic Games – winter and summer – though it is the summer Games that are the most prestigious. De Coubertin's idea was that the Games could be used to bring the people of the world together in friendly competition. He hoped that this might help prevent war and develop more international friendship.

The Olympics in the past have been used to promote the good side of sport. All competitors were amateurs, competing purely for enjoyment, and the winner's medal had no real monetary value. Sportsmanship was the central point of the Games, and before competition started all the athletes took the Olympic Oath.

The IOC organise each games every four years, choosing the host city and coordinating funding. Most of the IOC's income now comes from selling the festoon (the five-rings symbol) to international companies and from television fees.

Each participating nation must have a national Olympic body that takes responsibility for promoting the Olympic ideals in their own country. In the UK this is the British Olympic Association.

15.9.1 Problems at the Olympics

Berlin, 1936

This was called the 'Nazi Olympics' and was the first Olympic Games where politics was openly evident. Berlin had been awarded the Games in 1931 but by 1936 Adolf Hitler's Nazi party had taken over Germany, and Hitler wanted to use the Games to show the world how powerful Germany and its people were.

Hitler believed in the supremacy of the 'Aryan' race ('true' Germans, blond-haired, blue-eyed and muscular): they would dominate the Games and show that the German race was superior to all others. Unfortunately for Hitler, a young Black American athlete called Jesse Owens dominated the Games, winning four gold medals. Owens was the only athlete not to receive his gold medals from Hitler, who left the stadium in disgust. Three years later Hitler's aggression led to the start of the Second World War.

Mexico City, 1968

Two main problems affected these Games. Mexico was a very poor country and many people felt that the huge amount of money needed to put on the Games would have been better spent helping to develop the country. Mexican students were the most active in opposition to the Games. They held a number of demonstrations, the final one being 10 days before the Games were due to begin. Over 10 000 people marched to the Square of the Three Cultures in Mexico City. Aware of the impact such a demonstration could have in the world's media so close to the start of the Games, the Mexican authorities reacted strongly, sending in the army to surround the demonstrators. A fierce battle developed, at the end of which 260 people had been killed and several thousand injured. Amazingly, the Games went on with no further trouble.

The next political problem occurred within the Olympic stadium. In America in the late 1960s Black civil rights groups had been protesting about the lack of opportunity for Black people and the racist attitudes in American society. With the world's media watching, two young Black American athletes used the medal ceremony to show their support for the

*Tommie Smith and John Carlos giving the Black Power salute
at the 1968 Mexico Olympics*

Black Power movement. In the 200 m Final Tommie Smith took gold and
John Carlos took bronze. As they stood on the medal podium listening to
the American national anthem they bowed their heads and each raised one
gloved hand in the Black Power salute. Both were expelled by the US
Olympic Association and immediately sent home.

Munich, 1972 – the terrorist Games

During the Games Palestinian terrorists stormed part of the Olympic
village, taking several Israeli athletes as hostages. There had long been a
serious disagreement between Palestinian groupings and the Israeli authorities over the ownership and control of disputed land.

The German police attempted to stage a dramatic rescue but things
went wrong, ending in the deaths of nine athletes, a policeman and five terrorists. Many felt that the Games should be abandoned in honour of the
athletes killed, but the IOC decided to carry on – so, they said, showing
that no terrorist groups could stop the Games.

Montreal, 1976

Again there were two main problems associated with these Games. The
Canadian government underestimated the costs and ran out of money
before all the facilities were completed. Indeed the Canadian people are
still paying via their tax for the 1976 Olympics. After this, the IOC let more
commercial companies get involved in the Games so that they had financial backing.

The Montreal Games were boycotted by several African countries, who
were unhappy that New Zealand had been allowed to compete in the
Games even though their rugby team had continued to play against South
Africa.

Moscow, 1980

Boycotts also dominated these Games. In December 1979 the Soviet Union had invaded Afghanistan. To show that they did not agree with this, the following countries did not go these Olympics: the USA, Canada, West Germany, Japan and Kenya.

Los Angeles, 1984 – 'tit for tat'

Because the USA had led the boycott of the Soviet Olympics in 1980 the Soviet Union led a boycott of the 1984 Games. No Eastern bloc countries competed in these Games.

Seoul, 1988

Another Games dominated by the feud between the political systems of communism and capitalism. Korea is a divided country, the north being a communist state, the south capitalist. Seoul (in South Korea) was awarded the Games by the IOC but North Korea applied to stage some of the events. The IOC refused and North Korea and three other communist countries boycotted the Games.

The 1988 Games were also the first to allow professional performers into the Games, so ending another Olympic tradition. Most of this was to do with the inclusion of tennis as an Olympic sport.

Barcelona, 1992

Generally a very successful Games. No-one boycotted the Games and through the development of the commercial side the Games made a profit. South Africa was allowed back into the Olympic movement after abolishing Apartheid. The Soviet Union was replaced by the Commonwealth of Independent States and West and East Germany were joined as one team.

Atlanta, 1996 – the centenary Games

These will be remembered for the hype and glamour, a terrorist bomb and the organisational problems that hindered athletes and spectators alike.

Many people felt that the centenary Games should really have gone back to Greece, home of both the ancient Olympics and the first modern Games, but the IOC chose Atlanta. Atlanta's other major claim to fame is that it is the home of Coca Cola, the Olympic movement's biggest sponsor.

The Americans claimed that these would be the best Games ever but problems with transport systems and the very hot weather meant there were lots of complaints. The lowest point of the Games was when a terrorist bomb exploded in the middle of a music concert for athletes and fans in Centenary Park, killing several people and injuring many others.

> ### Key revision points
>
> *Sport at European level follows a decentralised pattern. European legislation is increasingly having an impact on sport – examples include the Bosman case and tobacco sponsorship. There are two basic models of European sport: the Eastern European model – state control – and the Western European model – autonomous control. Sport throughout Europe follows a pyramid structure. European bodies such as UEFA control the individual sports. These in turn form international bodies (such as FIFA) that control world championships. The 'live' nature of global games can result in their being used as a stage for protest. Sport can be manipulated by states for propaganda purposes.*

KEY TERMS

You should now understand the following terms. If you do not, go back through the chapter and find out.

Bosman case
Boycott
European Charter for Sport for All
Festoon
FIFA
Grass-roots sport
IOC
Olympic Oath
Propaganda
Sporting federation
UEFA

PROGRESS CHECK

1 What are the reasons behind the increase in world club competitions?
2 Sport at European level follows a decentralised pattern. What does this mean?
3 Name three of the five functions the EC believe sport performs in Europe.
4 How does EC legislation affect the provision of sport in Europe?
5 How can sport be used for propaganda purposes?
6 Explain what is meant by the pyramid structure of sport in Europe.
7 What is the role of UEFA in European football?
8 How does the organisation of European sport differ from the organisation of sport in the USA?
9 Explain what a boycott is in the context of sport.
10 Why do global games tend to attract protest?
11 What were de Coubertin's ideals behind the setting up of the modern Olympics?
12 What is the role of the IOC?
13 How does the IOC generate most of the funds it needs?
14 Using examples, describe how some groups of people have used the Olympic Games to stage political protest.
15 How are the EC rules on tobacco sponsorship going to affect sport?

Chapter
16
Sport in society and the pursuit of excellence

Learning objectives

- To understand the role of sport in society.
- To know the way sport reflects the society in which it is played.
- To be able to compare sports in different cultures.
- To understand the concepts of excellence.
- To investigate different strategies in the pursuit of excellence.

Hurling – Ireland's national sport

Sport is a universal activity, played all over the world. In this chapter we discuss how countries have used sporting success to further political ideals and show how good *their* country is, and how this attitude has often affected the most important world sporting events such as the Olympic Games. We also investigate the concept of excellence in sport and the methods different countries have used to achieve it.

16.1 Sociological aspects of sport

Sport in the 1990s became a cultural phenomenon of great magnitude, its influence permeating all aspects of our society. Sport is a compulsory element of our education system, it dominates all forms of media and is increasingly becoming an important section of our economy.

Sport can provide a useful focus for studying different societies. Roberts, Sutton Smith and others have developed the field of *sports sociology*. They foster the view that the games played by a society reflect the values inherent in that society. Sports are also used to teach younger members of the society these values. In other words, sport reflects the society in which it is played.

A particular sport can become an extensive reference for the country or society it is played in. Each game has its own history and pattern of development and this evolution is closely linked to the development, history, geography and values of the country in which it is played.

Take the Gaelic game of hurling as an example. This invasion-type game (see Chapter 11) is only played in Ireland, but is the largest spectator sport in the country. By studying the game we should be able to pick out characteristics of its play and structure that can be linked to the country (Table 16.1). Hurling reflects closely the wider values and traditions in Irish society and remains an important expression of the culture.

Definition

SOCIETY

The structural composition of a community of people.

CULTURE

The way the society functions and its traditions and beliefs.

SPORTS SOCIOLOGY

The study of human social behaviour in a sports context.

Table 16.1 *Linking the characteristics of sport to society – hurling*

Characteristics of sport	Societal links
Robust, physical game	Traditional link with hard/rural work, history of violence
Large pitch	Rural nature of Ireland, allowing traditional large-scale, 'mob' games
Few rules – players can hit, kick or throw the ball	Sport that has retained traditional rules, little change – strong traditional culture
Unique to Ireland	Reflecting Ireland's peripheral geographical position on the edge of Europe – not much mixing. Lack of status meant that, unlike England, Ireland imported rather than exported sports

Football also makes an interesting study. All countries play the game of Association Football to very similar rules, yet it is amazing how different countries impose their own style on this universal game. This is most evident during the World Cup, when we see the flamboyance of the Brazilians clash with the tactical brilliance of the German team or the exuberance of the Cameroon team.

Sport is a reflection of society and many issues (such as class, gender and race) have an effect on sport. Sport follows the trends of society and a number of patterns can be identified. These are described below.

ACTIVITY

This type of analysis can be an interesting way of researching the role sport plays in culture. Try to find some video clips of different sports from other countries and see if you can identify aspects of the country it is played in. Perhaps these questions may help: Why is Australian Rules football only played in Australia? How have the West Indies adapted the English game of cricket to suit their own independent culture? What parallels are there between American Football and American society?

16.1.1 Sociological theories

One recently developed theory is that of *centrality*, which suggests that the dominant roles in sport such as coach, captain, play maker are undertaken by people in the dominant sections of the society in which the sport is played. The sections of the community that are in the minority either numerically or in terms of status, often immigrant or lower-class people, are underrepresented in these roles. For example, in American Football there are very few Afro-Caribbean Quarterbacks and in the UK we have no professional managers in football from ethnic minorities.

Often these anomalies are related to *stereotyping*. This has a great effect in sport on the selection of players and positional decisions. The issue of discrimination in sport will be developed further in Chapter 17.

16.1.2 The role of sport in socialisation

Socialisation is the way humans adjust to their culture, the process through which we become participating members of society. During socialisation we acquire our personalities and decide on the roles we will take on in later life.

Sport, especially physical education since it is compulsory, is an important vehicle for transmitting the values of the wider society. Physical education is used at school to develop a range of social skills such as cooperation and communication as well as the practical aspects of fitness and motor skills. Sport allows individuals to express themselves and to experiment with different roles and activities.

Sport may also lead to *social mobility* for certain people. In countries where sport is more liberal than the society at large, underprivileged members of that society can use sport for social recognition and to gain wealth. Sport attracts members of the lower classes because through hard work they can be generously rewarded – and there are many role models to emulate.

16.2 A comparative view of sport

Comparative studies of sport have developed from the sociological base. The emphasis of these studies is on the structure and organisation of sport in other countries and on identifying the aspects we should introduce to our own system. This is an important issue for the present British sports

---

Definition

CENTRALITY

A theory which suggests that the dominant roles in sport – such as coach, captain, play maker – are undertaken by people in the dominant sections of the society.

Definition

SOCIALISATION

The way humans adjust to their culture

Definition

SOCIAL MOBILITY

Gaining in social status and income.

Emergent cultures select sports and work hard to achieve world status

organisation because we would appear to be losing our traditional dominance in international sport.

A truly comparative study would view individual countries, but we will confine our study to just four groupings of countries and the ways they develop sport:

- emergent cultures
- the Eastern Bloc cultures
- the New World democratic cultures
- the American model.

16.2.1 Emergent cultures

These are the *developing countries*, such as the African nations. In these countries modern sport has often been introduced by previous colonial powers and in the main has replaced the indigenous activities. With their new-found independence, the people have used sport as a process of nation building.

The success of countries such as Kenya in athletics, the West Indies in Cricket and Brazil in football has shown that developing countries can take on the developed world and often beat them.

These countries face the problems of limited resources and little infrastructure, but through selection and channelling in only a limited number of sports they are able to compete on the world stage. The model of sports development in these countries is shown in Table 16.2.

Table 16.2 *An emergent model of sport*

Integration	Sport unites the country by bringing together different races, areas and tribes
Defence	National Service gives a chance for selection. The strict regime is suited to training and development of talent
Shop window	Sporting success puts the country onto the world stage
Selection	Concentrate on limited number of sports, usually the ones suited to the environment or the physique of the people

Many emergent countries have now introduced elite sports systems aimed at increasing the chance of gaining gold medals. Often the armed forces act as sports nurseries and screen for sports talent (Kenya is a good example of a country in which the army plays an important role in fostering sports talent).

Performers that do reach an elite level have the opportunity to earn a great deal of money and often move to Western countries, where the opportunity to gain higher reward is greater.

16.2.2 The Eastern Bloc cultures

Definition

EASTERN BLOC

Former communist countries found in eastern Europe.

Although now only a historical grouping since the communist system disintegrated in the early 1990s, this culture, dominated by the Soviet Union, is worth study because of the phenomenal sporting success Eastern Bloc countries achieved in a short time scale.

In countries such as the Soviet Union and German Democratic Republic sport was completely state controlled. Every aspect – from selection to training and diet – was coordinated by the central government. The shop window was the objective, although in this case it was the political system that was on show (see Figure 16.1). As Riordan states 'Every win for the Soviet Union was a win for the Communist system' – and if this win was against an American performer or team, then the political emphasis was maximised.

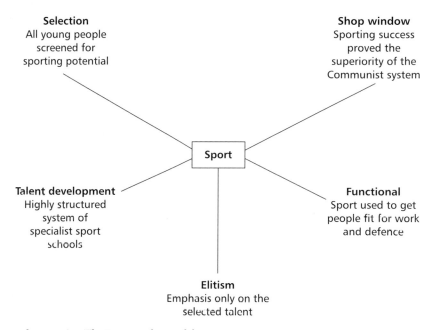

Selection
All young people screened for sporting potential

Shop window
Sporting success proved the superiority of the Communist system

Sport

Talent development
Highly structured system of specialist sport schools

Functional
Sport used to get people fit for work and defence

Elitism
Emphasis only on the selected talent

Figure 16.1 *The Eastern Bloc model*

In all Eastern Bloc countries sport played a very important role. Success came as the result of a carefully structured system that tested the entire population and fed the talented through sports schools and training centres to national teams.

Although much of their success has been put down to the widespread use of drugs, this alone would not account for the level and rate of success. Performers in these countries had the best facilities, coaches and support available. Another important point is that sport in these societies reflected the egalitarian ideology of the system, which fostered the idea that everyone in society was equal in status. Although in practice this was not strictly true, in sport everybody had an equal chance of success. If you were identified as having talent in a sport you were selected, no matter what your race or background. This ensured that the state had the widest possible base to select from.

16.2.3 New World democratic cultures

By this title, we mean societies such as Australia, South Africa and New Zealand. These are cultures with European origins and in the main former

British colonies. Most are under 200 years old and, after achieving independence, developed into advanced thriving societies.

In a few sports such as cricket and rugby these countries vie for world honours. Australia in particular is a world leader in an ever-increasing number of sports. South Africa, until recently left out of international sport because of Apartheid, is quickly redeveloping its sporting talent and is again emerging as a powerful force in rugby, cricket and athletics.

What these countries have in common, apart from a shared colonial history, is a culture of 'Bush Ethos'. The environments remain harsh and the people have had to work hard to develop and expand. Being young countries they lack the traditions and history of the Old World and have consequently needed to find new ways of expressing their emotions. Sport has more than filled this role: it is often seen as a substitute for the higher forms of culture in Europe. It is no cliché to say that in these societies sport is a religion.

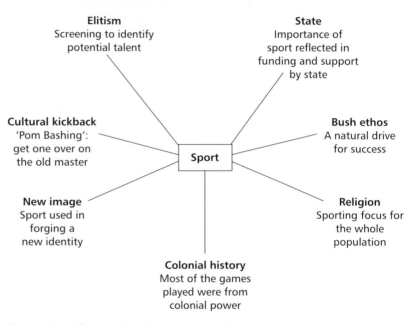

Figure 16.2 *The New World democratic model*

The other drive is again a form of shop window, although here the focus is different. The ambition of all these new cultures is to beat their old colonial powers – in particular England. Their sportsmen and women seem to have an extra edge to their approach, are driven by the win ethic and do not appear to be restrained by our more traditional values and ethics. To them, *winning* is important: it reflects struggle and hard work – the values that are inherent in their societies.

It is interesting to note that a lot of Australia's success can be linked to a 'Soviet'-style programme of state funding and selection. The Australians have made good use of comparative sports study, adapting many successful methods from around the world but predominantly from the old Eastern Bloc countries.

All young people are now screened for sports talent, the results being fed into a national computer system which then suggests the best sport for the youngster to follow. All talented performers are offered state sponsorship and through the extensive clubs system and chain of national sports centres are nurtured and groomed for international success. The results have been outstanding and as the programme has expanded into football and other sports, Australia can now rightly claim to be a sports superpower.

Sports testing

The Australian Institute of Sport has recently introduced a system of sport talent-spotting, which they call *Sports Search*. Sports Search was originally devised as a way of increasing participation in sport but is now an effective means of identifying talent. It is aimed at children in high school of 11–15 years old, and it is hoped the project will visit all of Australia's 3200 high schools. Each child will undertake a series of physical tests which will rate them for size, shape, agility, endurance and explosive power. This information will be fed into a computer and each student will be matched to their ideal sport. The school will follow this up by ensuring that each student has the opportunity to take up the sports he or she is best suited to.

> **Definition**
> ### SPORTS SEARCH
> *A sports selection programme used in Australian schools to give children a 'best fit' sport.*

16.2.4 The American model

America (according to the Americans) is the world's number one nation in all terms, the superpower now without the Soviet Union and with nobody to beat. America's sports are the most technically advanced in the world, its sports stars are the richest in the world, and in a number of sports the Americans are undisputed world champions. What is interesting is that America's major sports are not really played anywhere else in the world – America is so far ahead that it can hold World Championships in American football and baseball, in which only American teams compete!

Like Australia, the USA has colonial links, but these were cut much earlier in the country's development and for many years the USA developed in planned isolation from Europe. During this time its sports developed, adapted from the old European games but modelled and changed to suit America's new image. In fact so American were these new sports of baseball, grid iron and basketball that even with extensive backing they have never really developed elsewhere.

The sports are high scoring and action packed to maximise their entertainment value. They reflect American culture in that the aim is to win – the win ethic is what drives all American people and this fuels the so-called 'American Dream'. The American model is outlined in Figure 16.3.

But it is the commercial aspect of American sport which makes it so different. Every level, from professional national teams to the local high school football teams, is run as a business. The influence of television is total and most sports in the USA rely entirely on the money generated

> **Definition**
> ### AMERICAN DREAM
> *The idea of rags-to-riches success, best personified in the* Rocky *films, where a nobody becomes World Champion overnight.*

American football – a sport that reflects the culture in which it is played

Figure 16.3 *The United States model*

through television deals and advertising revenue. Sports stars in America are millionaires; most professional teams will have a number of players on multi-million dollar annual contracts. Many stars, like Michael Jordan, make even more money through sponsorship deals and endorsements.

There is a flip side to this: sport in the USA is extremely elitist. In athletics, for example, there is not even one amateur club where 'Joe Public' can train. For most Americans sport is something you watch on the television and not something you actually play. The television also dictates the rules – for example, American Football has evolved into a constant stop–go staccato pattern to allow companies to screen advertisements every five minutes.

Many of these trends are beginning to filter into British sport, and it may be very difficult for us to prevent Americanisation of our sport.

> *Definition*
>
> ## AMERICANISATION
>
> *Where American trends and attitudes invade traditional culture.*

Key revision points

Sport plays an important role in modern societies, reflecting the wider values and traditions of the society. Different countries play different sports, and also play the same games differently. Centrality is a sociological theory which states that the dominant roles in sport are taken by the dominant section of society. Emergent cultures select and channel athletes into a limited number of sports to ensure success. In the Eastern Bloc cultures the state controls sport for political gain. The New World democratic cultures use sport as a focus of national identity and to gain status over the Old World. In the USA sport is seen as a commercial commodity and is driven by the win ethic. In all cases, the shop window is the aim.

16.3 The pursuit of excellence

Sebastian Coe and his colleagues, in their book *More than a Game*, state that 'Champions are made, not born.' In this section we will discuss how champions are developed and the issues that are related to excellence in

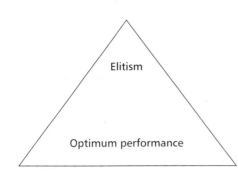

Figure 16.4 *The sports pyramid*

sport. Excellence is an important current issue in the UK. Many people have recorded the fall in our sporting standards and in sports such as tennis, where our players were among the elite, we are now slipping down the rankings.

We must first try to define what we mean by 'excellence'. In fact, the word has two meanings, immediately causing a dilemma which we, as sports scientists, need to face. The two meanings can be viewed as two sections of the sports pyramid (shown in Figure 16.4).

ACTIVITY

What makes a champion? Write down the key factors that create excellence in a performer. Use the following headings to help you:

ability, practice, equipment, coaching, sports science support

---

ELITISM

Activities confined to an exclusive minority, usually the best.

OPTIMUM PERFORMANCE

Sporting excellence should be the target of every individual.

16.3.1 Elitism

In elitism the emphasis is on a few, the best, performers. The tendency is to look for the most developed and to ignore the rest. We have already seen this approach in the emerging cultures discussed in the previous section. The best example of this approach was seen in the German Democratic Republic, a country with a population of only 16 million which managed to be in the top three for sports such as athletics, swimming and boxing. The whole sports system of this communist country was geared up to selecting and developing champion performers, but this was at the expense of the rest of the population.

16.3.2 Optimum performance

In contrast to elitism, the optimum performance model asserts that sporting excellence should be the target of every individual. The society acknowledges that each person has a potential and that the sports system should help everyone fulfil this objective. This model has been used in physical education in the UK, where the aim has been to try to develop in all participants a feeling of achievement. This is reflected by the vast range of activities we undertake in school and the lack of specialisation.

It has been argued that this system has a great disadvantage in that it will not lead to the development of talent on the level required for international success.

Very few societies are concerned with the optimum performance model because it doesn't bring the short-term responses that they crave or because they do not have the finance or resources to allow every member of the population the chance of success.

If we acknowledge that in the main it is the first model that is most relevant in modern sport then let us investigate more closely the issues in the development of excellence.

16.3.3 Development of excellence

Three key stages may be identified in the development of sporting talent:
1   Selection of talent
2   Development of talent
3   Providing support for performance.

The actual methods used differ from country to country, but increasingly a number of policies are being followed by most. A lot of the these have been adapted from the Eastern European model of sports excellence, pioneered by the Soviet Union and the German Democratic Republic from the 1950s onwards.

Selection

Selection is the start of this process, identifying individuals with the potential to become champions. The pyramid theory of sports development suggests that the wider the base then the greater the number at the top of the pyramid. The aim of the selection process is to make the base of the pyramid as wide as possible.

In the old Soviet Union this was achieved by screening every child in the education system for sporting potential. At first this would involve gross motor skills but later more specific skill tests, physiological and psychological tests were used to identify talent and channel it into the appropriate sports. This latter aspect is perhaps a debatable issue – many argue that is wrong for young people to specialise too early because it can lead to problems such as physiological 'burn out'.

Australia has recently implemented a system of screening every child at high school level using sport-related tests. The results are put into a computer which predicts which sport they are most suited to. In most cases this is the sport they will be directed towards. In the UK we have tended to keep away from this approach. Performers tend to specialise later in their development, and the general view is that it is still better to develop skills and experiences in a range of sports.

Talent development

Stage two is again a crucial aspect. The children selected are coached, instructed and nurtured to become champions. In many countries this process is achieved through the education system, predominantly in sports schools.

Sports schools

Sports schools are found in most European countries and are often controlled by the state. They allow young people to develop their sporting potential while continuing with academic studies. They usually have high-quality facilities and specialised staff, the advantage being that students get more time to practice their skills and the atmosphere of excellence encourages their development.

The Soviet Union was the role model in the field of sports schools. After selection, students were filtered up the sports pyramid through city sports schools, regional boarding schools and (the ultimate aim) the national training centre.

In America a slightly different method of development is followed. Sport is viewed as such an important aspect of the American education system that all schools and colleges have extensive sports facilities and place a lot of emphasis on sports success. Students are offered sports scholarships which pay all their expenses, and are given a lot of time to practice. The best college players are selected by the professional teams each year during the annual 'Draft'.

In the UK the number of sports schools is increasing, but these are still few and of little influence. The best known was the FA school at Lilleshall, where the best 22 young footballers board and spend half a day at a local comprehensive school (players such as Andy Cole and Nick Barmby have progressed through the FA school), and the LTA Tennis School at Bisham Abbey.

Administration of excellence

The final part of the process is to provide support in terms of administration and funding. If athletes are to be successful they need full support, primarily financial aid to ensure that they don't have to worry about raising the funds to cover their training and competition expenses, which allows them more time to prepare for competition. Again there is wide variation in the method of financial support. In many countries the state funds the

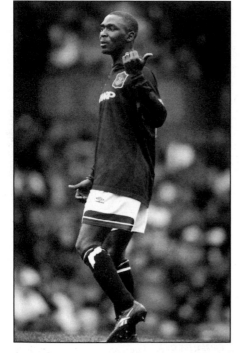

Andy Cole – a graduate of the FA school of excellence at Lilleshall

ACTIVITY

List four advantages and four disadvantages of basing performers in sports schools.

top athletes – in Australia, France and the old Soviet Union all top performers are paid grants that allow them to become virtually full-time athletes. In America talented performers are paid scholarships by schools and colleges or athletes are contracted to a professional team. We have already discussed how SportsAid in the UK tries to fund up-and-coming athletes – as yet there is little government input to sports in the UK (see Chapter 14 for more on sports funding).

Modern sports performers also require the support of an ever-increasing range of sports specialists (psychologists, dieticians, physiotherapists), as well as video and computer equipment to help improve technique. In the UK such service is now being developed in a number of National Sports Centres forming a national network, with the United Kingdom Institute of Sport (UKSI) as the central focus. The aim is to enable our international performers to use top-quality facilities for training. These now come under the Sports Council's World Class Performance programme, funded by the National Lottery. This Sports Fund has three levels:

- *World Class Start* – programmes aimed at developing talented youngsters.
- *World Class Potential* – assisting with the development of teenagers helping with educational support.
- *World Class Performance* – supporting our elite athletes through financial support and providing top class facilities through the UKSI.

Most other countries have similar national centres for the use of the national squads.

The national sports centres in the UK

Bisham Abbey, Bucks. Home of the LTA National Tennis Centre. Also has facilities for football, hockey, squash, golf and weightlifting. England's soccer and rugby teams use Bisham Abbey as a base for training.

Crystal Palace, London. International standard facilities for athletics, swimming, martial arts and up to 40 other sports. Used as a training base for the national athletics and swimming squads.

Holme Pierrepont, Nottingham. The national watersports centre, with international standard facilities for canoeing, rowing and water skiing and provision for many other aquatic sports. The centre also has a sport science and sports medicine centre.

Lilleshall Hall, Shropshire. Home to the Human Performance Centre and the National Sports Injuries Clinic. The British Amateur Gymnastics Association has also recently established a national centre here.

Plas Y Brenin, North Wales. This houses the National Centre for Mountain Activities and caters for a wide range of sports and outdoor pursuits.

Sport England plans to widen the provision of top-class national sports centres, establishing a national network by adding centres at Bedford, Bath, Southampton, Sheffield and Gateshead.

16.3.4 Constraints on excellence

We should now be able to identify aspects of sporting excellence from other societies that we could take and implement in the British sports system, with the aim of developing our sports potential – aspects such as setting up more sports schools, introducing state or other sponsorship schemes that will allow our sports performers to be able to train harder and concentrate more on their chosen sports.

However, it is not simply a question of transplanting practices from other societies. As we have already suggested, sport and the way it is administered and developed in a country reflects the values and culture of that country. There are several cultural constraints why we in the UK do not actively encourage excellence in sport.

Historical – We invented most modern sports and retain a status in world sport, so it is not important for us to excel.

Geographical – Our population is relatively small, so our pyramid base is much smaller than, say, the USA or China.

Ideological – Most of the world sports powers have a very nationalistic approach, where you are playing for the honour and status of your country, but we are patriotic rather than nationalistic. Similarly, we promote the recreational ethic rather than the win ethic, our heroes are Eddie the Eagle and the Frank Brunos of the world. We also tend to feel that winners are arrogant.

Socioeconomic – Participation in sport in the UK has had the middle-class tradition that taking part counts, not winning, and that sport should not be work.

What should we do to develop a more effective programme of sports excellence? The answer is twofold:

1   A large amount of *money* is required to fund such a programme – high-level facilities and equipment, coaches and the extensive back-up require a lot of funding. The National Lottery fund is proving to be a possible source of the money needed.

2   A more coordinated *administration* system is required. At the moment our sports system is too diverse at all levels; we need sports to come together to share aims and objectives for the overall benefit of British sport.

Key revision points

Excellence in sport has two meanings: elitism, which means 'all for the best – forget the rest' or optimum performance, where everyone has the chance to succeed. Most societies emphasise elitism as this produces champions, which can be used as a 'shop window'. There are three major stages in the development of excellence: selection, development and support. There is much diversity in the methods used by different societies.

KEY TERMS

You should now understand the following terms. If you do not, go back though the chapter and find out.

American dream
Americanisation
Centrality
Culture
Eastern Bloc
Elitism
Optimum performance
Social mobility
Socialisation
Society
Sports Search
Sports sociology

PROGRESS CHECK

1   In what country is hurling played?
2   Why is sport a useful focus for studying different societies?
3   Explain what is meant by the term centrality.
4   What role does sport play in socialisation?
5   Explain what comparative study is in the context of sport.
6   Give examples of three emergent cultures.
7   How can sport be used for social mobility by emergent athletes?
8   Name two countries that were in the old Eastern Bloc.
9   Using the Eastern Bloc as an example, explain what is meant by the term 'shop window'.
10 Give three examples of countries that are classed as New World Democratic cultures.
11 What are the moral arguments against the Eastern European model of early selection and channelling of young children into a particular sport?
12 Why has a country such as Australia placed so much emphasis on developing sports talent?
13 Explain the Sports Search programme undertaken in Australia.
14 Explain what is meant by 'American dream'.
15 Give examples of how British sport is being Americanised.
16 Explain the pyramid system of sports development. How does it make the development of sporting talent more efficient?
17 What are the two meanings of the term 'excellence'?
18 What are the three stages in the development of sporting talent?

17

Factors affecting participation in sport

Learning objectives

- To identify the benefits of regular exercise.
- To understand mass participation in sport.
- To be able to identify discrimination in sport and to understand what causes it.
- To investigate methods of overcoming discrimination.

Sport is a natural part of life, whether you are one of the elite competing for gold medals or just playing for fun and enjoyment. The opportunity to take part in sporting activity should be a basic human right; however, many people suffer constraints that prevent them from taking part. The aim of mass participation is to break down these constraints, whatever they may be, and to encourage as many people as possible to take up sport.

The Sports Council estimate that one in three people in the UK regularly take part in sport. In this chapter we look at the reasons why people take part in sport and recreation and also what constraints may inhibit people from taking part in an active lifestyle.

17.1 Why play sport?

After reading the early sections of this book you should now have some firm ideas about why sport is good for us. It promotes mental and physical health, it is a positive use of spare time and is an important emotional release.

Everyone should be able to participate in sport

ACTIVITY

Write a list of specific benefits to a person who regularly plays sport. Your list will mainly contain intrinsic benefits, but there may also be extrinsic benefits for the society as a whole if many of its members regularly participate.

Sport for all will also benefit the country as a whole: people will be fitter so there will be less strain on the health system; they will also be able to work harder and more effectively. Another, less positive, aspect is that people will be fit for war if the need arises.

In a sporting context there are also other extrinsic rewards – if more people are playing sport the sports pyramid discussed in Chapter 16 will have a wider base.

Many countries have set up mass participation schemes, often state sponsored, to encourage more people to take part in physical activity. Even in the decentralised British sports system, the Sports Council's 'Sport for All' campaign has had considerable state involvement, specifically in its funding.

The phrase 'Sport for All' has now become synonymous with the ideals of mass participation. The Soviet Union used the phrase 'massovost', while in France they have 'Sport Pour Tous'.

The whole emphasis in sport for all should be on promoting the intrinsic value of sport – too many people view sport as either something they had to do at school or something they see on the television which is far too advanced for them to try. The real point is that, as we have mentioned many times, sport is an extremely diverse area, involving many different activities and catering for every shape, personality and level of skill. Perhaps we need to use a few more realistic role models to encourage people to take up activities.

Every Sunday morning well over a million people play football in organised leagues. There are 125 000 voluntary sports clubs in Britain catering for six million members, and many more people regularly take part in sport and recreation outside any structural organisation – be it a kick around in the park or joining the 23% of the adult population that walk two miles or more each week. Mass participation, however, is still not a reality in Britain – even the most generous prediction by the Sports Council puts the figure at one in three of the population. The vast majority of people in Britain do not actively participate and, what is more worrying, the activity levels in young people (who were previously the most active group) are also drastically falling.

We now know that the claim by the Soviet Union that everyone undertook physical activity was a propaganda myth and that sport was confined to the elite. In America, a country with the resources to allow the optimum performance form of excellence discussed in the last chapter, participation levels are low – and falling. If we concentrate on the UK, although we know it is advantageous for us to promote and develop mass participation the success rate of existing programmes or their overall importance is limited. Again we can use sociocultural analysis to suggest reasons for the failure of mass participation to take off.

17.2 Constraints on mass participation

These may be analysed and classified in the same way as we classified the constraints on excellence in the UK.

Historical – In the past sport has been very closely linked to education, and many people's only sporting experience was through compulsory and often harsh physical education lessons. Many are put off sport for life.

Huge numbers of people take part in events such as the London Marathon every year

Geographical – Many areas of Britain are under-resourced in terms of sports facilities and – equally as important – qualified coaches, teachers and leaders.

Ideological – In our culture, sport has always been seen purely as a non-serious recreation: many other more important issues require attention before you turn to sport. Often at school academically bright students are encouraged to move away from sport so that they can concentrate more time on their studies.

Socioeconomic – Amateur/voluntary sport has had a rather middle-class image and the fact is that most of us in the UK must 'pay to play'. We have to pay club subscriptions, fees and facility costs, as well as providing our own kit and equipment.

Consequently, although there have been some successes we are still a long way from achieving sport for all. Marathon running has been one success – a previously minority sport involving serious athletes has over the last few years become a true mass participation event. Events such as the London Marathon or the Great North Run have captured the public's imagination and huge numbers of people have taken up running purely for the intrinsic rewards of finishing the course. At the same time, however, these events have remained high quality in terms of excellence, with serious runners racing at the front while thousands plod on behind with the only aim of finishing. Other sports could take many pointers from these events in developing the right formula for mass participation.

ACTIVITY

Why has running become such a success in terms of getting people involved in physical activity?

Key revision points

Mass participation means maximising the potential for all sections of a community to take part in physical activity. 'Sport for All' is the campaign set up by the Sports Council to foster mass participation in the UK. Taking part in physical activity has many benefits for both the individual and society. Benefits for the individual are classed as intrinsic. Benefits for society are classed as extrinsic. Mass participation is not yet a reality for most countries. A sociocultural analysis can be used to provide some reasons for this.

17.3 Discrimination in sport

In this section we will see again how closely sport reflects the society in which it takes place. In many societies groups are divided by sociocultural variables which lead to *discrimination*.

In the last section we highlighted the fact that many people do not have equal access to sport, often as a result of discrimination due to a cultural variable.

17.3.1 Cultural factors

Five main cultural factors lead to discrimination in sport:
- gender
- class
- race

Definition

DISCRIMINATION

One section of a community is disadvantaged because of certain sociocultural variables.

- age
- ability.

Unfortunately we do not have the space to investigate fully each of these areas, but to help students gain a sound grasp of each area we suggest further and more specific reading at the end of Part 3. In this chapter we will identify the common variables leading to discrimination in sport and briefly outline the areas highlighted above.

Discrimination can be said to affect the following areas in sport:

- provision
- opportunity
- esteem.

Provision

Are the facilities that allow you to participate available to you? We have already suggested that in the UK there is a shortage of facilities and those that do exist are often sited in particular areas. Living in an inner-city area would discriminate against you because there is little provision in these areas. Equipment is also required, which is often expensive – those on low incomes may be discriminated against unless equipment is available free or can be hired cheaply.

Opportunity

There may be barriers to an individual's participation in an activity. In the UK most sport takes place in the voluntarily run clubs, which are often elitist organisations. Clubs work on membership systems and membership is controlled either by the ability to pay the fees or, in cases such as some golf clubs, election to the club membership. This often closes membership to certain members of the community.

Another consideration for the individual is whether they have the time to play. Women in particular are often faced with this problem. The demands of work and family often mean that women have little leisure time, which accounts in some way for the low levels of female participation in sport.

Esteem

This is concerned with the societal view of individuals. In many cultures societal values dictate that women should not take an active part in sport, or if they do it should be confined to 'feminine' sports such as gymnastics and not 'macho' pursuits such as football or rugby. These judgements are based on the traditional roles men and women have taken in the society and may be very difficult to break.

Stereotypes and *sports myths* are also societal variables that lead to discrimination. Often minority groups within a community are labelled as having certain characteristics or traits, and this can lead to them being steered into certain sports or positions and away from others.

One good example in the UK is the current lack of Asian footballers in soccer. Much research has been done into this area and programmes are now being set up to try to address the imbalance but the main problem is that, in our societal view, Asians are not potential footballers.

Stereotypes and myths can become 'self-fulfilling prophecies' – even the people they discriminate against come to believe they are valid and conform to the stereotypes by displaying their appointed characteristics and choosing the sports that fit them. In doing so they are reinforcing society's view. It is only recently that a number of women have broken this system by taking up football and rugby, and it is hoped that the success of the women's England Rugby team will start to change the views of society.

Let us now look briefly at the groups identified above and suggest key areas that lead to discrimination.

ACTIVITY

The British media are still reluctant to devote a lot of space or time to sports such as women's rugby. What cultural constraints may be causing this?

Definition

STEREOTYPE

A group of characteristics that we believe all members of a certain section of society share, usually based on very little actual fact.

SPORTS MYTHS

Stereotypes may lead to myths in sport, and this is where people are discriminated against. Common sports myths are that 'Black people can't swim' and that 'Women will damage themselves internally if they do the hurdles'. Again, myths are based on very little truth, but often become an important aspect in selection and opportunity.

17.3.2 Gender

Each year 33% of all men participate in some form of sporting activity, whereas only 10% of women do. As women make up over 50% of the British population this points to some form of discrimination.

Women's role in society is seen as needing to conform to a set image, referred to as 'femininity', and consequently the amount of and type of sport they play must adhere to this trait guide. There have been many myths about women and sport (see the definition box opposite) and although, thankfully, these have now been largely displaced, many people still hold some faith in them. Other problems concern time – women, due to the demands of work and family, tend to have much less leisure time than men, and even when they do have time they are often physically exhausted.

ACTIVITY

Try to get hold of a variety of newspapers from the same day and go through the sports pages. Make a record of all the sports covered and the gender they are concerned with. What do you conclude? Look through the television listings for the same day and compile an inventory of how much sport is on – and which gender.

17.3.3 Class

This discrimination is related to the history and tradition of sport. The upper classes have traditionally had the most leisure time, which they filled with exclusive sports such as hunting. The middle classes, which grew up during the industrial revolution, rationalised and then controlled sport, imposing their values, specifically amateurism, on our modern sports. The working classes were allowed to participate in sport, but only after they had finished their work – increasingly, spectatorism filled their time.

The main discriminator is money – sport has always cost money and, although many people now have more disposable income, sports such as polo, golf and tennis still require considerable expense.

17.3.4 Race

The UK is a multicultural nation, with a great mixture of races. A major discriminator is still the colour of a person's skin, and this is an area where stereotypes and myths dominate. We discussed in Chapter 16 the concept of centrality, which affects all minority groups in our culture.

Often there is a double effect, as the minority groups also tend to be in the lower income groups.

17.3.5 Age

In the UK your age is a very important factor in how much sport you play. The General Household Survey found that the age group with the greatest participation in sport was the 16–24 year olds, with 61%. After this the rate drops dramatically – only 16% of people aged 60 or more take part in any exercise.

In our society sport is definitely the domain of the young, and in many sports you become a veteran at 35! Other societies, such as Japan, encourage participation to continue throughout life, and there are over 70 rugby leagues in Japan. Other programmes, such as masters events and the Golden Olympics, are also attempting to make sport a true 'life-time' recreation.

17.3.6 Ability

This covers two areas: your ability in a particular sport and how generally able you are. People with disabilities have, until recently, had little

Lifetime sports such as golf can be played by all ages

ACTIVITY

Do a quick survey of your school/college and local sports facilities – do they provide access for differing abilities? When were the facilities built? Is there any correlation between when they were built and the facilities they provide?

opportunity to take part in sport. Nearly all the facilities were built solely for the able-bodied. Opportunity for disabled sportsmen and women is now increasing and all new sports facilities provide access for people of all abilities. The media have played an important role in this, and events such as wheelchair basketball, the Paralympics and the London Marathon have done a lot to put forward the case of disabled athletes.

Disabled people need to participate in sports as much as able-bodied people

Bodies such as the British Paralympic Association and the British Sports Association for the Disabled promote sport for the disabled but they remain a minority and only in a few sports such as bowls can disabled people compete on an equal basis with able-bodied competitors. The International Olympic Committee do now allow a small number of disabled events during the summer games.

The other area mentioned above – that of your ability in a particular sport – can also prove to be a discriminator. Most clubs/teams are elitist in their structure; they allow only the most talented players, often selected through trials, to play. Those who are not particularly talented are left with few alternatives. In some sports, such as football, it may be possible for less able players to join a 'lower' league such as pub football, and rugby clubs often run social teams.

Even in schools this causes a dilemma. Who do you pick for the school team – the best players, or do you give all those who want to play or attend practices a chance? For many children a chance to play for their school team will be the pinnacle of their sports career. If, as we discussed in the last section, we should be promoting excellence for all, then we should try to give as many people as possible the chance to enjoy sport.

ACTIVITY

List four advantages and four disadvantages of making your team less elitist and giving as many as possible a chance to take part.

> *Key revision points*
>
> *Discrimination in sport arises from sociocultural variables. The five main areas of discrimination are gender, class, race, age and ability. The three elements in sport that are affected by discrimination are provision, opportunity and esteem. Stereotypes have an important influence in sport, affecting access and selection. In sport, stereotypes often lead to myths and self-fulfilling prophecy.*

KEY TERMS

You should now understand the following terms. If you do not, go back through the chapter and find out.

Discrimination
Esteem
Opportunity
Provision
Sport for All
Sporting myth
Stereotype

PROGRESS CHECK

1   What is the aim of mass participation in sport?
2   What benefit would sport for all bring to the health service?
3   'What's your Sport?' was a Sports Council campaign – aimed at whom?
4   How does mass participation fit the concept of the sports pyramid?
5   How many people do the Sports Council claim participate in regular sport?
6   How might a person's experience at school affect their level of participation in sports as adults?
7   What do we mean by the term 'sporting myth'?
8   How can a person's socioeconomic status affect the amount of sport they play?
9   List five cultural factors that may lead to discrimination in sport.
10   Give examples of how provision may cause discrimination.
11   How can a sports club be elitist?
12   What type of sports fit a feminine stereotype?
13   Give examples of sports we might associate with the upper class.
14   Using examples, explain what is meant by stereotyping in sport.
15   How can a person's age affect their access to sport?

Chapter 18 *Deviance in sport*

Learning objectives

- To recognise deviance in sport.
- To investigate the concept of sportsmanship.
- To investigate the concept of gamesmanship.
- To understand the use of performance-enhancing drugs in sport.

> **Definition**
>
> ### CHEATING
>
> *Breaking the rules of sport.*

> **Definition**
>
> ### UNWRITTEN RULES
>
> *Sometimes referred to as 'the spirit of the game', unwritten rules are values and ethics which we expect all sportsmen and women to follow.*

Ben Johnson – banned from competition for taking drugs to enhance his performance

> **Definition**
>
> ### SPORTSMANSHIP
>
> *Conforming to the written and unwritten rules of sport.*

Deviance in society is where an individual or group breaks away from the expected norms of the society, drifts away from the structural and functional rules. A example is the criminals who disobey the rules of society.

Sport also has its rules and deviance occurs when participants break these rules. We call this *cheating* and this is an important issue in modern sport. The main concern at present is the vast range of cheating – drug abuse, bribing officials and technological cheating in sports such as Formula One motor racing.

Cheating is not a new concept – we know that the ancient Olympians took tonics to try to increase their performances. Some people would argue that cheating is an important element in sport and that without it sport would be dull.

Sport has many written rules but also *unwritten* rules, and these make investigation of deviance more complicated.

ACTIVITY

Can you write down five ways people can cheat in sport? Why do you think they cheat?

18.1 The concept of sportsmanship

Sport relies on *sportsmanship*, people conforming to the written and unwritten rules of sport. The idea of *fair play* means that you treat your opponent as an equal and, although you want to beat them, you will do so only by adhering to the rules and a code of conduct that has been developed in the sport through tradition. This includes shaking hands and cheering the other team off at the end of the game.

To cheat not only destroys the game but also detracts from your personal achievement. A win through cheating is a hollow victory as, although you may gain the extrinsic rewards, you will not gain the more fulfilling intrinsic ones.

But is this concept of fair play outdated? It certainly remains an important part of British sport but for many people the overriding factor is to win – at all costs. Governing bodies such as FIFA try to foster sportsmanship by giving out Fair Play awards. It is interesting to note that at the 1990 World Cup England had the honour of winning the Fair Play Award, but only reached the semi-final – which perhaps reinforces the American cliché that 'Nice guys finish last'!

Sport does rely on some form of mutual respect between opponents because often it involves high-speed contact with lethal 'weapons', and to disregard the rules could cause serious injury.

Definition

FAIR PLAY

Treating your opponent as an equal and abiding by the rules of your sport.

Definition

GAMESMANSHIP

Where you use whatever means you can to overcome your opponent.

18.2 Gamesmanship

The alternative dynamic in sport is known as *gamesmanship*, where you use whatever means you can to overcome your opponent. The only aim here is the win, and for most people it is not a question of breaking the rules – more bending them to your advantage.

Many sports stars of the last few years can be classed as 'gamesmen'. For example, John McEnroe used to disrupt his opponent's concentration by arguing and abusing himself, the umpire and people in the crowd, and Boris Becker was recently disqualified from a tournament for similar gamesmanship.

Gamesmanship has now become an acceptable part of modern sport and unfortunately the mood is changing from 'we shall play fairly' to 'if you can't beat them, join them'. The other aspect of gamesmanship is the 'hype' that surrounds the build-up to an event. Primarily for the advantage of the media, this hype is also used by competitors to 'out-psych' or intimidate their opponents.

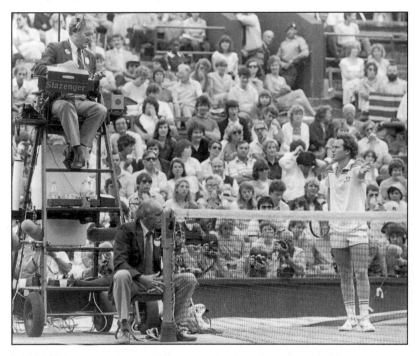

John McEnroe – a sportsman with a reputation for using gamesmanship as a means of winning

18.3 Drugs in sport

Drug abuse has been one of the main areas of deviance in sport during the last few years. It is not clear whether the actual level of drug taking has gone up or whether we now know more about it because testing systems have improved. It is also very difficult to decide where the line should be drawn between illegal and legal substances – many athletes have tested positive but claim that all they took was a cough mixture or other such product which can be bought over the counter.

Drug taking is the ultimate in gamesmanship – taking something to increase your performance and increase your chances of winning. There is a range of performance-enhancing drugs that athletes may take. Most originated as genuine medical treatments but their side-effects have been used by athletes to improve their athletic performance illegally. The range and availability of these types of drugs are constantly increasing, making control very difficult.

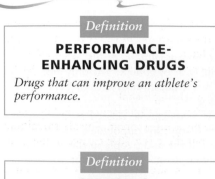

> **Definition**
>
> ## PERFORMANCE-ENHANCING DRUGS
>
> *Drugs that can improve an athlete's performance.*

> **Definition**
>
> ## STEROIDS
>
> *Artificial male hormones that allow the performer to train harder and longer.*

> **Definition**
>
> ## BLOOD DOPING
>
> *Removing blood after training at high altitude. The blood is stored and then reinfused shortly before competition in order to improve the aerobic capacity by increasing the number of erythrocytes. Blood doping is very difficult to detect.*

The huge increase in the rewards of winning may have meant that the temptation to take drugs became too great for many athletes to bear. For example, Ben Johnson felt the risk was worth while – even though he was stripped of his 1988 Gold medal and banned from competition for several years he continued to make money from his fame.

Most media attention has been focused on the use of *steroids*. These artificial male hormones allow the performer to train harder and longer and have been difficult to trace in the past as they are not actually performance-enhancing drugs. Athletes tend to take them in the closed season when they are building up fitness. A breakthrough in detection of these drugs was the decision to test athletes at any time during the year, meaning illegal activity could be detected even in the closed season.

The very fine line between what is legal and illegal causes many dilemmas for both the performer and authorities. A sprinter can legally take ginseng, although it contains substances that have advantageous effects. An athlete can train at high altitude to try to develop the efficiency of their blood system, but *blood doping* is illegal.

A substance is only illegal if it is on the International Olympic Committee's list of banned substances. It may be possible that athletes with access to highly qualified chemists and physiologists may be able to keep one step ahead by taking substances that have not yet been banned.

ACTIVITY

In the table is a list of drugs commonly used illegally in sport to improve performance. Try to find out what effect each has and give some examples of sports in which they might be used.

Substance	Effects	Sport
Amphetamines		
Caffeine		
Anabolic steroids		
Blood doping		
Beta blockers		

18.4 Violence in sport

Violence is also a growing element in modern sport. In some sports the mutual respect that we mentioned above may have disappeared. For

Violence in sport is another form of sporting deviance

example, in rugby we have seen 'stamping', deliberately kicking an opponent on the floor, which often means the victim has to leave the field, in American Football the aim of the defence is to 'sack' the quarterback – the more damage you can inflict, the more effective your defence has been – and in soccer we have the 'professional foul' – in which an attacker is deliberately knocked down to prevent him scoring a goal.

Once again it is usually the result that drives such actions; without a key player the opposition is not going to be as big a threat. A professional foul in football may result in a penalty – but there is a 50% chance of the goalkeeper saving it.

Deviance may be occurring more in modern sport as the rewards become so much greater – the win ethic has definitely begun to dominate high-level sport where the result is often seen to justify any means of achieving it. The problem escalates as amateur sportsmen – and, more importantly, children – are influenced by what they see professionals doing. Could it be that sporting etiquette is dead and that the gamesman has replaced the sportsman?

Key revision points

Deviance is going against the values and ethics of sport, breaking the rules and codes. Rules can be written or unwritten – the letter or spirit of the game. In cheating the drive to win overrides the idea of fair play: the recreational ethic of sportsmanship comes up against the win ethic of gamesmanship. Drug abuse, taking chemicals in order to increase performance, is one form of deviance. Violence, also a form of deviance, can also be used to gain an unfair advantage.

KEY TERMS

You should now understand the following terms. If you do not, go back through the chapter and find out.

Blood doping
Cheating
Fair play
Gamesmanship
Performance-enhancing drugs
Sportsmanship
Steroids
Unwritten rules

PROGRESS CHECK

1 Give three different examples of how people can cheat in sport.
2 Give three reasons why people might cheat in sport.
3 Suggest three methods sports organisations have introduced in an attempt to prevent cheating.
4 Give examples of fair play in sport.
5 Why is a win by cheating said to be a 'hollow' victory?
6 How does FIFA try to promote sportsmanship?
7 Suggest why the occurrence of gamesmanship may have increased over recent years.
8 Give examples of what is meant by the unwritten rules of sport.
9 What is meant by the term 'performance-enhancing' drugs?
10 Give three examples of the use of performance-enhancing drugs in sport.
11 Who decides that a drug is illegal in sport?
12 Explain the use of 'stamping' in rugby.
13 Explain, using examples, what is meant by the term 'professional foul'.
14 Why do gamesmen make bad role models?
15 Gary Linneker was a sportsman, John McEnroe a gamesman. Explain the difference.
16 What incentives make an athlete turn to drugs as a means of improving performance?
17 Cheating in sport means breaking the written and unwritten rules in sport. Explain what these mean.

Sport and the media

19

> *Definition*
>
> **MEDIA**
>
> *A form of mass communication, usually comprising the press, television and radio, although it can also include cinema. The media has a direct influence on the values and morals of a society because it reaches such a large proportion of the population.*

'Sport is not a requiem mass. It is entertainment. If you go to a soccer stadium, you see the teams run out and the match. TV gives the viewer a VIP seat . . . Technology enlarges the story you are telling.' (Dave Hill, Head of BSkyB Sport)

The most important influence on sport in the 1990s is the media. Its impact began in the late nineteenth century with the newspapers and extended into radio coverage in the twentieth century. The radio helped to develop major sporting occasions such as the FA Cup and the Derby into essential elements of our culture. In the 1950s television transformed many sports into entertainment packages. In the 1990s satellite added another dimension to sport and made it into a truly global commodity.

19.1 Media and sports funding

The presence of the media has turned sport into a commodity that can be bought and sold. Television companies pay out huge amounts of money to cover sports, and advertisers and sponsors back sport because of the exposure they will get in the media. Individuals train and prepare for sport in the knowledge that the media will give them a stage on which to present their talents – and also gain wealth.

Many sports have either been adapted to suit the needs of television or have changed their structure to attract television coverage. In order to survive a sport needs the media spotlight because without it it will be left behind. In 1994 The Hockey Association paid Sky Television to screen games each week in the hope that it would attract sponsors and other television companies to a sport that has been eclipsed by other games such as rugby and football.

There is a direct link between the funding of sport and the media. Media coverage brings sponsors and advertising to a sport, which are now essential for a sport to remain viable. Companies sponsor sports mainly as a means of cheap advertising, a way of getting into the public's living room. This is referred to as sport's 'golden triangle' and is becoming increasingly essential in the success of sports events. For some companies, like the tobacco firms, sport remains one of the few areas where they can still openly advertise. However, recent European legislation is due to phase out all tobacco sponsorship in the next few years.

> *Definition*
>
> **SPORT'S GOLDEN TRIANGLE**
>
> *The association between sports event, sponsorship and the media.*

The problem for sports such as hockey is that a vicious circle exists – to attract sponsors you need media coverage, but to gain media coverage you often need the funds to pay performers so they can become highly skilful and make your sport more attractive to the media. This is outlined in Figure 19.1.

The influence the media, and specifically television, has over sport is epitomised by the Olympics. This great event is controlled by American television companies, who pay well over $400 million for the exclusive rights to screen the Olympic Games. This kind of financial influence gives

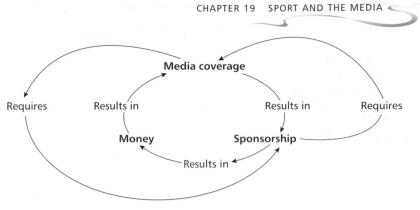

Figure 19.1 *The influence of media coverage on sport*

the companies control over many factors – for example, we are now used to having to stay up very late to see key moments such as the 100 m final so that it fits in with the peak viewing time in America.

Other new innovations include *pay per view*, where viewers have to pay a one-off fee to their cable or satellite supplier in order to watch a particular sports event. This has already been successfully trialed with both boxing and football and looks set to become a regular feature. Another development is the launch of channels specialising on particular sports or sports clubs – Man U TV is already available to fans and offers them 24-hour programming about their favourite football club.

>
> *Definition*
> **PAY PER VIEW**
> *Viewers pay a fee to watch a particular programme.*

19.2 Does televising sport lead to lower participation?

Actual participation in sport appears to be falling, and it has been suggested that the amount of sport now available on the television may have influenced this – people don't play sport because they're too busy watching it. However, a number of studies (in particular The Wolfenden Report) have found that, although watching television is our most popular pastime (roughly 25% of our leisure time is spent in front of 'the box'), there is little to link television watching and participation in sport. Indeed, television may actually have a positive effect, in that watching sport on the television often stimulates people to take up sports.

This effect is very noticeable when British teams are successful in world events such as the Olympics. During the last few years ice skating, hockey and gymnastics have all witnessed upsurges in popularity when Britons were seen on the television winning medals.

The one negative effect televised sport does appear to have is on spectatorism, where the lure of a 'live' game on the television and the unpredictability of English weather often makes staying home preferable to going to the stadium. Football clubs can now demand very large fees from television companies (in 1995 Sky paid £70 000 per game for Premiership Football), much of which is as compensation for loss of spectators. Cricket and rugby league have also been affected this way.

The media, and the press in particular, have turned sportsmen and women into celebrities, which may be beneficial in terms of potential earnings but which also means that they become 'public figures' and their every move, both on and off the pitch, is scrutinised. There is a general emphasis on sensationalism in the British press where stories (or 'exclusives') are an essential part of the ratings war.

All forms of the media are guilty of concentrating on the critical elements of sport – the action replay questioning an official's decision, or viewing a bad tackle or a violent incident from every possible angle. The use of edited highlights, in which only the goals or action is shown, can also give a rather one-sided view of sports.

193

Modern technology means that no corner of a sport can remain 'hidden'. We now have cameras in the cricket stumps, in the pockets of a snooker table, on cars, giving the armchair spectator the 'real' view. In some cases this has been very beneficial – many of the deviant practices discussed in the last chapter are more closely scrutinised and many sports now use video evidence to pick out any foul play the referee missed in the heat of the game.

ACTIVITY

What are the benefits of television technology being made available to sports officials? Are there any disadvantages?

19.3 An analysis

The mass media reflects its culture and may also actually shape that culture in fostering values, particularly in establishing and maintaining stereotypes. In general, the mass media will associate itself with the popular view and in sport this will be represented in the most popular sports.

Even in the quality papers several sports dominate the sports pages – and these will tend to be male-dominated sports often associated with gambling. However, there are some exceptions to this – Channel 4 has successfully introduced a number of ethnic and minority sports to the UK such as sumo wrestling, kabadi, women's football, wheelchair basketball and, most effectively, American football.

Much of the sociocultural elements in sport we discussed earlier will be evident in the media: there tends to an emphasis on the dominant culture and its sport, to the detriment of women and ethnic minorities. Sensationalism often feeds on stereotypes and national prejudice. Headlines such as 'We'll Blitz the Frogs' or 'Keagans' Masterplan to Beat Krauts' are blazed across the back pages when our national teams compete. Warlike terminology is often used in reporting sport – you will often see the words 'battle', 'bombarded', 'defence/attack', 'blitzed', 'sniping' in headlines – perhaps reinforcing sport's historical links with war (see Chapter 11).

ACTIVITY

Repeat the newspaper analysis you did in Section 17.3.2, but this time make up a table showing the amount of space devoted to different sports. Compare a tabloid newspaper with one of the broadsheet papers.

Definition

KABADI

A 'tick' like game, played to a high level in Asia.

Definition

SENSATIONALISM

Where the media exaggerates stories about sports stars.

ACTIVITY

As sports scientists we take a more analytical view than the media. Here are some areas of study you could develop.

Television – BBC 1, BBC 2, ITV and Franchises, Channel 4, Satellite channels.
- How is sport presented on each of these channels?
- How will the 'ratings war' and increased rivalry between channels affect sport in the future?

The press – Hard, tabloid, daily, local, weekly, national, local.
- How does the emphasis on sport reporting differ in each of these types of paper?
- Which papers lean towards sensationalism?
- Do papers provide a balanced view of sport? If not, identify groups that are discriminated.

The radio – Local, national, BBC, commercial, Radios 1, 2, 3, 4 and 5
- How does the emphasis change in each of these stations?
- How does radio's coverage of sport differ from that of the television?

The arts – Literature, painting/sculpture, music, dance, cinema, theatre.
- Can you list any examples of sport represented in these media?
- How is the history of sport linked to the arts?

Premiership football – a league exclusive to Sky television

Definition
SUPER LEAGUE
The new league competition created by Sky for rugby league.
MERCHANDISING
The sale of commodities such as hats, shirts, mugs, bedspreads that bear the team's name.

19.4 The future

Sport has become an important cornerstone of the media and each side feels it has the upper hand, although it would appear that the media is slowly beginning to take over power in sport. We have already mentioned that the American networks now own the Olympics, and Sky Television has changed football in the UK from a traditional Saturday game into an almost daily event in order to secure maximum viewing potential. In 1990 Sky paid £305 million for exclusive right to Premiership football for five years. At the time the sale of Sky dishes was low but the capture of England's premier football league led to a huge increase in sales. In 1996 Sky paid a further £670 million to retain their hold on football until the millennium. Rugby league is another sport transformed by satellite television – in 1996 Sky television bought exclusive rights to the game for £85 million, although there were a number of conditions. The game had to forget 100 years of history and change from a winter sport to a summer game to accommodate television schedules, the leagues were restructured to form *Super League* and new clubs have been manufactured in non-rugby league areas in an attempt to widen the market. To aid the marketing all teams also had to invent nicknames that made them into *merchandising* commodities and in some way broke down the geographical locations of the games – hence we now have the Bulls v the Blue Sox rather than Bradford Northern v Halifax!

Rugby league – a game transformed to suit the needs of satellite television

There have been, and will continue to be, many positive rewards from this 'media-isation' of sport:
- Modern technology has transformed sport into a true art form – slow motion and multiangle approaches extol the aesthetics of every sport.
- It has generated huge interest in every aspect of sport, leading to the development of sports science, academic qualifications and a whole host of books, magazines videos and films.
- Our modern sports stars are well known and well paid, receiving much-earned rewards for their effort and dedication and generally providing us with excellent role models.

However, if we look at televised programmes such as *Gladiators* or *WWF Wrestling*, are we seeing the true future of modern sport? Glamour, razzmatazz and the quest for action may kill some sports and ruin others – the wrestlers are very athletic and highly trained performers but they are actors and have lost that essential element that all sportsmen and women posses. In some cases sport may be close to becoming pure entertainment.

Key revision points

The media is a mass communication system made up of the press, television, radio and cinema. The media, and especially television, has been the most influential element in the development of sport over the last century. It plays an important role in the funding of sport by paying to cover sport, by attracting sponsors and advertisers and by making performers into stars who can then attract wealth. Television may stimulate people to take up sport but it may also have a negative effect on spectatorism. The media influences society's views of sport, often fostering and reinforcing stereotypes. It has the power to make or break sports careers. In addition, reports in the media can distort the public's view of sport.

KEY TERMS

You should now understand the following terms. If you do not, go back through the chapter and find out.

Kabadi
Media
Merchandising
Pay per view
Sensationalism
Sport's golden triangle
Super League

PROGRESS CHECK

1 In what ways has the increased influence of television affected sport in Britain?
2 'Sport is now a global commodity.' Explain what this term means.
3 Why are sponsors willing to pay out large amounts of money to sports that are seen on television?
4 What role has Channel 4 played in influencing our views of sport?
5 How can the media sensationalise sport?
6 How has rugby league changed to suit television?
7 What effect does the media have in promoting role models?
8 How has the development of media technology helped sports officiate their rules?
9 How might WWF wrestling give us an insight into the future of sport?
10 Why has Sky been prepared to put so much money into Premiership football?
11 What types of sport do newspapers tend to concentrate their coverage on?
12 What role does the media play in the development of stereotypes?
13 Give three examples of the positive effect the media has on sport.
14 Give three examples of the negative effect the media can have on sport.
15 How has the influence of the media in sport affected the earning potential of sports stars?

Further reading

L. Allison, editor. *The Politics of Sport*. Manchester University Press, 1986.

D. Anthony. *A Strategy for British Sport*. Hurst, 1980.

J. Armitage. *Man at Play*. Warne, 1977.

D. Birley. *Sport and the Making of Britain*. Manchester University Press, 1993.

D. W. Calhoun. *Sport, Culture and Personality*. Human Kinetics, 1987.

E. Cashmore. *Making Sense of Sport*. Routledge, 1990.

CCPR. *The Organisation of Sport and Recreation in Britain*. Central Council of Physical Recreation, 1991.

S. Coe, D. Teasdale and D. Wickham. *More than a Game*. BBC Books, 1992.

R. Davis, R. Bull, J. Roscoe and D. Roscoe. *PE and the Study of Sport*, 2nd edition. Mosby, 1994.

Department of National Heritage. *Sport – Raising the Game*. 1995

J. Dumazeidier. *Towards a Society of Leisure*. Collier-Macmillan, 1967.

J. Ford. *This Sporting Land*. New English Library, 1977.

P. Gardner. *Nice Guys Finish Last*. Allen Lane, 1974.

R. Holt. *Sport and the British*. Oxford University Press, 1990.

B. Houlihan. *The Government and Politics of Sport*. Routledge, 1991.

J. Huizinga. *Homo ludens, a Study of the Play Element in Culture*. Beacon, 1964.

A. Lumpkin. *PE and Sport – A Contemporary Introduction*. Times Mirror, 1990.

T. Mason. *Sport in Britain*. Oxford University Press, 1988.

P. McIntosh. *Physical Education in England since 1800*. Bell and Hyman, 1979.

C. Mortlock. *The Adventure Alternative*. Cicerone Press, 1984.

H.L. Nixon. *Sport and the American Dream*. Leisure Press, 1984.

S. Parker. *The Sociology of Leisure*. Allen and Unwin, 1976.

J. Riordan, editor. *Sport under Communism*. Hurst, 1981.

G.H. Sage. *Power and Ideology in American Sport*. Human Kinetics, 1990.

W.D. Smith. *Stretching their Bodies*. David and Charles, 1974.

Sports Council. *How to Find out About the Organisation of Sport*. Sports Council Information Services, 1993.

Sports Council. *Into the 90's*. Sports Council Information Services, 1988.

Sports Council. *New Horizons*. Sports Council Information Services, 1994

G. Torkildsen. *Leisure and Recreation Management*, 2nd edition. Spon, 1991.

Web sites

www.olympics.org.uk

www.uksport.org.uk

www.ncf.org.uk

www.sports.gov.uk

www.ukathletics.org

www.physicaleducation.co.uk

www.wsf.org.uk

www.lta.org.uk

Exam questions: Anatomy, biomechanics and physiology

The questions below are typical of those that you might have to answer in your examination. Try answering each remembering that the number of marks available for each question gives you a clue to the type of answer required.

Maximum possible marks

1 Compare the structure of the hip joint with that of the shoulder joint in relation to joint mobility and joint stability.

4

2 The knee joint is used in the performance of many motor skills. Identify three key features of this typical synovial joint and say how they contribute to the overall stability of the joint.

3

3 a Describe the movements that occur at the ankle, knee and hip joints during the take-off phase of a jump.

3

   b For each of these joints, name a prime mover that produces the movement during the take-off phase.

3

4 Using the biceps curl as an example, show how muscles work as antagonistic pairs.

4

5 A person participating in physical activity has to be able to produce a wide range of strength and speed. Explain how the arrangement of muscle fibres into motor units allows the performer to produce various strengths and speeds of muscular contraction.

5

6 Using an example from physical education, show how the functions of either a fast glycolytic fibre or a slow oxidative fibre affect performance.

3

7 The bench press is commonly used to improve the strength of triceps brachii (and other muscles). Identify the type of contraction performed by triceps brachii during the upward phase of the bench press and say how and why the type of contraction changes during the downward phase of this movement.

3

8 Use your knowledge of balance to say why it is easier to perform a headstand than a handstand.

3

9 During a physical education lesson a student takes part in a multi-stage fitness test and manages to reach level 15.

   a Draw and label a graph to show the changes in the student's heart rate during the lesson.

4

   b Use your knowledge of how heart rate is controlled to explain the changes that would have taken place immediately before and during the fitness test.

6

Maximum possible
marks

10 During exercise it is important to maintain good venous return. Describe the
mechanisms involved in venous return.

4

11 Use your knowledge of the cardiovascular system to explain the importance of
an active cool-down after exercise.

5

3

12 Define the terms stroke volume, heart rate and cardiac output.

3

13 Identify three factors that affect cardiac output during exercise.

14 The medulla oblongata contains the respiratory, cardiac and vasomotor control
centres. These centres are responsible for controlling oxygen supply. Explain how
each control centre responds to an increased need for oxygen during exercise.

8

15 The velocity of blood changes as it passes through the circulatory system and the
blood moves slowest as it passes through the capillaries. How is this change in
speed achieved, and why does it take place?

4

16 As you start to exercise, up to 85% of blood flow is redistributed to the working
muscles. How is this redistribution of blood flow achieved?

4

17 Endurance athletes often train at altitude to help improve their aerobic capacity.
Identify two changes that occur to the cardiovascular system as a result of
altitude training and say how they affect aerobic capacity.

4

18 After a period of endurance training the heart becomes more efficient. Identify
the changes that take place in the heart as a result of training, and explain the
impact these changes have on stroke volume and cardiac output.

5

3

19 Outline the effect that an asthma attack has on the respiratory system.

20 As you start to exercise the amount of air that is ventilated by your lungs
increases. Use your knowledge of lung volumes to explain the changes that take
place during exercise.

3

4

21 Explain how the amount of air ventilated by the lungs is controlled.

22 Explain how the exchange of oxygen is achieved between the blood and muscle
cell at rest and how this exchange is accelerated during exercise.

6

Exam questions: Skill acquisition

The questions below are typical of those that you might have to answer in your examination. Try answering each, remembering that the number of marks available for each question gives you a clue to the type of answer required.

Maximum possible marks

1 Define the terms motor skill, perceptual skill, fundamental motor skill and cognitive skill. Give practical examples to illustrate your answers.

4

2 Choose a motor skill related to sport and classify it using the open/closed continuum. Justify your placement on the continuum.

4

3 Classical conditioning is related to the modification of stimuli. Explain this learning theory and relate it to skill acquisition in sport.

5

4 Reinforcement to ensure learning is at the heart of the operant conditioning theory. Explain, using examples from sport, how reinforcement can help in the learning of motor skills.

4

5 Motivation is important if skill learning is to take place effectively. What is meant by the terms intrinsic and extrinsic motivation? Give examples from physical education to illustrate your answer.

4

6 'The peak flow experience is enjoyed by only the very elite in sport.' Discuss this view by using practical examples.

6

7 Explain each of the elements in the diagram below, using examples from physical education.

8

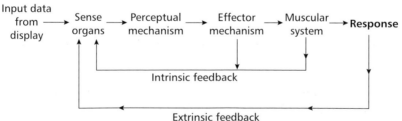

8 Define the terms serial and parallel processing.

4

9 Nedeffer (1976) identified two types of attentional focus: broad/narrow focus and external/internal focus. Describe both of these and relate them to examples from physical education.

6

10 Define the terms reaction time, movement time and response time. Using
    examples from physical education or sport show how a performer might cut
    down the time it takes to respond to a particular stimulus.

    6

11 Using a diagram, describe how the memory process affects perception in
    acquiring motor skills in sport.

    6

    3

12 What is meant by a motor programme, and how is it formed?

13 Explain, using practical examples, how feedback can motivate a performer.

    5

14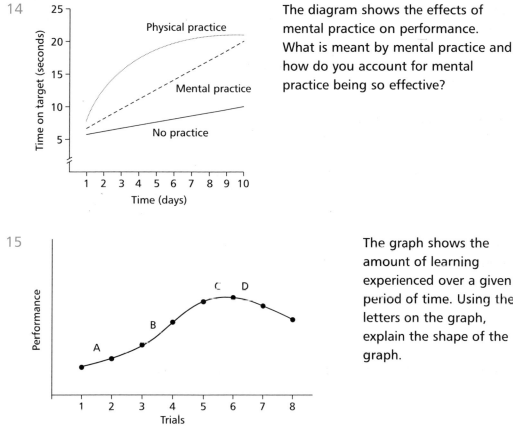

The diagram shows the effects of
mental practice on performance.
What is meant by mental practice and
how do you account for mental
practice being so effective?

    5

15

The graph shows the
amount of learning
experienced over a given
period of time. Using the
letters on the graph,
explain the shape of the
graph.

    4

16 What is meant by the plateau effect, and how might a teacher or coach seek to
    combat it in an athlete's performance?

    5

17 How would you ensure that positive transfer occurs in skill learning? Illustrate
    your answer with a practical example.

    4

18 What is meant by the whole and part methods of teaching skills? List the
    advantages and disadvantages of each method.

    6

19 When would you use mechanical guidance in the teaching of motor skills? What
    are the drawbacks of doing this?

    5

20 Name three different teaching styles used to teach motor skills, and state when
    each style is most appropriate.

    6

Exam questions: Sociocultural aspects of physical education and sport

The questions below are typical of those that you might have to answer in your examination. Try answering each, remembering that the number of marks available for each question gives you a clue to the type of answer required.

Maximum possible marks

1 Using a practical example, explain the main differences between an activity as a sport and as a physical education.

4

2 Discuss the idea that the concept of leisure involves the characteristic of escape.

3

3 What reasons can you give for the rise of the outdoor recreation movement during the industrial revolution of the nineteenth century?

4

4 'Do professional sports performers play?'
a Discuss the above question.
b What constraints in high-level sport might inhibit the concept of play?

4

4

5 What is the role of physical education in promoting life-time sport?

4

6 What added dimension does outdoor education offer the physical education programme in schools?

4

7 What constraints limit access to outdoor education in the UK?

6

8 Sport at the local level is provided by a range of organisations and facilities within the private, public and voluntary sectors. Outline the various types of organisation and facilities at this level.

9

9 Comment on the role that national sports bodies play in the promotion of Sport for All in the UK.

8

10 Sport in Europe tends to follow a decentralised pattern. Comment on the meaning of this and suggest historical reasons why this pattern has developed.

6

11 Traditionally, the member states of the European Commission have hosted a significantly large percentage of world sports events. Comment on the cultural and historical reasons for this.

6

12 Using specific examples, comment on how global games can be used for protest and propaganda purposes.

6

Maximum possible
marks

13 Comment on how the sociological theory of centrality can be applied in sport,
using examples in your answer.

4

14 Discuss how social mobility can be gained through sport.

3

15 Why do emergent countries appear to be so successful in global sport?

4

16 What were the motives for the state control of sport in the former Eastern Bloc
cultures?

4

17 Comment on the different ways that Australia and the USA have maintained
their colonial links with the UK through sport.

6

18 Can you identify elements of 'Americanisation' developing in UK sport?

5

19 Give reasons for the importance given to sport in the New World democratic
cultures.

5

20 Discuss the differences between the elitist model of sports excellence and the
optimum performance model of sports excellence.

6

21 Discuss the elements that aid the development of sporting talent.

9

22 What role can national centres of excellence play in the development of sports
excellence? Use specific examples in your answer.

6

23 Discuss the cultural and socioeconomic constraints that may inhibit the pursuit
of sports excellence in the UK.

8

24 Why should modern societies promote the ideal of Sport for All? Comment on
the benefits to the individual and wider society.

6

25 Discuss the cultural and socioeconomic constraints that may inhibit mass
participation in sport in the UK.

8

Revision guide: Anatomy, biomechanics and physiology

This guide summarises the most important areas covered in Part 1. By fully understanding everything below you will be better prepared to succeed in your examination.

The skeletal system

There are six types of synovial joint: ball and socket, hinge, pivot, gliding, condyloid and saddle. All synovial joints allow some degree of movement and share common features, such as a synovial membrane, synovial fluid, articular cartilage and ligaments.

- The skeleton is made up of 206 bones, comprising the axial skeleton and the appendicular skeleton.
- The skeleton provides support, protection and attachment for muscles, and produces blood cells.
- There are three types of cartilage: yellow elastic cartilage, white fibrocartilage and hyaline cartilage.
- Ligaments join bone to bone.
- Tendons join muscle to bone.

Joints and muscles

Movement takes place around a joint and at least one prime mover is responsible for each type of movement that can be produced at a specific joint. You need to know the name and location of the prime mover for each movement possible around the major joints outlined in Chapter 2.

- Elbow flexion – biceps brachii; elbow extension – triceps brachii.
- Radioulnar pronation – pronator teres; radioulnar supination – supinator muscle.
- Shoulder flexion – anterior deltoid; shoulder extension – latissimus dorsi; shoulder abduction – middle deltoid; shoulder adduction – pectoralis major; shoulder inward rotation – subscapularis; shoulder outward rotation – infraspinatus.
- Flexion of the trunk – rectus abdominis; extension of the trunk – erector spinae; lateral flexion of the trunk – external and internal obliques.
- Flexion of the hip – iliopsoas; extension of the hip – gluteus maximus; abduction of the hip – gluteus medius; adduction of the hip – adductor longus, brevis and magnus; inward rotation of the hip – gluteus minimus; outward rotation of the hip – gluteus maximus.
- Flexion of the knee – biceps femoris, semitendinosus, semimembranosus; extension of the knee – rectus femoris, vastus lateralis, vastus intermedius, vastus medialis.
- Plantarflexion of the ankle – soleus; dorsiflexion of the ankle – tibialis anterior.

Skeletal muscle

Skeletal muscle creates movement by actively contracting and shortening. The muscle is stimulated by a motor neurone. This stimulation results in each individual sarcomere decreasing in length as the actin and myosin filaments slide over each other. The nature of the contraction produced is a result of the fibre type recruited, the number of fibres stimulated and the frequency and timing of the stimuli.

- 1 A muscle is stimulated by a motor neurone. 2 The T-vesicles stimulate the release of calcium ions from the sarcoplasmic reticulum. 3 Calcium binds with troponin and then the troponin removes the tropomyosin from the binding site on the actin. 4 Actin and myosin cross-bridges can now form as the myosin head attaches to the active site on the actin. 5 ATPase acts on ATP to release energy. 6 The cross-bridges swivel, release and reform as the actin is pulled over the myosin; the muscle shortens. 7 Stimulation stops, the calcium ions are removed and the muscle returns to its normal resting length.
- There are three types of muscle fibre – slow oxidative fibres, fast oxidative glycolytic fibres and fast glycolytic fibres. The percentage distribution of these fibres is genetically determined.
- A muscle can act as an agonist/prime mover, as an antagonist, as a fixator and as a synergist.
- There are four different types of muscle contraction – concentric, eccentric, isometric and isokinetic.
- Gradation of contraction depends on the number of motor units stimulated, the frequency of the stimuli and the timing of the stimuli to various motor units.

The mechanics of movement

A basic kinesiological analysis needs to include three features: a description of the skill, an evaluation of both the joints and muscles used and the mechanical principles applied, and identification and correction of any faults.

- There are three different orders of lever: first-, second- and third-order levers. The greater the distance between the joint and the muscle insertion, the more strength can be generated. The closer the insertion is to the joint the better the range of movement.
- The longer the lever the greater the change in momentum and consequently the change in velocity that can be imparted on an object, e.g. a squash ball can be hit harder when the elbow is fully extended rather than flexed.

- The angle of pull refers to the position of the muscle relative to the position of the joint, measured in degrees. The angle of pull changes as the limb is moved and this affects the efficiency of the muscle's pulling force. Every joint has an optimum angle of pull.
- The effect that a force has on a body is influenced by: **1** the size of the force, **2** the direction of the force and **3** the position of application of the force.
- Motion (movement) will only occur if a force is applied. Motion occurs either in a straight line (linear motion) or around an axis (angular motion). There are three laws of motion, namely the law of inertia, the law of acceleration and the law of reaction.
- The centre of gravity of an object is the point at which the mass of the object is concentrated.
- The centre of gravity of a performer is continually changing as the body position changes.
- You are in a balanced position when your centre of gravity falls within your base of support. The lower the centre of gravity and the greater the base of support, the more stable a body will be.

Structure and function of the heart

The heart acts as two separate pumps, distributing oxygenated blood round the body and deoxygenated blood to the lungs. Deoxygenated blood returns to the heart via the pulmonary and systemic circulatory systems. The heart responds to the demands made on the body when exercising by increasing the heart rate and stroke volume to increase overall cardiac output.

- Cardiac output = stroke volume × heart rate. At rest is it about 5 litres.
- The cardiac cycle has two phases: systole, when the heart muscle contracts, and diastole, when the heart muscle relaxes.
- There are three mechanisms for controlling the heart rate – neural control, hormonal control and intrinsic control.
- The important components of the conduction system of the heart are the sinuatrial node, the atrioventricular node, the bundle of his and the purkinje fibres.

Structure and function of the vascular system

Five different types of vessel form the closed circulatory network that distributes blood to all cells. The distribution of the cardiac output is controlled by the vasomotor centre and is achieved by altering the flow and pressure of the blood. This is mainly brought about by opening or closing arterioles and pre-capillary sphincters.

- Arteries, arterioles, venules and veins have similar structure. Tunica interna (smooth inner layer), tunica media (smooth muscle layer), tunica externa (collagen layer). Capillaries are only one cell thick to allow diffusion.
- Blood pressure (measured in mmHg) = blood flow × peripheral resistance.
- Blood velocity is directly affected by the total cross sectional area of the blood vessels. Blood flow slows down through the capillaries as the total cross-sectional area increases to allow diffusion to take place.
- During exercise up to 85% of blood is distributed to the working muscles (the vascular shunt mechanism).

The respiratory system

The amount of air required by the body varies considerably, depending on the amount of oxygen used by the cells. This is why we have a 'working' volume of air (tidal volume) plus a reserve volume available (inspiratory and expiratory reserve volumes). The respiratory control centre works in conjunction with the cardiac control centre and the vasomotor control centre to ensure a co-ordinated response to oxygen demand and delivery.

- Muscles of inspiration at rest – external intercostals and diaphragm.
- Additional muscles of inspiration during exercise – sternocleidomastoid, scalenes and pectoralis minor.
- Expiration is passive at rest.
- Muscles of expiration during exercise – the internal intercostals, the obliques and rectus abdominis.
- The parietal pleura is attached to the thoracic cavity and diaphragm.
- Lung tissue is made up of millions of air sacs called alveoli, resulting in an extremely large surface area for diffusion.
- Air enters the lungs when the atmospheric air pressure is higher than the pressure of air in the lungs. This is achieved by increasing the volume of the lungs during inspiration.
- In a healthy individual physical performance is not limited by pulmonary ventilation.
- The partial pressure of a gas is the single most important factor that determines gaseous exchange between the alveoli and the capillary and the capillary and the cell.
- The rate of diffusion speeds up during exercise as the diffusion gradient increases, body temperature increases, the partial pressure of carbon dioxide increases and pH drops.

Revision guide: Skill acquisition

This guide summarises the most important areas covered in Part 2. By fully understanding everything below you will be better prepared to succeed in your examination.

The concept and nature of skill

- A motor skill is concerned with movement, and a skilful performer in sport is consistent and follows a good technical pattern.
- Some skills are fundamental to movement in sport, such as throwing and catching a ball. These are the platform on which to build more advanced skills.

Ability

- Abilities are underlying factors that help us to carry out skills in sport. Our abilities are largely determined genetically.
- There are two types of ability: psychomotor ability (the ability to process information – e.g. reaction time) and gross motor ability, which involves actual movement (e.g. speed).

Classification of skill

- To analyse skills we need to classify them. All classifications should view skills on a range of continua.
- Gross skills involve large muscle movements; fine skills involve small muscle movements.
- The open–closed continuum is concerned with the effects of the environment.
- The pacing continuum is concerned with the timing of movements.
- The discrete–serial–continuous continuum is concerned with how well defined the beginning and end of the skill are.

Classical conditioning

- This is concerned with modifying a stimulus to give a conditioned response.
- Pavlov described the process of conditioned reflex.
- This type of conditioning can help performers associate positive feelings, rather than negative ones such as fear, with an event or a particular environment (e.g. swimming).

Operant conditioning

- This involves the modification of behaviour. The work of Skinner is important here.
- Operant conditioning involves shaping behaviour and reinforcing that behaviour.
- Rewards are extensively used in the teaching of motor skills to reinforce correct movements.

Cognitive theories of learning

- These involve intervening variables, which are mental processes that occur between the stimulus being received and the response.
- These theories involve the performer understanding what needs to be done to perform a motor skill. Previous experience is important in this type of learning.
- The Gestaltists (a group of German scientists) established many principles related to cognitive theories of learning.

Motivation

- This involves our inner drives towards achieving a goal, the external pressures we experience and the rewards we receive. It also concerns the intensity and direction of our behaviour.
- Intrinsic motivation is specifically the internal drives to participate and to succeed.
- Extrinsic motivation is concerned with external rewards.
- Arousal represents the intensity aspect of motivation. Its effects can be positive or negative. The correct level of arousal is important if optimal performance is to be achieved.
- The drive theory describes the relationship between arousal and performance as linear. Learned behaviour is more likely to occur as the intensity of the competition increases. The formula often used to describe this theory is $P = f(H \times D)$.
- According to the inverted U theory optimum performance is reached at moderate arousal levels. Performance will fall under conditions of low or high arousal.
- The catastrophe theory takes into account both cognitive and somatic anxiety factors. The decline in performance under conditions of high arousal is dramatic, rather than the slow decline described in the inverted U theory.

Peak flow experience

- At optimum performance levels many top athletes appear to be in a 'zone' of emotional experience.
- Mental strategies can help to achieve this positive emotional response, which will motivate an athlete and enable them to cope with high levels of anxiety.

Information processing

- This views the brain as working like a computer. Stimuli enter the brain (input), decisions are made and a response occurs (output).
- The stages of information processing – stimulus identification stage, response selection stage, response programming stage.
- Serial processing is a type of information processing in which each stage is arranged sequentially, with one stage affecting the next.
- In parallel processing two or more processes occur at the same time but one does not necessarily affect the other.

Attentional control

- This involves concentration, which is important for motivation and skill learning.
- Nedeffer identified two types of attentional focus: broad/narrow focus and external/internal focus.
- In situations of high arousal there may be cognitive overload, when too much information is available.

Reactions

- Reaction time is important in the execution of skills and is the time between the presentation of the stimulus and the start of the movement. This affects response time.
- Hick's law states that choice reaction time is linearly related to the amount of information to be processed.
- The single-channel hypothesis states that the brain can deal with only one piece of information at a time. It is often referred to as the bottleneck theory.

Memory

- The memory process affects skill learning.
- Selective attention is important in filtering information so that only the important aspects are used.
- Information recently acquired is kept in short-term memory.
- The long-term memory is a store of information that can be used to perform skills. Motor programmes are stored here.
- Motor programmes are associated with open loop control. They are generalised memories of movements that can be used by making a single decision. No feedback is involved.
- Closed loop control involves the use of feedback to detect and correct errors in movements.
- Schema are items of information that are used to modify a motor programme. There are two types: recall schema and recognition schema. Variety of practice conditions will ensure the building of schema in the performer's long-term memory and assist in future performances.

Feedback

- This is information available to the performer during and after performance of a skill.
- Knowledge of results and knowledge of performance are the two main types of feedback. These can help with motivation and can reinforce movements.
- Feedback can also be used in setting goals, which can in turn affect future motivation and performance.

Learning curves

- These describe the relationships between practice and performance. Performance is seen as only a temporary measurement; learning is more permanent.
- Types of learning curve include positive acceleration, linear and negative.
- A plateau is a part of a learning curve where there is little or no change in measured performance. Strategies are needed to combat the plateau effect – e.g. regular rest intervals.

Structure of practices

- Practice must be well planned, taking into account the type of skill to be learned and the environment involved.
- If a skill can be split up, each sub-routine could be taught separately. If the skill is highly organised then it is best to teach the skill as a whole.
- Variation in practice will help in the construction of schema.
- Massed practice involves few rest intervals and works best with highly skilled athletes.
- Distributed practice involves rest intervals and can counter the effects of fatigue and the plateau effect. It works best with beginners.

Guidance

- Visual guidance is best used in the early stages of skill learning. Demonstrations are good examples of this type of guidance but should be accurate and highlight important cues.
- Verbal guidance should be used alongside visual and can be used to point out important coaching points.
- Manual and mechanical guidance are important in the early stages of skill learning. They combat fear responses and enable safe practice. Overuse of manual guidance can be detrimental to learning because the performer does not experience the true kinesthetic feelings of the skill.

Teaching styles

- Teachers and coaches should adapt their approach to the type of activity and the characteristics of the performer.
- Mosston's spectrum of teaching styles states that the more decisions that are made by the teacher, the more authoritarian the approach.
- Advantages and disadvantages or all styles are related to the performer, the teacher and the environment.

Revision guide: Sociocultural aspects of physical education and sport

This guide summarises the most important areas covered in Part 3. By fully understanding everything below you will be better prepared to succeed in your examination.

Conceptual basis of sport

You need to know the meaning of the following terms:
- Sport
- Leisure
- Play
- Physical education
- Outdoor education
- Physical recreation
- Outdoor recreation

You need to be able to characterise the key points for each of these concepts:
- Sport – physical activity; competition with a clear winner; strenuous and enjoyable.
- Leisure – free time; choice, not work.
- Play – freely undertaken; non-instrumental; informal rules and uncertain ending.
- Physical recreation – physical activity of a relaxing nature; limited organisation and outcome; active form of leisure.
- Physical education – occurs only in school, college or university; learning through bodily movement.
- Outdoor education – learning in the natural environment; novel activities that include challenge.
- Outdoor recreation – challenging activities in the natural environment.

Organisation of sport in the UK

You need to know the role of the following organisations:
- National governing bodies
- Sport England
- The sports councils
- CCPR
- NCF
- BOA
- Sports Aid
- Department of Culture, Media and Sport
- Countryside Commission
- British Sports Association for the Disabled

Make sure you understand their role in the funding of sport, promoting Sport for All and developing sports excellence.

Sport at the local level is provided by the private, public and voluntary sectors.

Organisation of European sport and global games

- Sport at European level follows a decentralised pattern.
- European legislation is increasingly having an impact on sport. Examples include the Bosman case.
- There are two main European sports models – the Western European model (autonomous control) and the Eastern European model (state control).
- Sport throughout Europe follows a pyramid structure. European bodies such as EUFA control the individual bodies, which in turn form international bodies that control world championships.
- The 'live' nature of global games makes them a stage for protest and propaganda.

Sport in society and the pursuit of excellence

Sport reflects the wider values and traditions of the society in which it is played.

You need to be able to understand that different cultures approach sport in different ways and you need to be able to characterise the key elements for these different cultural approaches:
- Emergent cultures – select and channel athletes in a limited number of sports to ensure success
- Eastern Bloc cultures – the state controls sport for political gain
- New World democratic cultures – use sport as a focus of national identity and to gain international status
- USA – sport is seen as a commercial commodity and is dominated by the win ethic.

Excellence in sport has two meanings:
- Elitism – 'Pick the best; ignore the rest'
- Optimum performance – everyone has the chance to succeed.
- Elitism is the most popular model because it creates champions – which bring shop window status.

There are three major stages in the development of excellence:
- Selection
- Development of talent
- Providing support

Factors affecting participation in sport

Mass participation is maximising the access to sport and recreation for all people.

- 'Sport for All' is a campaign set up by the Sports Council to foster sport for all. Benefits are individual (intrinsic) and societal (extrinsic).
- Discrimination is where one section of a community is disadvantaged because of certain sociocultural variables.
- The five main cultural factors that lead to discrimination are gender, class, race, age and ability.
- The reasons for discrimination can be summarised under three headings: opportunity (have people the chance to play?), provision (where can people play?) and esteem (what will I look like when I play?).

Deviance in sport

- Deviance in sport is breaking the rules and codes, both written and unwritten.
- Sportsmanship – where taking part is the key focus.
- Gamesmanship – winning at all costs is the main focus.
- Examples of deviance include taking performance-enhancing drugs and violence.

Sport and the media

- Media – mass communication, made up of the press, television, radio and cinema.
- Television is now a major influence on sport – funding, fostering popularity and reinforcing stereotypes.

Research project guidelines

In most of the examination specifications there is an opportunity to complete a research project as coursework. This is assessed and the results of the assessment go towards your final grade.

Examination boards differ in their requirements for a research project. There are, however, some general guidelines that you would be wise to follow for completing a project. Here are some important tips which will help you to obtain a good grade for your research project.

Projects often have a word limit. For example, for the AQA specification (used to be called a syllabus) at AS level for Sports and Physical Education the word limit is 1000 words. For the full A level (A2) a maximum of 2000 words is required. For the Edexcel specification the project must be between 1500 and 2000 words for AS level and up to 2500 words for the full A level (A2). Make sure that you keep within the limit. Examiners emphasise quality rather than quantity, so do not try to write up to the maximum allowed just for the sake of it. Be sure that you fulfil the minimum requirements.

Each specification has specific requirements. Make sure that you fully understand the structure required for your project. For example,
- **Edexcel** requires: Introduction, Literature review, Method, Results, Discussion/conclusions, Appraisal of the project, Bibliography, Appendices.
- **AQA specifications** require: Abstract, Acknowledgements, Planning, Observation/analysis/evaluation, Literature review, Method, Results, Discussion/conclusion, Bibliography, Appendices.

As you can see there is a great deal of overlap with these requirements, whatever the specifications (syllabus). Your choice of subject is largely dictated by your examination board, so make sure you understand what you can write about and what you cannot write about.

Planning

Include a coherent timetable of how you are going to develop the project and the relevance of the project. If you have to state a hypothesis (a statement about what you think the outcome of the project is going to be), make it clear and to the point – e.g. 'Exercise affects the mood of an athlete'.

The better your planning, the better your project. Do not be afraid of choosing several topics, doing background research and then choosing the one you feel you can cope with most effectively. Remember, the examiners are not expecting groundbreaking research. Keep your project simple!

Abstract

This is a short synopsis or summary of your project. It should contain enough detail for the examiner to know what you did, with whom and what the outcome was. Give a brief statement about your sample if relevant. An abstract should be only about 200 words long.

Literature review

This is demanded by some examination boards. Describe any relevant research or theories from books that deal with your subject. If you find that information about your topic is extremely thin you might be better off choosing another topic. Make sure that you keep a record of the books you have used, along with authors, publication dates and publishers for your bibliography.

Method

You should describe fully your research techniques and your reasons for using them. Be concise. Your procedure should be easily replicated and your research method copied by other people. The structure of the method can vary considerably, depending on the nature of your project but the following format is common:
- Design
- Participants/sample
- Apparatus/materials
- Procedure

Results

This section should include a clear presentation of the data you have collected. There should be some element of data analysis. Describe how you have analysed the data and include any statistical procedures that you have used. If it is possible, represent your data in chart and graph forms to give a visual representation of the data you have collected.

Discussion/conclusion

This may also involve an appraisal of your study – in other words, you may wish to criticise your project because of the methods you used or to praise your project because the methods worked well.

The results should be discussed in this section and if you have used a literature review you should try to link your results with the material in the review. Do your results agree with other findings or do they show something different?

Conclusions that you draw should relate back to your hypothesis and the aims of your study. Does the study prove your hypothesis or not? If your project does not show that your hypothesis is correct this does not mean that you score lower marks – the process of finding out is the important aspect of your research project.

Bibliography

This should be an alphabetical list by author and should follow the Harvard system. For example, if you used this book for your project you would record:

Honeybourne, J., Hill, M., Moors, H., *Advanced Physical Education and Sport* (2nd edition), Stanley Thornes, 2000.

Make sure that all the books and journals you have used are included in your bibliography.

Appendices

Materials used in your project (instruction sheets, tally charts, questionnaire responses, etc.) are usually put into the appendices. As you write your project, you can refer to material in your appendices.

Presentation

Just as in life many people judge on first impressions, the same can be said for projects. If a project looks like a professional piece of work, then it is only human nature to assess it as such. Write neatly and legibly – or, better still, word-process your project. If you do use a word processor, make sure that the spacing is either 1.5 or double spaced. A readable font helps – probably 12 point – and ensure that you use the spell-checker! A title page and a contents page referring to numbered pages also help to give the right impression.

Glossary

Abduction	Movement away from the midline of the body
Actin	A protein filament found within the sarcomere
Adduction	Movement towards the midline of the body
Aerobic respiration	The complete breakdown of fats and carbohydrates to carbon dioxide and water. This process requires oxygen
American Dream	The idea that in the USA anyone can move from rags to riches
Anaerobic respiration	The partial breakdown of carbohydrate to pyruvic acid. This process does not require oxygen
Angular motion	Movement around an axis
Antagonist	A muscle that works in conjunction with a prime mover. As the prime mover contracts, the antagonist relaxes and returns to its original resting length
Anxiety	The negative aspect of experiencing stress. It is the worry that is experienced due to fear of failure
Aponeurosis	A fibrous sheet of connective tissue joining muscle to bone or muscle to muscle
Appendicular skeleton	The part of the skeleton that comprises the upper and lower limbs, the shoulder girdle and the pelvic girdle
Arousal	The energised state, or the readiness for action that motivates a performer to behave in a particular way
Arteries	Blood vessels that always carry blood away from the heart
Articulation	The place where two or more bones meet to form a joint
Athleticism	A philosophy of physical, moral and challenging activities that fostered the development of character in young men. A term associated with sport developed in the public schools of England in the nineteenth century
ATP	Adenosine triphosphate. A form of chemical energy found in all cells
Atrioventricular node	A specialised node found in the atrioventricular septum that forms part of the conduction system of the heart
Attentional wastage	When a performer's concentration is misdirected to irrelevant cues
Autoregulation	The local control of blood distribution within the tissues of the body in response to chemical changes
Axial skeleton	The part of the skeleton that comprises the skull, spine and rib cage
Blood pressure	Blood flow × resistance. The resistance is caused by friction between the blood and the vessel walls
Bohr effect	A drop in pH causes oxygen to dissociate from haemoglobin more readily
Buffer	A substance, e.g. haemoglobin, that combines with either an acid or a base to help keep the body's pH at an optimal level
Bundle of His	Specialised bundles of nerve fibre found in the septum that form part of the conduction system of the heart
Capillaries	The smallest type of blood vessel. Their walls are only one cell thick. This is where the exchange of gases and nutrients take place
Cardiac output	The amount of blood ejected from one ventricle in one minute
Cardiovascular drift	An increase in heart rate during exercise to compensate for a decrease in stroke volume in an attempt to maintain cardiac output
Cartilaginous joint	A joint with no joint cavity but with cartilage between the bones of the joint. Examples are the joints between the vertebrae of the spine
Centre of gravity	The point where all the mass of an object is concentrated
Circumduction	The lower end of the bone moves in a circle. Circumduction is a combination of flexion, extension, abduction and adduction
Clarendon Commission	A royal commission set up in 1864 to investigate the great public schools
Classical conditioning	An unconditioned stimulus is paired with a conditioned stimulus to create a conditioned response
Cognitive phase of learning	The first phase of learning. Involves the performer discovering movement strategies

Cognitive skill	A skill that involves the intellectual ability of the performer
Concentric	A form of muscular contraction in which the muscle is acting as the prime mover and shortening under tension
Condyle	A large knuckle-shaped articular surface
Connectionist theory	See Associationist theories
Dendrite	A process of the motor neurone that carries the nerve impulse from the central nervous system to the cell body
Diastole	The relaxation phase of the cardiac cycle
Distal	Furthest away from the centre of the body
Distributed practice	Practice which includes rest periods between trials
Drive	Directed, motivated or 'energised' behaviour that an individual has towards achieving a certain goal
Drive reduction theory	When performance is perceived to be at its optimum, the performer experiences inhibition which demotivates
Drive theory	The relationship between arousal and performance is linear: as arousal levels increase, so does performance
Dual use	Use of a sport/leisure facility is shared by two sectors of the community
Eccentric	A form of muscular contraction in which the muscle is acting as the antagonist and lengthens under tension
Elitism	Activities confined to an exclusive minority
End diastolic volume	The amount of blood in the ventricles just before the contraction phase of the cardiac cycle
Epinephrine	A hormone. More commonly known as adrenaline
Erythrocyte	A biconcave disc containing haemoglobin that helps transport respiratory gases around the body. Also known as a red blood cell
Expiratory reserve volume	The amount of air that can be forcibly exhaled from the lungs in addition to the tidal volume
Extension	An increase in the angle around a joint
External respiration	The exchange of respiratory gases (oxygen and carbon dioxide) between the lungs and the blood
Extrinsic motivation	External factors which influence behaviour, such as rewards
Fasciculus	A group of individual muscle fibres bound together by connective tissue to form a bundle. Plural is fasciculi
Fibrous joint	A joint with no joint cavity and the bones held together by fibrous connective tissue. An example is the sutures of the skull bones
Field sports	Another term for country pursuits such as hunting, shooting and fishing
Fixator	A muscle which allows the prime mover to work more efficiently by stabilising the bone where the prime mover originates
Flexion	A decrease in the angle around a joint
Foramen	A hole in a bone
Forster Act	Passed in 1870. Made education compulsory for all children between the ages of 5 and 13 years
Fossa	A depression in a bone
Fulcrum	The fixed point that a lever acts around. In the body the joint acts as the fulcrum
Fundamental motor skills	Skills learned at a young age that are basic to many sports
Fusiform	A muscle shape, where the muscle fibres run the length of the muscle
Game cult	A way of thinking about sports which was exported around the world (see also Athleticism)
Gestaltists	A group of German scientists who established principles of perception and insight learning
Haematocrit	The percentage of blood cells in the total blood volume
Haemoglobin	A protein in red blood cells with a high affinity for carbon monoxide, carbon dioxide and oxygen
Hick's law	The more alternative responses that could be made, the longer the reaction time of the performer
Holy day	A religious festival, which gave people a day off work
Hyperextension	Continuing to extend a limb beyond 180°
Hyperplasia	An increase in the number of cells in a tissue
Hypertrophy	Where an increase in cell size leads to an increase in tissue size

Inertia	A body or an object is said to be in a state of inertia and needs a force to be applied before any change of velocity can occur
Insertion	The part of a muscle that is attached by connective tissue to a bone that moves
Insight learning	A performer learns through understanding rather than simply connecting a certain stimulus with a particular response
Inspiratory reserve volume	The amount of air that can be forcibly inspired into the lungs in addition to the tidal volume
Internal respiration	The exchange of respiratory gases (oxygen and carbon dioxide) between the blood and the tissues
Intrinsic motivation	Internal drives such as emotional feelings
Invasion games	Games in which the aim is to invade another team's territory – for example football
Inverted U theory	As arousal levels increase, so does performance, but only to a certain point, usually at moderate arousal levels. Once past moderate arousal level, performance decreases
Isometric	A form of muscular contraction in which the muscle increases in tension but its length does not alter
Kinesiology	The study of the science of movement
Kinesthesis	The information that we hold within ourselves about our body's position
Lever	A rigid bar that rotates around a fixed point. In the body bones act as levers
Life-time sports	Sports that can be played throughout life, generally ones that are self-paced or can be adopted
Linear motion	Movement in a straight line
Lombardian ethic	The idea that winning is the most important thing
Mass	The quantity of matter a body contains
Massed practice	A continuous practice period with very short, or no, rest intervals
Minute ventilation	The amount of air taken into or pushed out of the lungs in one minute. It is calculated by multiplying the number of breaths taken by how much air is inspired or expired in one breath
Model course	Established in 1902 by the War Office. Made military drill compulsory in all state schools
Momentum	The product of velocity × mass
Motor programme	A generalised series of movements stored in the LTM
Motor skill	An action or task that has a goal and which requires voluntary movements
Movement time	The time taken from the start of a movement to its completion
Multipennate	A muscle shape, where the fibres run off either side of small tendons that are attached to the main tendon
Myelin sheath	A fatty sheath that covers the axon of a motor neurone
Myocardium	Cardiac muscle tissue that forms the middle layer of the heart wall
Myoglobin	A protein substance found in the sarcoplasm of the cell. It has a high affinity for oxygen and helps transport oxygen from the capillary to the mitochondria
Myosin	A protein filament found within the sarcomere
Neuromuscular junction	The point where the axon terminal of a motor neurone contacts the sarcolemma of a muscle fibre
Newton	One newton is the force required to produce an acceleration of one metre per second per second on a mass of one kilogram
Open championship	Competition that is open to both professionals and amateurs
Operant conditioning	Actions are 'shaped' and then reinforced. The behaviour is manipulated, rather than the stimulus
Origin	The part of a muscle that is attached by connective tissue to a stationary bone
Ossification	The process of bone formation
Part method of training	A skill is split up into sub-routines for more effective teaching
Partial pressure	The pressure a gas exerts within a mixture of gases
Peak flow experience	The emotional response of an elite athlete whose performance levels are optimal
Perception	Interpretation of stimuli as part of information processing
Popular recreation	Sporting activities before the industrial revolution

Post 16 gap	The 60% drop-off in participation of sport among young people after they leave school
Precapillary sphincters	Found between the arteriole and the capillary. A sphincter is a ring of muscle that surrounds an opening and can effectively open up or close down the capillary
Prime mover	The muscle that is directly responsible for creating the movement produced at a joint
Private sector	Ownership of a facility is in the hands of private individuals or companies
Process	A prominent projection of a bone – for example, the spinous process of a vertebra
Profile of Mood States	The measurement of moods of those who participate in sport
Proximal	Nearest the centre of the body
Psychological refractory period	The delay caused by the increased information-processing time when a second stimulus follows closely after the first
Public sector	A facility in public ownership, usually administered by a local authority
Pulmonary ventilation	The movement of air into and out of the lungs
Purkinje fibres	Specialised nerve fibres found in the ventricles that form part of the conduction system of the heart
QUANGO	Quasi-autonomous non-governmental organisation
Rationalisation	A term associated with the development of sport that occurred during the industrial revolution, resulting in the codification and organisation of modern sport
Reaction time	The time between presentation of a stimulus and the start of movement
Reinforcement	The process which increases the probability of a behaviour reoccurring. Reinforcement strengthens the S–R bond
Reliability	Research that achieves consistency of results after two or more applications of tests
Response time	The time between presentation of a stimulus and completion of the movement
Romanticism	An artistic movement in the nineteenth century that encouraged all people to get into 'the great outdoors'
Sabbatarianism	The view that Sunday is a holy day of rest
Sarcomere	The smallest contractile unit of a skeletal muscle fibre
Shop window	Sport is used to show off a country
Single-channel hypothesis	This states that the brain can only process one stimulus at a time. It is often referred to as the 'bottleneck' theory
Sinuatrial node	A specialised node in the wall of the right atrium, sometimes called the pacemaker, that forms part of the conduction system of the heart
Socialisation	The process by which humans adapt and grow into their society
Stroke volume	The volume of blood pumped out of the heart by each ventricle during one contraction
Swedish gymnastics	Drill-type exercises based on the work of Ling. Emphasise style, grace and movement
Synovial joint	A fluid-filled joint cavity is surrounded by an articular capsule. The articulating surfaces are covered in hyaline cartilage. An example is the hinge joint of the knee
Systole	The contraction phase of the cardiac cycle
Tendon	A round cord or bank of connective tissue joining muscle to bone
Thoracic cavity	The area surrounded by the ribs and bordered by the diaphragm. The thoracic cavity is divided into two halves by the mediastinum
Tidal volume	The amount of air breathed into or out of the lungs in one breath
Transfer	The influence that the learning and/or performance of one skill has on the learning/performance of another
Validity	Research that has high internal validity is scientific and keeps unwanted variables to a minimum. Research that has high external validity can be generalised to the population as a whole
Vascular shunt	The redistribution of the cardiac output during exercise, taking more blood to the working muscles and less blood to other organs such as the kidneys and the liver

Vasoconstriction	A decrease in the size of the lumen of the blood vessel as the smooth muscle of the tunica media contracts
Vasodilatation	An increase in the size of the lumen of the blood vessel as the smooth muscle of the tunica media relaxes
Vasomotor tone	The continual low-frequency impulse received by blood vessels
Veins	Blood vessels that always carry blood towards the heart
Venous return	The flow of blood through the veins back to the heart
Vital capacity	The maximum amount of air that can be forcibly exhaled after breathing in as much as possible
Voluntary sector	Facilities run and administered by volunteers
Whole method of training	Teaching skills without breaking them down into sub-routines or parts

Index